RADICAL SOCIAL
WORI

Social work at

Edited by Mic

First published in Great Britain in 2011 by

Policy Press
University of Bristol
1-9 Old Park Hill
Bristol BS2 8BB
UK
t: +44 (0)117 954 5940
e: pp-info@bristol.ac.uk
www.policypress.co.uk

North American office:
Policy Press
c/o The University of Chicago Press
1427 East 60th Street
Chicago, IL 60637, USA
t: +1 773 702 7700
f: +1 773-702-9756
e:sales@press.uchicago.edu
www.press.uchicago.edu

Reprinted 2015

British Library Cataloguing in Publication Data
A catalogue record for this book is available from the British Library.

Library of Congress Cataloging-in-Publication Data
A catalog record for this book has been requested.

ISBN 978 1 84742 817 2 paperback
ISBN 978 1 84742 818 9 hardcover

The right of Michael Lavalette to be identified as editor of this work has been
asserted by him in accordance with the Copyright, Designs and Patents Act 1988.

Cover design by Qube Design Associates, Bristol.
Front cover: image kindly supplied by www.istock.com
Printed and bound in Great Britain CMP, Poole
Policy Press uses environmentally responsible print partners.

Contents

Notes on contributors

Roy Bailey was one of the two original editors of *Radical social work* (Edward Arnold, 1975) and the follow-up volume, *Radical social work and practice* (Macmillan, 1980). He has lectured in universities and colleges in Britain, Germany, Belgium, the US, Canada and Australia, though he has now retired from academic life. In recent years he has concentrated on his highly successful career as a folk singer and musician. In 2003, Roy, together with Tony Benn, was awarded Best Live Act at the BBC Radio 2 Folk Awards, for their hugely successful programme Writing on the Wall. In the 2000 Honours List, Roy received the MBE for 'services to folk music'. He returned this award (22 August 2006) in protest at the government's foreign policy.

Mark Baldwin is a senior lecturer in social work at University of Bath. His research interests include looking at the development of integrated health and social care services and Community Care policy implementation (particularly the part played by front line implementers and the construction of care management through different forms of knowledge). Mark is a member of the national steering committee of the Social Work Action Network.

Sarah Banks is Professor in the School of Applied Social Sciences, Durham University, co-Director of the Centre for Social Justice and Community Action and co-editor of the journal, *Ethics and Social Welfare*. She has a practice background in voluntary and statutory sector community development work and teaches mainly on professional qualifying programmes in community and youth work. Her publications include *Critical community practice*, with Hugh Butcher, Paul Henderson and Jim Robertson (The Policy Press, 2007).

Peter Beresford is Professor in Social Work at Brunel University. He is the Director of the Centre for Citizen Participation, Chair of Shaping our Lives, Visiting Fellow at the School for Social Work and Psychosocial Studies at the University of East Anglia, and a fellow of the Royal Society of Arts. He is also a trustee of the Social Care Institute for Excellence. Peter is a member of the SWAN national steering committee.

Iain Ferguson is a senior lecturer in social work at the University of Stirling and a founder member of the Social Work Action Network. He has recently published *Reclaiming social work* (Sage) and (with Rona Woodward) *Radical social work in practice* (The Policy Press)

Vasilios Ioakimidis is a lecturer in social work at Liverpool Hope University. He is currently editing a text on radical social work in Greece. He has recently published *Social work in extremis* (Policy Press) with Michael Lavalette.

Chris Jones is Emeritus Professor of Social Work at the University of Liverpool. He has written widely on social work education, poverty and inequality and state supervision, surveillance and control of marginalised communities. His book *State social work and the working class* (Macmillan) was originally published in the series Critical Texts in Social Work and the Welfare State which developed a number of radical social work themes in the 1980s. He is currently completing a book (with Michael Lavalette) on the experiences of young people on the Palestinian West Bank.

Mary Langan teaches social policy and criminology at the Open University. In the 1970s she was an inner city social worker and an active participant in the radical social work movement. She has written extensively on social work and social policy in a wide range of books and articles. She edited the Routledge social policy series The State of Welfare. As the parent of a boy with autism and severe learning disability, she has campaigned and written about the rights of people with disabilities and their families.

Michael Lavalette is Associate Professor of Social Work at Liverpool Hope University and a founding member of the Social Work Action Network. He has written on a range of issues within social work, social policy and sociology. With Iain Ferguson he has recently published *Social work after Baby P* (Liverpool Hope University Press), with Vasilios Ioakimidis he has just published *Social work in extremis* (The Policy Press) and is currently completing a book (with Chris Jones) on the experiences of Palestinian young people on the West Bank.

Laura Miles teaches on the social work programme at Bradford College. She is an elected national officer of the University and College Lecturers' Union with a remit to look at union policy and practice around lesbian, gay, bisexual and transgender (LGBT) issues.

Laura Penketh is a senior lecturer in social work at Liverpool Hope University. She has written on issues of 'race' and anti-racism in social policy and social work as well as on issues of women, gender and social work. She is the author of *Tackling institutional racism* (The Policy Press) and is currently researching alongside women in impoverished communities in both Liverpool and Chennai (India). She is a member of the SWAN national steering committee.

Jeremy Weinstein was a member of the Case Con collective, and worked as a social worker in Lambeth and Wandsworth before going to London South Bank University as a senior lecturer on the postgraduate social work programme. He remains a visiting fellow at LSBU and now works as a counsellor/psychotherapist running a low-cost counselling project and in private practice. Jeremy has researched/written on social workers as trade unionists, aspects of group work and more recently on the topic of loss and bereavement. His text, *Working with loss, death and bereavement: A guide for social workers*, was published by Sage in 2008.

Charlotte Williams is Professor of Social Justice and Head of the School of Public Policy and Professional Practice at Keele University. She is Visiting Professor at Liverpool Hope University. She has been a social work educator for over 20 years initially at the University of Wales, Bangor. She has written and researched extensively on equality issues and her publications include *A tolerant nation? Exploring ethnic diversity in Wales* (University of Wales Press) and *Social policy for social welfare practice in a devolved Wales* (Venture Press).

Acknowledgements

I would like to record my thanks to a number of people who helped pull this volume together.

First I'd like to record my thanks to Roy Bailey – not only for his role as co-editor (with Mike Brake) of the original *Radical social work* book which inspired so many working in the social work field, but also for agreeing to write the foreword to this book and agreeing to speak at the radical social work conference which was held at Liverpool Hope University in February 2010. He continues to promote radical alternatives to the iniquities of capitalism in his role as activist and folk singer for the movements.

Second I'd like to thank Karen Bowler at The Policy Press for her support for the project and all the contributors to the volume who met the tight deadlines and were all enthusiastic in their support for the project. I'm indebted to them all, but I would like to highlight two contributors in particular. Chris Jones has been a teacher, a friend and a comrade for a long time now. We have spent weeks together in refugee camps across the Palestinian West Bank and an immense amount of time discussing social work and social theory. Iain Ferguson has been a friend and comrade even longer. We met via involvement in social movements and our membership of the Socialist Workers Party, and there is hardly a day goes by without a phone conversation about social work, research, politics or issues concerning the Social Work Action Network (SWAN). Politics is never boring in the company of Chris and Iain; there is much fun and laughter that accompanies more serious debates.

Third, over the last few years I have been involved with SWAN and I am currently the national coordinator. SWAN has run some fantastic conferences and been involved in a range of campaigning initiatives. I'd like to record my thanks to those who have been part of constructing the organisation and helping to make it the open, vibrant campaigning network within social work that it has become. In particular I'd like to thank Rona Woodward, Kathryn MacKay, Barry Levine, Vasilios Ioakimidis, Mark Baldwin, June Sadd, Malcolm Jones, Mae Boyd, Phil Wheatley, Rich Moth, Bea Kay, and Debbie Saeed. Also, the work done by Linda Smith in South Africa and Lam Chi in Hong Kong has been immensely inspiring.

Fourth, I have been working on this book while being a member of the social work team at Liverpool Hope University. It is a small team working on a new degree programme but we all work to a shared vision of establishing a social work that is committed to social justice. Thanks for their support to Vasilios, Liz, Nicki, Gill, John, Wendy, Anne, Philomena and Maria.

Finally, there is one person who should have been thanked in each of the last three paragraphs above. Laura has contributed to the book, is on the SWAN steering committee and works at Liverpool Hope – but she has also decided to put up with me at home! For years she has carried on without complaint as I have disappeared to various political or SWAN meetings – often at the other end of the country! She supported me when I stood (and got elected) as a socialist anti-war councillor in Preston – and didn't complain when this took many hours of my time. As a political activist she has found the space for her own activity reduced by the demands made on my time – an embarrassing thing to admit from someone committed to women's liberation. We share a vision that another world is possible; a vision that, if fulfilled, will mean a better world not only for our children (Kristian, Olivia and Saskia) and grandchildren (Georgia and Isaac), but for everyone's children and grandchildren. It might not amount to much, but I'd like to take this opportunity to record my thanks and love.

Foreword

Roy Bailey

For 20 years I have done nothing but sing songs. In the songs I choose, I believe I am continuing the political work in which I have always been involved, either as a teacher, a lecturer, an academic or a folk singer.

In fact, sometimes the two worlds – of folk singing and social work – overlap. I was in Australia some years ago when a young woman came up and asked "are you the same Roy Bailey who produced the book entitled, *Radical social work*?" I said I was. She asked if I would be in town for the next couple of days. When I said I would, she replied "good, I'll come with my book for you to sign tomorrow." I was flattered and surprised!

This exchange leads me to ask, what was it about that book that made it so popular and left such an imprint?

Looking back, radical social work was formed out of events at the end of the 1960s. In 1968 I was invited to attend the initial conference known as The York Symposium. We were a group of criminologists and Social Theorists, critical of the positivistic approaches to the study of crime and delinquency that dominated such studies at the time. We eventually morphed into the National Deviancy Conference. We met regularly at York University hosted by Laurie Taylor and the Department of Sociology. We listened to many excellent presentations from sociologists and criminologists, including Stuart Hall, Laurie, Stan Cohen and others. These were exciting times.

After some time many of the participants argued that while listening to these albeit interesting contributions, we really were only talking to ourselves and not engaging with the world around us. Many responded by focusing their research agendas on problems and policies of the 'real world'. Some, like Jock Young, became involved in the 'new criminology'. Mike Brake and I turned our attention to social welfare and social work.

In 1967 I moved to Bradford University from Enfield College of Technology – which was, in many ways developing quite radical approaches to course development. At Bradford I was in a building shared by various departments of social science, including social work. The building was a 'shell' divided into prefabricated rooms with very thin walls! In my room, I was struck by the number of times I heard arguments between social work tutors and students – about the world in which we lived, about the politics of the new movements (for example, Case Con or Squatters) or the various models of social work within which students were expected to operate but with which they disagreed. And I was astonished by the number of times, it seemed to me, such disagreements were turned against the student with the words "have you always had a problem with authority?"

I thought this quite shocking. This was the 1960s; everything was questioned and nothing was taken for granted. So the idea that social work students couldn't question the ideas and theories of lecturing staff just struck me as unacceptable. I thought it would be helpful if students in this situation could quote from a social work reader. In the academic world it would give their ideas a degree of validity and, if nothing else, it would let them know that there were academics who shared their general outlook. To assert 'as so and so says' gave a degree of legitimacy to an argument. I invited Mike Brake to join me and we wrote a piece that was to become the Introduction to the book and we set out to look for a publisher. Eventually, the publishers Edward Arnold agreed that this was an interesting idea and that they would publish it.

Once we got the contract we then approached other writers and produced *Radical social work*. The book 'took off', not just in Britain but in the US, Europe, Australia and elsewhere. In retrospect I think this was because it was the first of a number of publications in a radical social work literature. There was clearly a need for books like this and we stepped into the vacuum. It was also partly because it reflected the various social movements of the time and how the ideas of these new movements were being taken up by a new generation of social workers.

Nevertheless, I think I can speak for all of us who wrote and contributed to the book – and for Mike Brake and myself in particular – when I say that the thought that 35 years later, people would still be interested in the book is not one that we could either have anticipated or, indeed, been able to comprehend.

What we did was legitimise the notion that we could criticise the psychodynamic model or framework that dominated social work theory and practice. Mike and I were concerned to locate that theory and practice within the wider context of a political economy. We raised the idea that it was possible for people to resist being stigmatised by social services, and to resist poverty being blamed on poor people. We hoped that social work in its understanding and practice might provide assistance to the victims of the worst excesses of a capitalist economy. We wrote, as the closing sentence in our introduction, 'we hope that the recipients of social work will themselves oppose stigma and stereotyping and resist all authoritarian attempts by the state to undermine their dignity.' I like to think that this is something which I continue to present in my solo concerts and when Tony Benn and I perform our programme, The Writing on the Wall. It is something which I see that the Social Work Action Network is continuing today.

I was hesitant but subsequently delighted to have been asked to address the conference at Liverpool Hope University and now to contribute this foreword to the collection that looks at the legacy, the relevance and the prospects of radical social work. In a world of growing inequality, welfare cuts, war and racism there has to be a space for a social work that has, at its heart, a commitment to social justice, meeting human need and equality.

Introduction

Michael Lavalette

This volume has been put together to mark – and indeed celebrate – the 35th anniversary of the publication of Bailey and Brake's (1975) *Radical social work*. Bailey and Brake's work has become one of the few great, seminal texts of social work in Britain. Today, even those hostile to the general direction of the argument presented in the book, are willing to concede that the book had a significant impact on debates over social work theory and practice in the 1970s and 1980s.

Reading the text today there is no doubt that some of the chapters are shaped by the language and concerns of the 1970s Left. But in its emphasis on the iniquities of the social structure of capitalist society, the challenge it posed to state directed bureaucratic welfare, and its emphasis on the public and social causes of private pain, it was contesting and reshaping many of the dominant assumptions of social work theory. In doing so, it was in contrast to previously dominant perspectives that saw social problems in terms of individual failing and moral ineptitude on the part of 'problem communities'.

As Roy Bailey points out in his foreword, the book was the first of a number of texts that offered a radical interpretation of social work theory, practice and intervention in the mid-1970s. Its publication reflected three significant and interconnected developments.

First, in the aftermath of the Kilbrandon (SHHD/SED, 1964) and Seebhom (1968) Reports, integrated social service/social work departments developed and created significant job opportunities for qualified workers. In response, higher education institutions expanded their social work course provision. Increasing numbers of social work students, however, then found themselves on courses where the traditional literature and theory base was found wanting. Psychological and medical accounts of clients and their problems were increasingly questioned and ridiculed by the new student cohorts (Jones, this volume). Instead students looked to new ideas that were emerging in the social sciences – ideas steeped in Marxist, feminist, countercultural and social constructionist perspectives that flourished in the early 1970s. Bailey and Brake put the book together to counter the traditional approaches to social work, to bring leading perspectives from the social sciences to social work and, by so doing, give students on courses the ammunition they needed to challenge the dominant theory base espoused on their courses.

Second, the book reflected, and in turn became part of, a growing radical critique of state directed welfare provision. It is worth remembering that the first critics of 'one-size-fits-all' welfare and the bureaucratisation of services came from the radical Left.

In the immediate post-war era 'social administration', both as a quasi-profession and an academic discipline, reflected a confidence that welfare professionals could administer and direct the welfare state and hence control and eradicate a wide variety of social problems and public ills. It encapsulated a belief that the welfare state in Britain had successfully managed to establish a 'third way' (long before New Labour and their supporters coined the phrase) between the anarchy of free-market capitalism (and the social problems that it created and had been exposed in the inter-war years: the 'five giants' of unemployment, poor health, inadequate education, impoverished housing and poverty) and the lack of freedom and authoritarianism of state directed 'socialism' (the reality of life under the state capitalist regimes of Eastern Europe). The suggestion was that the welfare state had established a fuller and more inclusive form of citizenship that combined freedom and democratic control, alongside the planning and direction of state resources to manage economic and social problems: Keynesian economics and the Beveridgean welfare settlement created a controlled and humane capitalist society (see, for example, Tawney, 1949/1964; Marshall, 1965 and Titmuss, 1974) and stood at the heart of the post-war broad political 'consensus' between the political parties.

By the mid-1960s this confidence started to wane. The 1960s witnessed the 'rediscovery of poverty' in the work of, for example, Townsend and Abel-Smith (1966). This undermined the complacency of the post-war state welfare system: despite the benefits 'safety-net', poverty had not been abolished (Kincaid, 1973). In major cities there was a severe housing crisis. The short-term 'solution' of prefabricated homes proved inadequate to the task, and in the private sector 'Rachman' landlords charged excessive rents for sub-standard housing (Lavalette and Mooney, 2000). The NHS had entrenched the power of doctors and physicians within the system and become an arena in which private pharmaceutical companies could generate vast profits (Widgery, 1988; Lister, 2008). It was also becoming clear that Britain's post-war migrant communities were facing discrimination within society, as well as within the welfare system and its institutions (Rex and Moore, 1967; Rex, 1975; Rex and Tomlinson, 1979). Further, as the film *Cathy come home* indicated, and as 'service user based research' like that of Simpkin (1979) and Mayer and Timms (1970) emphasised, state welfare bureaucracies treated working-class clients with contempt. The welfare state had not undermined class divisions or inequalities in society, and the promises of a post-war 'New Jerusalem' were increasingly seen as being wide of the mark (Timmins, 1995).

To cap it all the 1960s witnessed the growth of 'stagflation' in Britain (low levels of economic growth accompanied by inflation) which a simple reading of Keynes suggested was 'impossible'. In Britain, the Labour governments (1964–70) of the period came under pressure from global financial markets and faced a number of 'runs on the pound' as the markets tried to exert pressure on the government's domestic economic policy. The government's response was to devalue sterling in the hope that this would boost exports and employment. The British economy was struggling in comparison to its nearest competitor economies, and matters deteriorated when the long post-war boom came to an end in 1973–75. During this period, the first major post-war economic crisis began to affect the global economy.

In this context radical critiques that located welfare provision within existing capitalist social relations (and that emphasised the ways in which social policy and welfare reinforced, rather than undermined, all manner of oppressions) developed. These analyses looked more critically at the historical development of state social policy and the continuities and contradictions within different forms of welfare delivery. They analysed the way(s) in which welfare provision:

- developed to meet certain functional needs of capitalism (Saville, 1957/58; Gough, 1979; Lavalette, 2006a);
- reproduced 'social control' mechanisms and were as much about 'control' of populations as they were about 'social care' (Novak, 1988);
- emerged from a contested political arena and reflected the impact of political and social struggles over the distribution of resources (Saville, 1957/58; Lavalette and Mooney, 2000); had an impact on dominant regimes of accumulation (O'Connor, 1973; Gough, 1979).

An intellectual climate was developing that challenged both existing social work theory but also, more widely, the context within which social work, as a welfare activity, was located.

The third element which framed the background to both the book and the radical social work movement was the surge in social movement activity in the period. These movements brought forth new ways of thinking about, and engaging with, the world. In the US in the early 1960s, the civil rights movement and the anti-war movement gradually merged as black troops in Vietnam protested against the disproportionate number of black troops killed and injured in the theatre of war. They challenged the fact that they were expected to fight and die for 'democracy' in Vietnam, but faced racism and discrimination when they returned home (Branch, 1988, 1998, 2006). Things came to a head during 1968, when the United State's claim that they were fighting on behalf of the South Vietnamese against a minority communist terror force was blown apart during the Tet Offensive (Neale, 2001). In the aftermath of Tet there was a surge in the anti-war movement globally and this became a spark for a whole series of movements that grew to challenge the dominant order.

The year 1968 was a remarkable one which launched a wave of social protest that was to last until the mid-1970s (Tarrow, 1994). The Student Movement, the Women's Movement, the Gay Liberation Movement and the Black Movement all shook the US establishment. The 'Prague Spring' brought a challenge to East European state capitalism – and helped establish, for many at least, that an alternative was needed east and west; that there should be illusions in neither Washington nor Moscow. France was rocked by the biggest General Strike in history, and in Northern Ireland students led marches demanding 'one person, one vote', proclaiming 'class not creed' as they campaigned against the political iniquities and corruption of the Orange State (McCann, 1974; Farrell, 1980). Slightly later in the 'protest wave' there was major industrial conflict in Italy (1969–74) and Britain (1972–77), a popular rebellion that brought an end to fascism in Portugal (1974), and the revival of industrial militancy that marked the dying days of Franco in Spain (Harman, 1988).

In this context, it is not surprising that for the young students and new social workers active in these movements, existing social work theory and practice had to be challenged. It was part of the establishment; it pathologised and blamed working-class clients for their poverty and marginalisation from social life (Ferguson, this volume); it reflected dominant assumptions about women's role in society and the importance of maintaining 'family values' and dominant familial forms (Penketh, this volume); it treated lesbian, gay, bisexual and transgender people as if they had a psychiatric disorder (Miles, this volume); it was shaped by 'social control' concerns and disdain for those with whom it worked (Lavalette and Ioakimidis, this volume); it was concerned with establishing and maintaining 'professional distance' from service users (Beresford, this volume); and as a 'profession', it was ambivalent towards social worker trade unionism and collective trade unionism as a response to the problems faced by workers in the field and service users in the communities (Joyce et al, 1988).

It was in this context that more radical forms of social work began to gain a voice and a hearing among sections of social work students, academics and practitioners (Weinstein, this volume). It is worth, however, emphasising two points. First, radical social work in the 1970s was always a minority current within the field and was always stronger in certain regions of Britain (London and Yorkshire, for example). Second, radical social work wasn't homogeneous. Like the movements of the time, there were different currents: a Marxist/ socialist strand; those whose political practice drew more heavily on the autonomous traditions within the movements (such as feminism); and those who were more influenced by the lifestyle politics of the hippie counterculture.

Nevertheless, through forums like *Case Con*, through involvement in social work trade unionism, and through engagement in Claimant and Tenants Unions, a collective, campaigning social work began to emerge; one that located clients' problems within the context of unequal societies. But there were also debates within the movement. For example, if radical social work prioritised collective and community-based work, what should/did workers do when dealing with individuals or families facing particular troubles? What was the social worker's role in short-term intervention? Was there a distinctive radical social work method? What was 'professional' about social work – and was professionalism something to be defended or disparaged?

These questions were addressed in part by the chapters by Leonard (1975) and Cohen (1975) in the Bailey and Brake collection. Cohen in particular is scathing of what he terms 'authoritarian Marxists' who 'make people expendable' and 'write off all short-scale intervention' (1975, p 92). The object of his scorn was the notion that radical work was only concerned with collective and community campaigning for social change. As he argues, if radical work is to be more than a minority current of political campaigning it has to address issues of what social workers do in their daily interactions with service users.

Thirty-five years on, radical social workers would probably be more confident in addressing these issues. Few would argue that there is a specific radical social work method (in the narrow technical sense). Community-based strategies and group working clearly allow practitioners to 'collectivise' social problems and look at their structural and oppressive features – the public causes – at the heart of the problems. But radical practitioners can also be involved in quality, supportive casework that involves advocating on behalf of, and alongside, service users. There are some methods that radical workers would find hard, if not impossible to implement (for example, the use of cognitive behavioural therapy), but surely the key element is the *orientation* of the practitioner as they undertake good quality work: whom they involve in work processes and how they communicate and keep service users informed; how they 'speak truth to power'; how they fight for service user's rights and needs and how they locate (and explain) the problems service users and workers face in the context of local and national power structures. Any such orientation also involves a perspective about the social worker, as a worker, who, as a trade union member, looks to collectivise workplace problems, and fights within the union to ensure that it takes up political campaigning in defence of services and service-user needs.

If the first half of the 1970s Britain witnessed a series of significant industrial disputes in the shipyards, docks and mines, and in the printing and building industries (Darlington and Lyddon, 2001), the second half of the decade was marked by campaigns against Labour's welfare cuts. Between 1976 and 1979 there were significant real term cuts in social welfare spending and campaigning shifted towards defence of services (Clarke, 1993).

At the end of the 1970s the rebellion of the low-paid against Labour's austerity measures produced the 'Winter of Discontent'. Many of those on the radical left hoped it presaged a return to worker militancy but, instead, the election of the first Thatcher government marked a significant turning point and a ruling-class offensive against trade unionism, local 'socialism' within the councils, state-provided welfare and poor people. After a series of major confrontations between 1980 and 1985, the Conservative government managed to inflict expensive and socially divisive defeats onto the steel workers, dockers, printers and – most importantly – the miners.

Social work also found itself under attack. It was increasingly depicted – both by government ministers and the media – as the cause of 'welfare dependency', of 'failed' hippie values, of 'political correctness' and a culture of being 'soft on crime' (Penketh, 2000). In short, social work was portrayed as a 'failed profession' (Clarke, 1993; Langan, 1993) and the radical social work movement gradually dissipated. Yet many of the themes initially raised by the movement (for example, anti-racism, a commitment to anti-oppressive practice and advocacy approaches) remain embedded within social work, in theory if not always in practice, in a way that was not the case pre-Bailey and Brake.

If the 1980s were, generally, a period of retreat and defeat for progressive social movements, the 1987 election marked a watershed year for welfare (Lavalette and Mooney, 2000). In the aftermath, the Tories introduced the Education Act and the NHS and Community

Care Act, both of which introduced internal markets, league tables, targets and market principles in social care and educational delivery. The growth of managerialism underpinned the extension of market forces into social work. This further squeezed the potential of social work to act as a positive force for change, and increased demoralisation and alienation among frontline workers who found themselves overstretched, overworked and performing tasks which many felt clashed with their value base (Jones, 2005). Marketisation and managerialism also brought significant changes to the social work labour process. Practitioners found themselves with less time to build working relationships with service users, and were themselves increasingly regulated and controlled – not only by managers, but by managerial authority embedded within computer systems that were unfit for any social work task. Increasingly, the de-professionalisation and de-skilling of social workers reduced their role to one of being 'purchasers of care packages' within the care market system (Harris, 2003; Ferguson and Lavalette, 2009; Harris and White, 2009). This led to a crisis within social work – as many practitioners questioned the role of the social worker in a political climate that prioritised targets over meeting service users' needs (Lavalette, 2007).

Yet the attempt to introduce a 'neoliberal' form of social work has, in the long run, opened up such disillusionment and discontent within the profession that it has created a space for the rebirth of radicalism in social work. Further, it can be argued that the potential is greater than it was in the 1970s. Then, the radical social work movement was a minority current within social work, but today the neoliberal assault is such that many more social workers feel that the restrictions of managerialism and marketisation have an adverse impact on their ability to do the job in the way in which they think it should be done. Levels of disillusionment are evident in studies undertaken by Unison related to children and family teams and adult team workers (Unison, 2009, 2010), in the Community Care review of social worker attitudes to the modern social work business (Carson, 2009a, 2009b; Mickel, 2009), and in academic studies such as those by Jones (2005), Harris (2003), Harris and White (2009), and Sue White and her colleagues at Lancaster University (White et al, 2009). For radical social work to take advantage of this situation, however, it must offer solutions to the crisis which social work faces, and be able to draw on sources of hope that include a vision for a better world. So, what are the plausible alternatives?

First let's look at the resources of hope – for a regeneration of radical social work theory and practice. The end of the 1990s saw the birth of a new global social movement the 'anti-capitalist' or global justice movement. This was a movement against the impact and consequences of neoliberalism. It focused on third world debt and the role of the international financial institutions on the global south; the effect of the privatisation of public services (through such devices as the General Agreement of Trade in Services) on public services; the consequences of market deregulation on the environment; the plight of refugees and people 'without papers' across the globe, and the consequences of a philosophy of 'there is no alternative' (to the market and global neoliberalism) on working conditions and state welfare provision.

The significance of the movement was the result of three elements. First, the 1990s were dominated by notions that we had reached the 'end of history' (in Fukuyama's (1989) oft-quoted phrase); that capitalism had won the cold war and there was now no systemic alternative to global capitalism. The birth of the movement at Seattle in November and December 1999 opened up questions about the alternatives to the dominant economic paradigm – captured in the slogan 'Another World is Possible'.

Second, the movement was global. It included anti-privatisation movements in Africa, labour and political movements in opposition to existing governments in Latin America, the Dalit movement in India and, in Europe, it marked its birth at a series of major demonstrations against the leaders of the G8 and other gatherings of the world's leading representatives of the economic and political system.

Third, the movement has generated its own 'organic intellectuals'. The movement posed a series of questions about the nature and priorities of the world. It produced a series of contributions from people as diverse as Naomi Klein, Susan George, Mike Davis, Michael Albert, George Monbiot, Kim Moody, Slavoj Zizek Alain Badiou, Walden Bello, Toni Negri, Michael Hardt, Emir Sader, Alex Callinicos and Gilbert Achcar. Some of the writers have devoted their energies to the strategies and tactics of the movement, some to social criticism of the modern world and the impact of neoliberalism on the lives of the poorest, and some to broader questions about the role of the individual in society, the meaning of equality and social justice, the environmental crisis, the modern era of imperialist wars, and the possibilities of an alternative world. The traditional anti-intellectualism within much state social work and social work education in Britain means that social work theory has not fully engaged with these new ideas and perspectives, but would undoubtedly be enriched by any such critical engagement.

The 'anti-capitalist' movement that started in Seattle in 1999, has since deepened and merged with global anti-war movements, international campaigns in support of Palestinian rights and with the movement against climate change. Over a decade after it 'burst onto the scene' the movement has changed, but it is still a powerful mobiliser on the streets of the world's capitals – and continues to pose questions about the world in which we live.

The first 'resource of hope' therefore is in the theories and practices of the global justice and anti-war movements that force us to address global injustices and inequalities and think about the alternatives – locally, globally and countersystemically.

Our second resource of hope must be in revitalising our existing collective organisations. In Britain this means the trade union movement. There is no doubt that trade unions are contradictory and frustrating organisations, but in recent years there has been a shift away from trade unions as mere vehicles for addressing issues of pay and working conditions, towards a more political campaigning unionism. Things can move in different directions of course, but the unions have involved themselves in anti-war activities, anti-fascist campaigning and agitation in defence of services.

Britain's latest government, the 'Con–Dem' coalition, has announced its intention to introduce some of the most vicious cuts in welfare and social service budgets since the 1980s (and on some interpretations since 1930). Such cuts will have a significant and detrimental impact on social workers (many of whom will find their jobs under threat, the intensity of their work increasing dramatically and the resources available for work with service users severely restricted), and on those for and with whom we work. Here, political trade unionism and the collective organisation of social workers in defence of jobs and services provides another 'resource' and a means of addressing the crisis that is about to hit us.

Finally, social workers, social work academics, service users and students also need their own campaigning network that is able to respond quickly to social work and service user specific issues. Such an organisation should run in conjunction with the main trade unions (and is certainly not an alternative to them). The Social Work Action Network (SWAN) in Britain has the potential to fulfil this function.

SWAN developed out of the *Social work manifesto* that was written by Jones, Ferguson, Lavalette and Penketh (Jones et al, 2004), as a response to the growing crisis in social work. It was followed by a series of meetings across the country in 2004/05 around the theme 'I didn't come into social work for this', where frontline workers gathered in a free space to discuss the crisis on the 'frontline'. Then, in Easter 2006, close to 300 workers, academics, students and service users gathered at a conference organised around the theme: 'Social work: a profession worth fighting for?' The conference ended by formally announcing the creation of SWAN.

Since 2006, SWAN has grown, and the annual conference regularly brings over 300 delegates to debate issues affecting social work, social care and the welfare state. There are now local and regional groups across the country, in Glasgow and Edinburgh, Yorkshire and Lancashire, Birmingham, London, Bristol and Wales. SWAN organised three successful campaigning conferences around the attack on social work in the aftermath of the death of 'Baby P', as well as a large conference to mark the 35th anniversary of the Bailey and Brake book.

As well as organising conferences, SWAN is also an 'action network'. In the aftermath of the death of 'Baby P', when social workers found themselves under attack in the national media, it was SWAN that established a 'counter petition' and organised meetings in defence of the workers involved (www.socialworkfuture.org). In the aftermath of the Israeli attack on the Gaza Freedom Flotilla in 2010, it was SWAN that organised a pro-Palestinian meeting at the International Federation of Social Work/International Association of Schools of Social Work conference in Hong Kong, and moved and passed a motion at the IASSW congress expressing solidarity with the Palestinian people (www.iassw-aiets.org). On a day-to-day basis SWAN works closely with Unison, is an affiliate of Unite Against Fascism and the national Right to Work Campaign, and has been involved in various campaigns in defence of asylum seekers (Glasgow, Manchester and London). It has also campaigned against fascists working in local social service agencies (Bristol and the South West), and in support of striking social workers (Liverpool), striking care workers (Wigan), and victimised social work trade unionists (South Yorkshire). SWAN also has a developing network of international supporters – including a very strong 'chapter' in Hong Kong!

SWAN is a developing organisation. Its aim is to challenge the impact of cuts and neoliberalism on social work, social care and the welfare state. It is committed to anti-racist and anti-oppressive practice, to service user engagement and involvement, to strong links with relevant trade unions, and to participation in all those movements which hold within them a glimpse of a better future and a more humane world. SWAN is attempting to rethink the radical social work project for the 21st century; this book is a small contribution to the project.

ONE

Case Con **and radical social work in the 1970s: the impatient revolutionaries**

Jeremy Weinstein

Introduction

As I start writing this chapter I have in front of me a copy of Bailey and Brake's *Radical social work* (a deceptively slim and succinct book, published in 1975), and also a pile of rather frayed copies of *Case Con*, 'the revolutionary magazine for social workers', the first copy of which appeared in 1970, the last in 1977. Both the book and the magazines shared a social and historical moment and were engaged in the same struggles but they stepped on the stage at slightly different times and played somewhat different roles: *Case Con* with all the energy of the beginning of the decade, *Radical social work,* published and coming to prominence, perhaps, just as the mood was beginning to shift, presaging the triumph of Thatcherism from whose dark shadow we are seeking still to distance ourselves.

The prime purpose of this chapter, then, is to explore the experience of *Case Con*, both as the quarterly magazine and as an aspiring organisation of radical social workers, and to proceed to see how this complemented and/or competed with the Bailey and Brake book in the development of radical social work in the 1970s.

Philip Larkin famously observed that 'Sexual intercourse began/In nineteen-sixty three' (1988, p 167) and similarly for the radicals of the late 1960s and early 1970s there was an arrogant assumption that the revolution in social work started with us. But, as Ferguson and Lavalette have pointed out, there was 'a radical kernel' (2007, pp 11–31) within social work from its very beginnings: in the Settlement movement of the Victorian period and within the work of the pioneers of the labour, feminist and socialist movements. Sylvia Pankhurst took the experience she gained from the suffragette movement into her anti-First World War agitation which included practical support in terms of providing food and milk distribution to the women and children in the working-class communities in the East End of London (Davis, 1999). George Lansbury, also in the East End, held a similar balance, working with the individuals ground down by poverty with organised opposition to the Poor Law, a fight he took to its logical conclusion when, as leader of Poplar Council, he was imprisoned rather than implement policies he found unjust (Lavalette, 2006b). Clement Atlee is best known as the Labour Prime Minister who introduced the welfare state. It is interesting that one chapter in his autobiography is entitled 'Social work and politics' in which he talks about organising soup kitchens for striking dockers and their families and campaigning against the Poor Law (Ferguson and Lavalette, 2007). All these individuals managed the tension of combining advocacy and support for individuals within the system as it was alongside collective action against the abuses of that same system.

Having given all due honour to these pioneers it has to be acknowledged that in the subsequent period social work as a profession busied itself with more prosaic affairs. As the welfare state took hold in the 1950s/early 1960s the prevailing ideology was that, in the words of the Conservative Prime Minister, Macmillan, 'we'd never had it so good'. All the major political parties found themselves agreeing that the welfare state was working so, if poverty was disappearing, then social problems had to be the result of dysfunctional problem families or individual pathology. In such circumstances it seemed common sense to see, as one influential writer put it, that the social worker was 'post political man' and we were engaged in constructing our own professional domains as children's officers or psychiatric social workers, etc. (Halmos, 1978). The very success of the profession, however, also showed up its flaws and pretensions.

Initially the Seebohm Report (1968) was seen as a great triumph for the developing profession: it recommended that all the different fragments of social work, the children's officers, the psychiatric social workers and the welfare department, be brought together into one organisation built on the promise of politically powerful, preventative and community-based services. The excitement and optimism was reflected at the 1972 British Association of Social Workers conference when Barbara Castle, a minister and then a radical icon of the Labour Left, declared: 'If you will build a new Jerusalem we will give you the bricks' and got a standing ovation (Simpkin, 1979, p 14); while Chris Jones (in this volume) remembers the relief and excitement that came with the government decision that this work was explicitly the role of social workers rather than being subsumed within the health sector.

With this reorganisation came growth and the demand for new recruits, many of whom were graduates who had been part of the '68 student rebellions. One social services director, later embroiled in the 1979 social workers' strikes, claimed that revolutionaries had infiltrated social work to act as sleepers, emerging when the time was ripe for revolution (Smart, reported in Crine (1979). In truth the new recruits were well-meaning idealists, 'runaways from commercialism' (Pearson, 1975b, p 139) and many stayed liberals while others were radicalised by our disheartening experiences and this brought us into the orbit of *Case Con* which could articulate our anger. Thus the cover cartoon of *Case Con* (Autumn 1973): a hopeful and smartly turned out young man stands before a grand front door with a welcome mat, potted plants and a big bold sign reading 'COME AND JOIN US, NEW POST-SEEBOHM GENERIC AREA BASED MANAGEMENT ORIENTED SOCIAL SERVICES'. But the front door is just a front, propped up by a single post and behind it is a little hut labelled 'temporary office' with workers despairing among unanswered telephones and piles of papers.

Indeed, the paint was hardly dry on the new offices when social workers faced the first of the notorious child abuse inquiries, Maria Colwell, and the witch-hunting press headlines. We were unprepared and deskilled in the face of the mounting expectations of the public and other professionals. Going into the community raised issues that were beyond the remit of social workers: bad housing, alienating schools, hostile police, unemployment.

Meanwhile, in the wider world, the complacent belief in increasing prosperity was giving way to economic crisis and the response was a fighting labour movement with ship yards occupied to stop closures, successful miners' strikes and the freeing of the Pentonville dockers (see Harman, 1988). This spirit was echoed in the communities with claimants' unions, squatters' groups, tenants' associations, anti-psychiatry groups, and the burgeoning women's movement. At that time there was the powerful Black Power slogan, 'if you're not part of the solution, you're part of the problem' and we were part of the problem if we expected clients to fit into the system rather than changing the system to meet client needs.

So *Case Con* burst into this conflicted and confusing world. The name itself was a provocation and a criticism, it played on the term 'case conference', the 'con' of groups of concerned professionals sitting around a table and reducing structural problems to individual 'cases', a form of victim blaming.

Figure 1: Area-based management

'Professionalism' was identified here as a major enemy, not only putting barriers between social workers who had been on training courses and those who had not, but between all workers and their clients when, in fact, we shared the same struggles. This was captured in the cartoon on the cover of the women's issue (Spring 1974), that shows a block of flats named 'SELF CONTAINED CAPITALIST DEVELOPMENTS UNLIMITED' and with, in each flat, a lone woman struggling with children and domestic duties and asking herself 'why can't I cope like the others do?' In the corner of the cartoon is a little social services office with a woman slumped in front of her desk – with again the unanswered phone and the pile of papers – and also asking 'why can't I cope?'

Figure 2: Women's issue. Each caption reads *What's wrong with me? Why can't I cope?*

'Professionalism' meant careerism and social control of both clients and fellow workers, again represented in a cover cartoon from April 1973 which has the caption 'THE MANAGEMENT OF NEED, OR ONE DAY YOU'LL BE IN MY PLACE'. There is a flight of stairs, at the top is an authoritative-looking man giving instructions to the next in line, this second man has one face smiling up in an ingratiating way and the other passing on the instructions to the person below him and so it goes through the tiers of management, down to the social worker who admonishes the client who then turns on her toddler child.

So what we needed to do was to reject authority and find instead new ways of living and relating, both personally and professionally. In this context it is interesting that Roy Bailey (Foreword, this volume)

Figure 3: The management of need

explains that part of the inspiration for starting on the *Radical social work* text came from overhearing social work lecturers fielding the critical questions from students by accusing them of having an 'authority problem'.

Subsequently *Case Con* covered the stories of several social workers who faced losing their jobs because they challenged, in various ways, the better judgement of their managers. One of the more persistent cases was that of Myra Garrett, a prominent member of *Case Con*, and she expressed this very well when she wrote 'I believe that as social workers our experiences with authority are reflected in our dealings with clients. Each instance of deference without principle to higher authority, or avoidance of conflict for personal gain, corrupts us and increases the likelihood of our demanding the same from our clients' (Garrett, 1973, pp 5–6).

While we could all come together in defence of Myra, this did raise a wider question about the exact relationship between social workers and clients and the resulting discussions revealed the various strands within this developing radical body. For libertarians, many clients were seen as positively deviant, a countercultural revolutionary vanguard, with the potential to turn the values of society upsidedown. For those more influenced by Marxism, the people we worked with were certainly oppressed, 'not clients but workers' as Simpkin put it (1979, p 450), and there was the potential for their consciousness to be raised through struggle. Nonetheless there was some caution around the idea that you could be a 'revolutionary social worker'. Thus, on the cover cartoon for *Case Con* (Spring, 2005) entitled 'ON THE JOB – WHAT'S THE DIFFERENCE?' the cartoon shows two social workers, one denim clad, bearded and with pamphlets by Marx and Trotsky in the back pocket, the other is suited and bespectacled, with a shoulder bag overflowing with magazines from the Tavistock and one entitled *Social work yesterday*. Between them is a young man who declares 'I don't care which of you puts me away.' In the corner is the statement, 'Go direct to children's home, do not pass "go", do not collect £200.'

What seemed more immediate, irrespective of what was happening with clients, was that all social workers confronted the everyday experience of their workplaces. *Case Con* dubbed the new generic area offices 'Seebohm factories', a peculiarly powerful piece of political shorthand, if they were factories then we needed to work within them as workers, as trade unionists. The director and area officer were not colleagues, all part of 'one big team', but straightforward bosses. It also meant that we could work within unions, already existing structures, and did not have to forge new organisational frameworks to link up with clients' needs and problems.

In reality the doctrinal differences between the libertarians and the Marxists tended to be perhaps more important to those most centrally involved in *Case Con*, on the editorial collective or attending the

Figure 4: What's the difference?

conferences, than to the wider audience, those social workers who identified with a more general anti-authoritarian mischief making and bought the occasional magazine to enjoy the bravado of the comic covers or browse the articles. Certainly the content of the magazines was very broad.

Taking one copy at random, number 14, Winter, 1974, there are reports about social work students, one individual is being victimised by his university and there are more general concerns about availability of student funding. There are announcements about groups in the wider movement, for example, At Ease, an advisory service for disaffected soldiers and a journal for Marxists in medicine. An article covers the launching of a rank-and-file trade unionists' conference and there are reports about protests, one in Brixton by the claimants' union, another is an occupation of an electricity showroom after squatters had had their supplies cut off and there is a major occupation of the empty monster office block in London, Centre Point. The housing theme is continued in an article about the Tower Hill rent strike in Liverpool. Main articles urge social workers to challenge their practice when caught up in the racism of the immigration laws and another about our work with gypsies. A column, clearly modelled on Private Eye's 'Pseuds corner', is called 'Professionals' corner' and cherry picks articles from *Social Work Today*, the journal of the British Association of Social Workers (BASW), to illustrate their pretentiousness. A fuller article comes from a new *Case Con* sub group, 'on the job', and addresses the dilemmas of isolated activists, with a struggling union branch and no tenants' associations, etc. to relate to. They sell *Case Con*, become identified as the office 'pet red' 'but when it comes down to their actual work with individual clients act, and are seen to act, little differently from the most traditional of their colleagues'. Focusing on *Case Con* as an organisation there is a report back from the most recent national conference and the naming of nine regional organisers spread across the country and there is a wish for greater involvement by readers although this comes with a rather bad-humoured comment. The fact that the magazine is four pages shorter than normal 'reflects a lack of responsibility on your (the reader's) part in not writing articles appropriate for inclusion'.

Subsequent issues, as decided at a national conference, took up specific themes. The first was focused on women's issues (Spring 1974), then children (Summer 1974), training (Autumn 1974), gays (January 1975), community work (September 1975) and residential work (January 1976). Interestingly there was no specific issue about 'race' and social work.

So we can see that the magazines reflected a potent mixture of theory and activism. A fairly continuous theme is homelessness with squatters supported when they resisted the bailiffs and on occasions families were sheltered in social work offices to prevent their children being received into care. Memos were leaked when councils threatened cuts of funding to 'difficult' voluntary groups or told us not to refer to a women's refuge because they squatted clients.

On the ground people reacted to circumstances as they arose. Thus as trade unionists we protested against cuts, frozen posts, low pay, poor office accommodation. We argued that we were workers, not martyrs (as the badge declared during the 1983 residential workers' strikes) and that employers should not rely on exploiting the social worker's sense of vocation and fall back on a professional vocabulary that equated a social worker's protest with 'acting out', and a social worker's support for a client's position, as 'collusion'.

If one can risk claiming a general mood, there was a sense of social workers feeling that they could take risks and push boundaries, we were filled with 'revolutionary impatience when we felt that history was breathing down our necks' (a quote from the French Marxist and soixante-neuf revolutionary Daniel Bensaid, cited by Callinicos, 2010b). But if our revolutionary impatience sustained us at the height of the struggle it may also have led to the sudden decision in 1977, after 25 issues, that *Case Con* would dissolve itself and become, instead, a new magazine, *Public Con*. The aim was to launch a wider magazine, moving from trying to build, as it were, socialism in one industry to the wider world of public services. But the magazine never appeared. So *Case Con* had no presence in the social work strikes for more pay in 1978/79 or the subsequent residential workers' strikes of 1983.

Before rushing too far forward in the story of 'what happened next', however, we need to explore the symbiotic relationship between *Case Con* and the book *Radical social work*, for it was the spirit that *Case Con* generated which allowed *Radical social work* to find an audience and without *Radical social work*, and some of the texts that followed it, the ideas that helped shape *Case Con* could not have endured.

Both the magazine and the book had some important similarities. Both used the spirit and experience of the 1960s to shape the same, sharp challenge to the prevailing ideology of social work. Both were explicitly Marxist and *Radical social work* carried, as an appendix, the *Case Con* manifesto with its confidant socialist conclusion:

> Until this society, based on private ownership, profit and the
> needs of a minority ruling class, is replaced by workers' state,

based on the interests of the vast majority of the population, the fundamental causes of social problems will remain. It is therefore our aim to join the struggle for this workers' state. (*Case Con* manifesto, 1975, p 147)

Radical social work's explicit Marxist analysis was further evidenced in Bailey and Brake citing, in their opening chapter, the Communist Manifesto of 1848 and going on to explore the contradictions of social work within the welfare state. They do not shy from the 's' word, arguing that 'a socialist perspective is, for us, the most human approach for social workers' (1975, p 9). There is also the caution or cynicism of approaches presented as 'radical' so that the chapters in *Radical social work* unpicking community work (see Mayo, 1975, pp 129–43) or welfare rights (Cannan, 1975, pp 112–28) would have nods of approval from most *Case Con* readers and supporters.

There are, however, also differences. An obvious one is that *Case Con* was never just a magazine, its aim was to be an organiser with activists writing and selling copies, developing the arguments in the light of their experiences, setting up conferences and local groups, however transitory these often proved to be. This meant that the articles were necessarily brief, written by social work practitioners, 'rank and file workers' to use the terminology of the period, and I cannot remember any involvement of academics in the writing of the magazine or at the conferences. In *Radical social work,* of the nine contributors, six are listed as senior lecturers or professors and while there is always an important place for intellectuals in working-class movements, this does seem a significant shift in emphasis from activism to academia. At the very least it meant that the arguments take on a more lasting feel, both because they are between hard covers, and as chapters they are longer, more theoretically developed. And, distanced from the immediate struggle which, in any case, is fading in its promise as the decade moves towards its end, there is also a change of tone, for where *Case Con* is scathing about social work *Radical social work* presents a more considered role.

Thus Pearson's reference to how, when we chose/choose social work as a profession, it is a statement about 'commitment… curiosity … compassion' (1975a, p 20) and 'collectivity' (1975, p 44) and he describes what we find, having qualified, smacking of 'the grief of failed hope' and 'bad promises' (1975, pp 33–4). These words, as sharp as any of the *Case Con* cartoons, resonate down the years into the cry of the SWAN manifesto, 'We didn't come into social work for this.' And while *Case Con* tended to highlight the high peaks of collective action, the strength of the book lies in the authors' reflection on the daily mood of social workers, the detail of 'how misunderstanding occurs' (Rees, 1975, pp 62–75) and the sorts of acts of individual rebellion, of professional sabotage and middle-class banditry (Pearson, 1975a, pp 13–45). The book is also clear that casework is not always 'a con', social work skills can be a part of the process of building up self-esteem so that we can then have the strength to understand our alienation in terms of our oppression (Bailey and Brake, 1975, p 9) or Friere's 'group conscientization' (Leonard, 1975, pp 46–61). This is summed up in the important statement: 'Our aim is not, for example, to eliminate casework, but to eliminate casework that supports ruling-class hegemony. To counteract the effects of oppression, the social worker needs to innovate a dual process, assisting people to understand their alienation in terms of their oppression, and building up their self-esteem' (Bailey and Brake, 1975, p 9).

In Cohen's article, he includes in his 'manifesto for action', the case for 'the unfinished' intended to keep 'open the relation between revolution and reform' and based 'on what does not yet exist' (1975, p 92).

This demands a level of ambiguity which would have been beyond most *Case Con* activists and provides a fascinating read now as we, with the wisdom of retrospection, know what was happening in the wider world as the 1970s came to their end. The failures of the anti-cuts campaigns, following the Labour government's acceptance of the punitive terms set by the International Monetary Fund, suggested that this would be a tough time for those working within the social services, and this was reinforced by the protracted, weakly led (at the level of the national leadership) and isolated fieldworkers' strikes of 1978/79. Unfortunately we were just one more example of the industrial disputes that were 'heroic failures', the predominantly Asian women at Grunwicks, the firefighters and, of course, the low pay strikes followed by the election of the Thatcher government in 1979.

Although trade unionism continued around anti-cuts campaigns, the residential workers' strike of 1983 etc. and beyond, these actions were far more defensive and muted. This led to the movement diversifying. One strand was represented by social workers getting more alongside their Labour councils, as professionals developing neighbourhood patch work, as union members developing alternative plans and, then, with the mounting attack from the Conservative government, being seconded by the 'new left' councils to their anti-rate capping units. But by being co-opted in this way many activists lost their separate identity as trade unionists, became distanced from the sense of the inherent conflicts between managers and workers. Many of the strategies for patch work were grandiose and vulnerable to cuts and this initiative became largely discredited. The coming of rate capping, which saw off the various 'socialist republics of....' and the abolition of the GLC, signalled the clear limitations to the potential for radicalism within town halls (Weinstein, 1986).

Identity politics also became prominent as marginalised groups campaigned to join the profession and win it to a new perspective, thus the move into social work by black workers and their largely successful challenge to transracial adoption. Women also developed a more consciously feminist practice. While these initiatives were important in challenging inertia and conservatism, present within both mainstream social work and the radical tradition, identity politics could also lead to an atmosphere of moralising and rivalries between the contested hierarchies of oppression, with individuals feeling either self righteous or guilty. Sivanandan (1990) is eloquent in his analysis of how the mosaic of difference cut across the horizontal of class leading to a fragmentation of the oppressed with white working-class heterosexual males being excluded even when they themselves may have drawn little or no obvious benefits from the system. This was reinforced by the retreat of the Central Council for Education and Training in Social Work when faced with the accusation of 'political correctness', and surrendering the concept of 'institutional racism' (Penketh, 2000, p 19). The emphasis on improved practice for clients began to give way to concerns for equal opportunities for staff and the horizons of social work narrowed.

This conservatism and caution was not the whole story of course, a significant exception being the events that unfolded, in Lambeth, around the death in 1984 of Tyra Henry, a 22-month child killed by her father. In the face of an immediate media pack hunt, and demands from the chair of the social services committee, that 'heads will roll', the union did everything it could to prevent the scapegoating of the individual social workers. Action included unanimous votes of no confidence in the director and the entire social services committee, walk-outs, demonstrations and picket lines, all resisting the establishment of a public inquiry until its terms of reference included not just a scrutiny of the professional responsibility of individual social workers but also the wider context, such as the lack of resources. It was a difficult campaign, sustained over a full three years, led by the social services shop stewards committee and having to manage the divisiveness within the union where some black workers accused the union of racism since the chair of social services was a black woman challenging white social workers who had 'let another black child die'. It was, however, ultimately successful. As one commentator angrily acknowledged it had been able to put 'a ring of steel' around the social workers and, for a while at least, subsequent child death inquiries took heart from this example and argued for broader perspectives (Weinstein, 1989). All victories should be remembered and celebrated but this one is especially important given the current period that has seen the sackings of social workers involved in such cases as 'Baby P' and Victoria Climbié.

So, having been brought to the current period, what is the lasting significance of the radical social work of the 1970s? For some, any revisiting of *Case Con* and/or rereading *Radical social work* is the social work equivalent of watching *Life on Mars*, being bemused by the crudities of the 1970s and the certainties and possibilities that we advocated, and seeing how fleeting these actually were. It is important to note, however, the significant victories, times when we punched above our weight. *Case Con* had a part, along with the *Cathy come home* docudrama, in stopping children being taken into care because of homelessness and the sustained campaign against emergency standby duty led to permanent out-of-office-hours teams. At the same time we should neither idealise nor take what was then argued as a template for now. We need to acknowledge the problems even if not going as far as the conservative critics, Brewer and Lait, who sniped that we were 'second-rate graduates in second-rate sociology' who were 'without clearly defined jobs [and] ... not very busy' (1980, p 106). Other voices were rather more sympathetic if still critical and rather patronising in tone, noting that 'the issues were always too big for *Case Con*' (Brown and Hanvey, 1987, p 19) or that radical/Marxist social work could not fulfil 'the apostolistic role for social workers in the task of social transformation' (Yelloly, 1987, p 18).

But of course we knew that. *Case Con* was able to develop as it did because it was part of a lasting wider spirit of the 1960s and the buoyant labour movement of the early and mid-1970s and we could not be immune from the subsequent downturn in the industrial struggles and the onslaught of Thatcherism.

So the radical social work we create today is also part of the social and political context and this is a contradictory world for us. On the one hand the sharp awareness of the wider injustices of society, most obvious in the continuing and growing gaps between the poor and the grossly privileged within the UK and the world as a whole, means that a radical critique of capitalism is perhaps more widespread, even mainstream, than ever it was in the 1970s. The movements linked to the anti-war and anti-racist campaigns and environmentalism have created very many 'impatient revolutionaries'. It should, therefore, make it easy (or easier) to link the call that 'another world is possible' to that of 'another social work is possible'. At the same time it is harder for social workers to find a way of translating that belief into action. The workplace is far more constraining than in the 1970s, with its emphasis on market-driven targets rather than one-to-one, therapeutically driven work with individuals. If one does want to challenge policies or practice this is hard when trade union structures are weaker and the employment of agency staff encourages a sense that if you do not like where you are working you simply change jobs rather than staying put and organising for change. On the other hand we now have, for the first time for generations, an organisation in SWAN that provides a voice for discontent and challenge that is more sophisticated than *Case Con*. Where there was an indiscriminate labelling of 'professionalism' we can now distinguish this from 'managerialism' and 'neoliberalism'. This means that we do not need to reject the potential of our work, not seeing much need for social work in the socialist future for which we were fighting, but rather join SWAN in the claim that ours is 'a profession worth fighting for'. Where in *Case Con* the major theories that we tended to be committed to came from Marx, Lenin and Trotsky, and we had to wait for the *Radical social work* text to bend the stick here, we are now better able to be socialists and to value the interventions we might make. We may have some reservations with Thompson's argument that the original radical critique has become the 'essential building blocks' (2006, p 7) for mainstream current practice but there is some truth here. Anti-discriminatory/anti-oppressive practice, recognising the sociopolitical content of a client's life, working with service user groups, the expectation that we empower the people with whom we work: all resonate with the original critique even if it may have lost some edge in the translation. Where once we had a voice that seemed to be predominantly, in *Case Con*, that of basic grade social workers or, in *Radical social work*, of academics, SWAN provides a space available to both, alongside the involvement of service users. And, perhaps, most of all SWAN has the potential to move far more quickly than in the past, thus with 'Baby P' the website allowed for the distribution of a petition, then the development of an on-line discussion which in turn led to the publication of a pamphlet (Ferguson and Lavalette, 2009).

What I still value about *Case Con* was its ability to join humour with passion with sharp argument and which was linked to an organisation which allowed us to learn from each other, that offered solidarity to counter the isolation of difficult times. We needed that then, we need it now and we are in the process of building this in SWAN.

TWO

The best and worst of times: reflections on the impact of radicalism on British social work education in the 1970s

Chris Jones

Introduction

The 1970s was an extraordinary decade for British social work with repercussions that have decisively influenced its subsequent development. The decade opened with social work being rewarded with its own state agency, with social work and no longer medicine as the lead profession. It ended with a nationwide strike of social workers in targeted areas of the country. It was a decade of unbelievable optimism for social work, but also the stuff of nightmares. At the beginning of the 1960s, New York social workers remarked on the hats and gloves worn by their visiting social work students from the LSE, all of whom were women and thought further noteworthy because they bought their own silver tea set with them on the liner from Britain. By the end of the 1970s the tabloids caricatured social workers as long haired, bearded Marxists or dungaree-wearing lesbians!

To explain these extraordinary developments it is necessary to recall the turmoil of this decade. The 'people' were active both in Britain, continental Europe and the US, some, such as students, more so than others. Fundamental questions stretching from foreign policy (especially Vietnam and then Chile and South Africa) to gender, 'race' and sexuality were being asked and leading to new mobilisations and awareness. Trade unions such as the National Union of Mineworkers demonstrated how organised militancy could bring down a government (the Heath government of 1970–74). The people were not only active but they were confident. Social work was not immune from these convulsions of protest and questions whether it concerned the oppression of women, blacks, workers, or gays and lesbians.

The British welfare state that had enjoyed a period of unparallelled growth since 1948 became a significant site of action. By the 1970s it provided employment for thousands of new graduates emerging from an expanded higher education system following the creation of the polytechnics. State social work was a case in point with the creation of local authority social services departments which demanded thousands of new workers. In the nine years between 1967 and 1976 the number of social workers employed in local authority social services grew from 6,063 to 16,523 (HMSO, 1972/76). Among the new recruits and entrants into social work, as well as those employed in nursing, teaching and community health services, were many who engaged with and were affected by the wider political context of protest and questioning. It was a potent source of radicalism and informed the emergence of rich and often cross cutting networks of radical teachers, nurses, doctors, dentists, probation workers, architects, midwives and social workers (see London–Edinburgh Weekend Return Group, 1979).

For social work education, the expansion of state work with its resultant demand for more professional courses (met mainly by the polytechnics) seemed to offer a wonderful future. With the acceptance of the Seebohm Report as the basis for a unified social service in England and Wales (and Kilbrandon for Scotland), coupled with the passing of the 1969 Children and Young Persons Act, it appeared as though professional social work had at last arrived and its future and worth acknowledged and secured. Courses could be expanded and created, and with the provision of local authority funding for students guaranteed, a major hurdle to recruitment had been overcome. Funding for students with a virtual guarantee of a reasonably paid job on completion made social work an attractive proposition. This was certainly the case for me and my fellow students when, in 1972, we opted to do social work as part of a four-year degree in social sciences.

Nevertheless, it was not an entirely straightforward decision especially if you were on the political left. Many of our social science tutors and comrades were surprised and critical of our decision on the grounds that social work was no place for left-wing students. For them social work epitomised reformism and conservatism and in the words of one 'was more suited to middle-class girls from the home counties' than for socialists. Moreover, as we were told and came to see for ourselves, state social work was not only one of the most class specific of the state's welfare agencies, but had never enjoyed any degree of popularity among the working-class poor who constituted its primary client base. One will search in vain, at least in Britain, to find any popular working-class demand for more social work or social workers. But we were not dissuaded and many of us saw social work as providing a job where we might be able to use our degree and felt that there was room within the social democratic welfare state to act in ways which could both expose the cruelties of contemporary capitalism as well as improving the position of our clients.

Social Work Education in the Early 1970s

As we and many other radical students were to discover, social work courses were peculiarly vulnerable to the influx of the 'new' students and many were ill-prepared for the subsequent onslaught. A number of factors played a part, one of which was its intellectual feebleness. Even by 1970, social work was viewed by much of the social science and wider academic community as hardly worthy of a presence in a university. It was seen as primarily low level vocational training better suited to colleges of further education among the plumbers and hairdressers. In the then university sector social work was not universally available and where it was offered it was often through extramural departments which rarely had much contact with the 'proper' social science disciplines and departments. Between 1974 and 1978 I visited a number of long-standing university social work departments which were isolated and tucked away in portacabins or, in one case, above a shop, all physically isolated from the rest of the university. Such environments not only isolated social work academics but led to rather introverted staff groups who cherished their professional identity hence closing them off further.

Neither were the professional courses helped by their reliance on non-professional social science colleagues to teach units in social policy, sociology and psychology. Such teaching was often unpopular among these social science academics. Many social science departments, especially in the polytechnic sector were expanding their undergraduate provision and saw 'service' teaching on social work courses as diverting them from their principal objectives. More troubling for the social work professional tutors, however, was the impact of countless new radical currents on the main social science disciplines from the mid-1960s onwards: currents that came to be felt in all the main disciplines which underpinned social work education including psychology, sociology and social policy. Hence through the late 1960s and early 1970s, some of the 'service' teachers began to introduce more critical and challenging course content – about the nature of poverty, class inequalities, gender and 'race' oppressions, deviancy, feminism, radical psychology, and so on – which were increasingly in tension with the professional elements of the social work programme.

The influx of a different type of student combined with the increasingly critical and challenging content of some of the social science input on professional courses were significant drivers of the radicalisation of some social work courses during the 1970s. Social work teachers were also having to confront increasing numbers of graduate students who in their first degrees in social science were both familiar with and thirsty for the new critical currents in social science, including psychology, and were impatient and intolerant of much of the professional content of their courses. I remember all too well how outraged we were as social work students to hear our professional lecturers promulgate views of poverty as though they were manifestations of pathological personalities and inadequate mothering; of how the well-functioning family with the mother at the hearth was the ideal and how clients were both devious and childlike. It really was so much stuff and nonsense and a million light years away from what we were discovering about class inequalities and the reproduction of poverty and disadvantage under capitalism.

We enjoyed taking on social work and it inspired us to read widely and deeply well beyond the confines of our social work reading lists which never included Marcuse, Althusser or Marx. I have to be careful not to exaggerate here, but my memories of that time included a thirst to learn about the characteristics and dynamics of British capitalism, the role of the state and the manner in which it was sustained. We believed that knowledge was power which provided us with powerful weapons in our battles with social work tutors. This proved to be the case in many instances as our social work tutors were often woefully informed.

I became especially interested in the history of British social work only to discover that the few histories which did exist were simplistic and naïve. They were accounts of an honorable occupation driven by concern and love for the poor highlighted in the lives of selected heroines and heroes from Octavia Hill to Eileen Younghusband. They made no sense and seemed outlandish in comparison to the historiography of E. P. Thompson and Eric Hobsbawm among others. At the time social work history provided a classic example of the Whiggish view of history with the social services departments of the 1970s being seen as the latest marker on a road of evolutionary progress from the time of the monasteries in medieval Britain! There was nothing comparable to Stedman Jones' book (1971) which located the emergence of modern social work with the formation of the Charity Organisation Society in London in 1869 as one fragment of the ruling class's reaction to the threat of urban squalor and poverty; a reaction moreover that was vociferous in its opposition to state welfare intervention and developed its casework methods in the belief that destitution was the consequence of individual moral weakness.

These failings were not only confined to its professional histories but were evident in every aspect of the professional social work curriculum from social work methods, social work theory, values and so on. There were at that time no great struggles over finding placements and nor were students at all confident in challenging the perspectives of practice teachers who exercised considerable power over them: the students depended on their teacher's positive report in order to qualify. This is not to say that practice was immune from the various strands of radicalism impacting on social work education. Indeed such were the tensions that the Council for Training in Social Work (CTSW) (the validating body prior to the Central Council for Education and Training in Social Work (CCETSW)) published a discussion paper in 1971 for practice teachers which warned them of the challenges they were now likely to face from students and advising them how to respond. In true social work fashion it advises practice teachers to treat radical students as though they were turbulent adolescents:

> [S]tudents on most courses nowadays are familiar with new concepts about conflict and consensus, and some see conflict rather than co-operation as the only solution to certain social problems. This viewpoint may well be having a considerable and unexpected impact in some agencies. Teaching on organisations theory may also impose further strain on some fieldwork teachers, agencies and students. Close links and full exchange of information between tutors and fieldwork teachers are essential if possible clashes between agencies and students are to be anticipated. This is different from conflicts which are inherent in social situations, in departments, in the authority of fieldwork teachers and attitudes towards social action. All the foregoing pose fresh problems about students' obligations to adhere to agency policies, especially in the early days of a placement when they may not always see what is constructive in a given agency. It is vitally important that student's educational experience should engage their enthusiasm for social reform and social action, and help them to understand better the range of social problems and the complexities of reform. They should be given opportunities to express, examine and analyze their criticisms of social workers and social agencies. They also need help in seeing their tendency to stereotype,

> in analysing their own professional roles and in coming to terms with acting as representatives of the agency 'warts and all' in which they are working. (CTSW, 1971, p 19)

Without doubt the placement was a trump card in the hands of the course teachers and where their power was strongest. To fail a placement meant to fail the course. But unlike the academic requirements the criteria for success was largely subjective and based on the practice teacher's assessment as to suitability and competence (Michael, 1976). As a student the lack of clear criteria meant that you could never be sure of the outcome and in the end it seemed to depend largely on whether you pleased your practice teacher. Of course, there were practice teachers who were also active in progressive campaigns and issues and supported their students to ask critical questions of agencies and to work in new ways with clients which were not predicated on the assumption that they were deficient and inadequate. But there were many more who were not sympathetic and took offence at what they saw as the arrogance of the students and the manner in which we trashed and challenged their practice-based authority. As far as many of these were concerned, students were coming out of the universities and polytechnics with their heads in the clouds and needed reining in. Tensions between practice and 'theory' have a very long history in social work education and continue to play out today, but in these years it was especially acute. I sometimes wonder if the aggressive anti-intellectualism I used to encounter among too many local authority training officers has its foundations in these years.

In the academic settings however, social work tutors in courses across the land were on the defensive. The so-called knowledge base of social work was revealed to be little more than an eclectic mixture of any social science which supported British social work's long-established conservative perspective. Brian Heraud for example had pointed out the ways in which social work courses in the early 1960s prior to the radical upsurge drew on sociology which 'is mainly concerned with questions about family life and that this is the main reason for having sociology in the course' and that there was 'a lack of concern with the whole field of social control' and its overall 'perspective was eclectic and functionalist' (1967, pp 14–16). Similarly the influential educationalist Brian Simon said in a lecture to social work teachers, that while he did not dispute their attempt to synthesise the various approaches to understanding people and society he was critical of what he saw as their attempt to 'integrate mutually exclusive theories' which 'emulsified' differences and led to superficial eclecticism (1967, pp 16–17). Indeed, superficial eclecticism seems a highly apt description for much of social work theory both then and now!

Freudian psychology in particular was plundered to support social work's insistence on the primacy of personality and family in terms of successful socialisation and for 30 years or more had come to dominate social work methods and knowledge. NeoFreudians such as Bowlby with his maternal deprivation thesis had iconic status for social work. There can be little doubt that it was psychoanalysis which gave social work both here and across the world its scientific patina and vocabulary so critical to its claim for professional recognition. But here again, social work was selective, choosing to emphasise only those elements of Freudianism which supported its underpinning conservatism, neglecting entirely works such as *Eros and civilisation* in which Freud drew attention to how toxic social and political environments can distort human development. And the highly influential (at the time) works of Fromm and Marcuse which sought to take forward the living theories of both Marx and Freud were notable by their absence from the reading lists of all but a few social work courses.

The problems confronting the social work academy were also compounded by social work itself becoming an area for critical social science commentary. Social scientists associated with the Fabian Society such as Peter Townsend and Adrian Sinfield led the way with their withering critique of the 1968 Seebohm Report and its proposals for a unified family-based social work service. They saw the Report as little more than a victory for the social work profession with little hope that it would be beneficial to clients. From the National Deviancy Conference (including many of the contributors to Bailey and Brake, 1975) social work was critiqued for its capacity to aid in deviancy amplification and its clearly paradoxical position as a state strategy that combined both care and control. Then there was Handler's (1968) widely read article from *New Society* which revealed the coercive and bullying character of childcare social work. And so it went on.

These attacks coming from a range of sources and disciplines overwhelmed many social work courses and their professional teachers. So much of its acclaimed knowledge base was so crudely constructed that it collapsed like a house of cards in the face of sustained intellectual challenge. Their cause was not helped in that many of the professional social work lecturers obtained their position in the academy by dint of their practice experience rather than because of their intellectual prowess. If there was any intellectual strength at all, it was clustered in only one or two places, such as the LSE and Manchester University, where there was a deep-rooted attachment to Freudian theory and especially psychiatric social work. By and large the courses most committed to psychotherapeutic approaches tended to resist more strongly the challenges from the students and those who queried its legitimacy.

Elsewhere the wider use of hack psychotherapy as a means of defusing the challenges backfired badly. Those of us who persistently challenged the prevailing social work orthodoxies were commonly told that we were 'immature' and that our concerns were in fact 'presenting problems' that masked our (largely unconscious) anxieties about confronting the inner realities of both clients and social work itself. In other words they tried to 'casework' us. I suspect that the social work students at Sussex spoke for many when they wrote to *Social Work Today*:

> The ideology of the Sussex course emphasised the importance of the students' autonomy and responsibility to develop their own approach to social work and appeared to offer a democratic structure in which this could happen. Over time we found that this model of democracy was severely restricted by a rigid power structure which allowed only as much student self-determination as was approved by the tutors. As soon as we attempted to go beyond the limits of this structure our actions were interpreted in terms of our individual pathology. Far from helping us to develop, this merely made us feel impotent and intensely frustrated. (Letters, *Social Work Today*, 15 February 1977)

That this was also how they expected us to work with clients made it all the more derisory. Their refusal to take us seriously and their attempts to undermine us individually simply enraged us and encouraged many of us to sharpen our critiques further. Moreover it revealed one of the fundamental divides between all the various radical currents and the social work establishment. For us one of the defining aspects of our radicalism was our solidarity with clients in particular and the oppressed in general. Whereas when it came to clients all we heard from the social work profession was difference, pathology and inadequacy.

The impact of these various radical streams on social work education and courses during the 1970s elicited responses at both the local and national level. As a student, it was the local which preoccupied us with a wide range of demands concerning course content, assessment and selection. This was the time when social work courses had a great deal of autonomy to determine their programmes. The new validating body, CCETSW, was nothing like as intrusive as its successors became and in its *Guidelines to social work training rules*, published in May 1976, it claimed to be concerned only with setting broad parameters for the content of courses and it was up to the educational institutions to work out the curriculum. Employers had no formal role and were confined to allowing their staff to take part in selection and practice teaching.

A few courses emerged, notably at Bradford and Warwick universities, and the Polytechnic of North London, which embraced rather than rejected the demands for a more critically informed social work education. Many of the teachers on these exciting courses became influential in shaping what became known as radical social work, notably Peter Leonard and Paul Corrigan at Warwick, Hilary Rose, Geoff Pearson and Jim Kincaid at Bradford and Elizabeth Wilson and Crescy Cannon at North London. Their writings became invaluable and were widely read and discussed. Few of these came from a social work background. Peter Leonard was the exception at the time, at least in terms of being the only senior figure within social work education to embrace radical social work. It is little different today with the current British social work professoriate demonstrating no vision and more concerned with 'getting by' than being the awkward squad which is demanded given the current depths of poverty and disadvantage.

The few radical courses were at one end of the political spectrum; most fell somewhere in the middle and floundered around in their attempts to pacify our demands. I recall that we stopped the social work tutors on our course from asking applicants to the course whether or not they attended communion regularly! But my overwhelming memory of the time was the sense that the tutors had capitulated. Our social work theory course was rewritten with its pseudo-Freudianism removed from the core to be replaced by what we were told was a 'systems' approach. It was never clear to us whether the tutors understood what they were talking about, but we received it as 'anything goes' – nothing was ruled in nor out. If we wanted to take a community or structuralist approach to any issue this was fine just as a traditional casework approach would be equally appropriate. It was a model that had no intellectual coherence or justification but seemed to serve because it put an end to classroom battles especially over casework. In the meantime, it was from our other courses in the sociology of deviance, sociology of 'race' and social policy that we were gaining our education. It was in these courses where we were able to discuss power and the ways in which professionals manipulated and distorted the lives of their clients. Kincaid (1973) and Coates and Silburn (1970) revealed the intimate connections between capitalism and poverty and pointed to explanations far more convincing than any we could find in Perlman (1957) or Beistek (1957), our standard texts. Laing (1965) and Cooper (1971) turned our so-called psychology inputs on their head and shed light on family dynamics which made a mockery of so many fundamental tenets of social work practice and 'theory'. And threading through it all was a resurgent feminism which carried more in its wake than probably any of the other radical currents, at least with respect to social work.

It was a feminism that was ferocious in its attacks on Bowlby's maternal deprivation thesis and revealed the manner in which mainstream social work was fundamentally sexist in its focus on mothers and blamed working-class mothers in particular for any number of social problems ranging from delinquency to mental illness, unemployment to welfare dependency. It highlighted the interconnectedness of patriarchy and professionalism, especially illustrated by medicine (*Our bodies ourselves*) and noted how social work – despite its association with women – was now being captured, at least in senior positions, by men. And not least, as with so many of the other radical influences, it stood for solidarity with clients and castigated social work for its stance of professional disdain and distance.

It is important to recall that these were dynamic years with a great deal of activity taking place across a broad spectrum of politics. Radicals rarely confined themselves to single issues and could well be involved in a *Case Con* workshop over one weekend and the next week out on picket with the miners. It was also a period when left-wing parties formed and broke apart with some frequency. Consequently the radical streams took many forms and were subject to any number of influences and trends. Moreover, it was not only dynamic but also localised. Social work radicalism in the workplace especially through National and Local Government Officers Association (the then trade union for local authority social workers) was much more likely in the large cities and the well-known examples of the period included Islington, Camden, Birmingham, Manchester and Leeds among others. These were the places that attracted the radical students and practitioners. In many other parts of Britain radical practitioners were often very isolated and had little chance to connect with some of the radical movements and their activities.

The state responds

It is all too easy when writing about past events to impose a sense of order which suggests a coordinated and effective state response when the reality was much more confused, messy and incremental. This was certainly true for social work education in the 1970s. Nevertheless, notwithstanding the variety of responses it is possible to discern some key themes, the most significant being that the state in all its guises and agencies was aghast at the notion of there being a social work profession which included critical, radical and problematic strands. Something had to be done.

Especially pressing was the issue of what kind of social work education was now needed in the changed context of there being large state social work agencies following the Seebohm and Kilbrandon reorganisations. It was a question that increasingly exercised the newly created state social work agencies and was informed by their growing conviction that social work courses were no longer fit for purpose. They were not providing the sort of social workers they wanted. Of course the radical turbulence on many courses was an important factor in this questioning and during the national social workers strike of 1978/79 some directors claimed that radical courses such as the one at Warwick were directly responsible for the militancy of the strike. In a letter to then minister of state responsible for social services, David Ennals, the Tory MP Anthony Steen (more recently famous for his expenses in Totnes!) wrote that one of the main reasons why social workers who are 'dedicated to the deprived have turned against them' [by striking] was due to their 'indoctrination by militant left-wing and Marxist lecturers on training courses' (*Liverpool Echo*, 17 October 1978). And in Birmingham:

> Councillor Banner Adkins, chairman of Birmingham social services committee, would give no details of the blacklist [of radical courses they had compiled] but said that information was being sought in an attempt to connect courses with the recent protests over social services policy in the city. Councillor Adkins was reported in the Birmingham *Evening Mail* as saying, 'I think the universities are very much to blame for all this. We spend about 6,000 pounds to send a social worker for two years training and at some universities they come under political influence. We have known that this goes on at certain universities like Warwick.' (*Social Work Today*, 14 November 1978, p 3)

These comments echoed the widely publicised Gould 'report' of 1977 in which he warned of extensive Marxist penetration of higher education, in particular on social work and teacher training courses. For Gould this was especially worrying as both these areas were responsible for acting on behalf of the state – 'guardians of social trust' – and ensuring the appropriate socialisation of children and clients (Gould, 1977). Both this report and the comments of those who sought to blame left-wing indoctrination for the radicalism and activism of students were highly exaggerated and were more a matter of seeking a convenient scapegoat for the upsurge in radicalism. Nevertheless, true or not, they were influential in framing the agenda that something had to be done about social work education.

Social workers in Camden standing shoulder to shoulder with squatters to prevent their employing authority from demolishing their homes; social workers in Birmingham publicly protesting the closure of children's homes or the proclamations in *Case Con* setting out our solidarity with clients were met with dismay by employers (Jones, 1983, ch 7). Moreover, the courses, which were supposed to help avoid such scenarios, were increasingly seen as complicit or at least ineffective. It was expected that students would receive an education that would legitimise the individualised family pathology approach of social work; learn how the well-functioning heterosexual family with the mother in the central role was the key to successful socialisation and individual realisation (and the converse of the problem family) and so forth. For the agencies, failure to inculcate the right sort of knowledge was further compounded by the courses' failure to ensure that qualifying students were prepared to subordinate their professional aspirations to loyalty to the agency. This became one of the mantras of the agencies, namely that social workers in state agencies were first and foremost officers of local government and as such their first duty was to show undivided loyalty to the local authority. On no account was it permissible for social workers to oppose their agency's policies publicly (see Jones, 1983, pp 120–2 for more details).

In the British context there was the added dimension that professional social work courses had for a long time been entrusted with the job of being the 'essence' of social work – the primary site for the reproduction of the profession and the principal gateway to employment. As I have detailed elsewhere social work education has historically occupied a key place in the development of the profession in Britain and the place where the professional light burns strongest (Jones, 1978). One consequence was that until the 1970s the agencies which employed social workers were largely content to leave responsibility for recruitment and training in the hands of courses and they had virtually no formal role in course design and content. Agencies were expected to play their part in the provision of placements but that was about it, although as noted above this was not without influence as a successful placement was an essential prerequisite to qualification. This was now to change.

The responses to these pressures were varied. Significantly, one of the first moves of CCETSW was to limit the role of the contributing social sciences and the non-professionally qualified social scientists who taught on courses. This was seen to be especially problematic on the four year degree courses where the social science input was significantly greater than on the two year non graduate courses and the one year postgraduate courses. In its second annual report CCETSW noted that agencies were increasingly questioning 'the academic disciplines that the students are being taught or even to suspect that the education they receive makes them difficult employees more concerned to change the "system" than to get on with the job. Clearly social work education must balance these changes' (CCETSW, 1975a, pp 38-9).

Some academic subjects were more of a concern than others. According to Brian Munday:

> Current theories in the sociology of deviance pose the greatest threat of all to social work students, with their clear message that society creates deviants for its own ends and that social workers are part of the system of social control, are used to create and amplify deviance rather than improve the lot of the deviant. The ideas of writers like Matza, Becker and Cicourel are intellectually fascinating and persuasive but quite ominous for social workers. (Munday, 1972, p 4)

Another tutor argued that such teaching was contaminating students and added that such 'undermining of professional commitments of novices in the field parallel[led] those of putting a viper in the cradle of an infant' (Wilson, 1974, p 9), an astonishing claim, but one that was probably felt by many tutors at the time. However, being located in higher education meant that social work had to accept the prevailing conventions of academic freedom and were not able to pick and choose who taught the contributory social science disciplines. What they could do, however, was restrict their role, and increasingly those without professional qualifications were squeezed to the margins. A position endorsed by CCETSW itself when it noted that:

> Staff attached to the course who are not social workers will not be expected to carry out comparable responsibility for the professional development of students, for example, arranging practical work placements, giving guidance to

practical work teachers, tutorial work, visits to placements where there is a special need, undertaking some practice teaching. (CCETSW, 1976, p 19)

From this period onward, and evident in every change that has been made to professional social work education since, we can see that the academic and intellectual content of the courses has been constrained and diluted in favour of content that emphasises the priorities of the agencies. As a former social services director in Liverpool told me and others in a discussion on his agency's expectations of the local courses, he wanted us to produce doers and not thinkers, and doers, moreover, who will do as they are told! Sadly this trend has been supported by much of the social work academy which has been only too pleased to marginalise challenging colleagues and course materials that make a mockery of so much so-called social work theory and methods.

In hindsight however, the most decisive response to the issue of difficult and querulous social workers was the creation of the Certificate in Social Services (CSS) in 1975. Launched as a parallel qualification to the Certificate in Qualified Social Work (CQSW), the CSS was targeted at the large numbers of day and residential social workers who had virtually no training. That it was a separate qualification and not integrated into the CQSW as a specialist route is revealing in that it indicated the lack of trust in higher education to deliver and the difficulties the agencies encountered when seeking changes to the CQSW because of the protections offered by higher education concerning academic autonomy and control.

For the first time a professional route into social work was removed from education and placed in the hands of the big state agencies. Indeed in almost every detail the CSS presaged what was to become of social work education as a whole by the end of the 20th century with employers having a significant role in every aspect of the courses from selection to course content and assessment. The CSS was managed by local consortia with the principal employing agencies taking the lead role and providing the full-time course managers who had considerable power. It also based the first two years in colleges of further education which were much easier to control and influence (than the polytechnics) and with long traditions of providing employer-determined courses. The final year was in higher education but not in the universities but the polytechnics. At that time the universities would not tolerate such an active role for non academic partners in course provision, assessment and delivery and were elitist when it came to so called 'sub-degree' teaching. The polytechnics were far more amenable.

It was also day release, with much of the programme delivered as work-based learning and very much designed around the day-to-day tasks of the agency. This had two major benefits, one being that students on the CSS courses had little exposure to the 'subversive' influences of student culture and activities as they were only in college for one day a week and with a completely full timetable that allowed no time for wider student activities. Second, the agency focus ensured that it was likely that the students would graduate not thinking of themselves as some kind of virtuoso professional with rights to any degree of autonomous practice. And finally, the agencies determined that the social science units and so-called 'difficult' academic components would be squeezed out:

> Although courses leading to the CSS will include the broadly based common unit, teaching will generally be more narrowly focused and more pragmatic than in those leading to the CQSW with their generic base. The former will not include equivalent study in the behavioural sciences and other academic subjects, given the time available and the limited opportunities to engage the services of academic staff from allied disciplines. (CCETSW, March, 1975b, p 18)

The CSS provided the eventual route for employers to gain a significant grip over social work education first by pressing for the CSS to be seen as an equivalent qualification to the CQSW for entry into professionally designated posts and then by amalgamating the two in the later Diploma in Social Work which inherited its structure and principles from the CSS and not the CQSW. That they should have succeeded reflected a seismic shift in British social work by reducing it and even defining it as a creature of the state social work agencies. All the questions about the nature of social work and its role and responsibilities were thereby resolved. With no pretensions to any form of professional independence, social work became that activity undertaken by state social work agencies. No other version mattered.

Previously social work had been fragmented across a variety of state agencies but now with reorganisation and unification the agencies were big and organised sufficiently to exercise their new power. They also had to come to terms with becoming something they had not envisaged. The Seebohm vision of a social work agency focused on preventive work with families with casework as its principal method was never realised and from the very beginning of their existence they functioned more like the 'dustbin' agency of the state's welfare system. It was not a matter of there now being a single phone number or office for the client to use as envisaged by Seebohm, but rather a single agency to which referrals could be made by other front line state agencies who wanted to offload their difficult users – whether long-term social security claimants, those in rent arrears, those with fuel debts, delinquents and the like. It was work which required surveillance and control more than time-consuming and expensive casework. These issues drove many of the changes to social work education with the control of radicalism and professional contamination being only complementary objectives.

There are of course other dimensions to this story which cannot be fully recounted here, including the capitulation of the social work academy to these new directions in British social work practice and education. Much of that particular story, in my opinion, is not honorable and revealed a profound intellectual and political vacuity within its senior ranks. Rather than commit themselves to fighting for a social work that had every right to be challenging and difficult given the extent of poverty and class inequalities which have dogged British society for centuries, it chose the road of servility. They chose not to have a social work that tried to speak truth to power but one that was to serve the powerful through its quiescence. As I came to discover when I eventually moved in these circles, fear was often the main factor which led to the professoriate's complicity in what became known as neoliberalism. To speak out about injustice, about the cruelties of our society were considered as just too dangerous. The agencies, I heard in countless meetings, were now so big and powerful that they would simply move away from higher education altogether and set up their own training courses. That we now have highly state regulated social work education in Britain is not simply a reflection of state power or neoliberalism but of a complicit senior social work academy which all too often was the implementer of reactionary change.

The legacy of this radicalism, however, remains potentially potent if we care to reflect and act on the ways in which it offered another vision for social work to the sterile and oppressive entity it has become today. It was a vision not only grounded in a commitment to social justice but was moving to a social work informed by a far superior understanding of the plight of clients and their continual reproduction under capitalism. It was a social work that was not afraid to learn and to think and saw how rigorous and deep analysis of society and its dynamics could lead to forms of practice which strengthened rather than undermined people. It was a social work based on solidarities and alliances and whatever our naiveties offered as ways of working that were far less likely to stigmatise and harm than is the case today.

Much of this was influenced by the more general radicalism of the late 1960s and 1970s whether feminism, gay liberation, civil rights or militant trade unionism. Without this context it is doubtful that there would have been any significant development of radical social work. It is only to be hoped that the renewed activism of the people which appears to be emerging now, whether it be in respect to climate change, global financial crises, war or anti-capitalism, will similarly provide the much-needed impetus to push forward a vision of social work that is free of the shackles of the past 30 years.

THREE

Social work and women's oppression today

Laura Penketh

Introduction

In the Bailey and Brake collection, there was no specific chapter on women's oppression, but the position of women in society and the ideas and perspectives of the women's movement were embedded within the book and formed a central part of the radical social work revival in the 1970s.

This chapter seeks to explore social work and women's oppression with a focus on gender and class. It will mainly discuss the lives of poorer working-class women who are overrepresented as service users in the social work sector, particularly in relation to childcare and child protection work. In doing so, it will assess the discrimination that women face in the labour market and from the state, and the impact this has on levels of poverty, inequality, health and wellbeing. The chapter will also analyse how welfare developments linked to the marketisation and privatisation of social provision have had a negative impact on the lives of poorer women. Throughout, it will challenge stereotypes of poor women that focus on individualistic and moralistic character deficiencies, and point to the key role of poverty and inequality in shaping their lives. Over the past 10 to 20 years, women and young girls have been subject to increasing levels of sexual objectification, and the chapter will also explore how this has reinforced discrimination within and outside the workplace, as well as having a negative impact on women's self-image and self-worth.

Historical overview

Historically, social work has been underpinned by powerful ideas regarding gender and class which have had an impact on women's role as both social workers and recipients of social care. During the

19th century, middle-class women who were active supporters and agents of philanthropy, intervened in the lives of working-class women, making moral judgements that affected their eligibility for charitable support (Lewis, 1986). Pivotal to this philanthropic activity was the role of working-class women as wives and mothers within the private sphere of the family. In this context, the supposed 'feminine' qualities and domestic management skills of poor women were scrutinised and used as a tool to reform working-class families. In the context of political and familial ideology during this period, women were seen as having a key role in socialising, controlling and re-moralising their dependants to fulfil their future roles as workers within a capitalist economic system (Mooney, 1998).

Political and family ideology established during the 19th century has been remarkably resilient in informing social welfare policies during the twentieth and into the 21st century, and has continued to apply the politics of gender by prescribing the 'natural' role of women as wives and mothers within the nuclear family. For example, during the 1980s the attack on lone parents (usually mothers) was informed by the view that single parent families were damaging for children and costly for the state. These families were socially constructed as living outside of the normative structure of society, and their welfare dependency, analysed from an individualistic and moralistic perspective, was linked to a rise in crime and anti-social behaviour. In contrast, the traditional family was constructed as a pivotal institution that would ensure social order. Public discourse and public policy were informed by naturalistic, essentialist and ahistorical understandings of marriage and the family. Here, an idealised view of marriage obscured the often negative and violent side of the family for women and children, and failed to address issues of dependency and power that disadvantage women both in the home and the workplace (Lentell, 1998).

These themes have resonance in Britain today in relation to arguments regarding 'Broken Britain' that blame marital breakdown and lone parenthood for the rise in antisocial behaviour. The Centre for Social Justice (2008) and Family Law Review (2009) argue that British children and teenagers who live in 'broken communities' lack morality, do not know the difference between right and wrong, and do not adhere to any rules. Political initiatives to deal with the problem involve 'carrot and stick' measures. The 'carrot' is a small tax credit (amounting to no more than a few pounds a week) to encourage marriage, whereas the 'stick' involves developments such as compulsory parenting classes.

Even during the post-war period when more progressive policies were pursued regarding state welfare provision, family policy was underpinned by implicit assumptions of women as carers and nurturers. Although women had been employed in munitions factories and as a land army during the war, when the war was over, state policy encouraged them to leave the workforce and return to the home (Woodward, 2006). The assumption was that in peacetime they would revert to their traditional and 'natural' role within the family. As Beveridge, the architect of the post-war welfare state said, 'In the next 30 years, housewives as mothers have vital work to do in ensuring the continuance of the British race' (Beveridge, 1942, para 117).

It was during the 1960s and into the 1970s that established assumptions and ideas regarding women's role in society began to be challenged. Women's issues achieved prominence as a result of the 'second wave of feminism' and the emergence of the Women's Liberation Movement. Feminists began to locate gender as a structuring principle of social policy and welfare provision, and started to deconstruct categories and concepts linked to women's inequality and oppression. For example, challenges were made to the assumption that it was women's 'natural' role to care for the needs of dependants within families, and the idea of the family as a safe haven was undermined as research began to reveal the alienation and despair that many women experienced within the nuclear family (Oakley, 1974), and the levels of domestic violence they experienced (Woodward, 2006). Women began to fight for control over their fertility and for abortion rights, as well as campaigning for more equal relationships within marriage. They had varying degrees of success in pursuing equality and liberation in these areas, particularly in relation to the legalisation of abortion (Orr, 2007).

There were also campaigns for equal pay, when female workers took industrial action on an unprecedented scale and were supported by key trade unions. This influenced legislative developments and in 1970 the Equal Pay Act was introduced, taking effect in 1975. The legislation was relatively weak in terms of what constituted 'like' work with men, and did not cover women who did not work alongside men. Also, the timescale regarding implementation gave employers years to find ways of evading the recommendations. Nevertheless, it did make a small but significant difference for many women workers. For example, in 1970, women's gross hourly earnings were 63.1% of men's, but by 1975 they were 72.1%, and by 1976, 75.5% (Orr, 2007).

Inequality and oppression in Britain today

As the 20th century progressed, and in the wake of the Women's Movement, it began to be argued that women had overcome inequality and exploitation. This was reflected in figures that showed, for example, how women were outperforming boys in education, could choose whether or not to have children, and could express their own sexuality. Yet, evidence reveals that women's lives are still characterised by inequality and oppression, as well as being subject to increasing levels of subjectification and commodification (Orr, 2007; Cochrane, 2008; Walter, 2010)

In the labour market, full-time female workers are still paid less than half as much as men in some parts of the UK, despite the fact that Britain has had an Equal Pay Act since 1975. On Equal Pay Day (30 October 2009), Woodroffe (2009), revealed that nationally, women earn an average of 17% an hour less than men for full-time work of equivalent value, which rises to 20% for women from minority ethnic backgrounds, and 36% for women who work part time. Britain has now slipped further down the international league table for gender equality and is ranked 15th out of 130 countries in the World Economic Forum's global gender gap index. The situation is worse when considering wage equality, with the UK now 78th in the world behind countries such as Egypt, Malawi and Malaysia (Williams, 2009). Of course, there are women in higher paid professional positions in society, but they often face a 'glass ceiling' as they climb the occupational ladder, and 'top jobs' are still a male preserve in government, parliament, the city and the judiciary. For example, before the general election of May 2010, only 19.3% of women were Members of Parliament, and 96% of executive directors of the UK's top companies were men (Cooke, 2008).

Katherine Rake, Director of Equality at the Fawcett Society, has voiced her fears that long-established rights that had seemed beyond debate are now under threat, and that levels of oppression against women are increasing. For example, in 2008, the Conservative MP Nadine Morris, campaigned to bring the time limit for abortion down from 24 to 20 weeks, and before the 2010 election, 86% of prospective Conservative MPs wanted a lower time limit than 24 weeks (Cochrane, 2008). Rake's concerns are also reflected in recent comments from prominent businessmen. For example, Theo Paphitis who appears on the Dragon's Den, stated that:

> [Women] get themselves bloody pregnant and…they always argue that they will be working until the day before, have the baby, go down to the river, wash it off, give it to the nanny and be back at work the following day. But sure enough, their brains turn to mush, and then after the birth the maternal instincts kick in. They take three months to

get it out of their system and get back to normal (cited in Cochrane, 2008).

Alan Sugar, who was appointed as a government business adviser under New Labour, responded to the fact that it is illegal for women to be asked at interview about their plans to have children, by saying "You're not allowed to ask, so it's easy – just don't employ them." In a survey of employers, 68% agreed with this sentiment (Cochrane, 2008).

While these comments relate to professional women, for working-class/poor women who make up the majority of social work service users, liberation is a more distant goal and oppression a more significant feature of their lives. It is working-class women who bear the brunt of increasing levels of poverty and inequality in society, and who are affected by cut-backs in social security benefits and welfare provision, and among women it is lone mothers and single female pensioners who experience the highest rates of poverty. For example, over half of lone parent households are poor and older single women have a 24% chance of living in poverty. Woodroffe (2009) notes how having children can be the start of a 'great gender divide' in the labour market. For example, just half of mothers with children under five are in paid work compared with nine-tenths of fathers, and interruptions to employment due to caring responsibilities account for 14% of the gender pay gap. This worsens for women from minority ethnic communities.

In relation to social security provision, women are more likely to be dependent on means tested benefits that do not provide an escape from poverty. This is partly the result of a punitive approach to levels of benefits, but also because the tax and benefit system still contains assumptions that reinforce the dependency of women on men. For example, pension entitlement is still based on continuous employment from 16 to 65 years of age, which discriminates against women whose working lives are interrupted as a result of caring responsibilities and changing family structures (Bellamy et al, 2006). However, women in the labour market are also vulnerable to poverty due to their overrepresentation in low-paid jobs, and can be worse off in work when benefits are lost, and the costs of childcare and work-based expenses are considered. In this respect women are often caught in a 'poverty trap' that prevents them from raising their living standards. Women have also been negatively affected by worsening conditions in the labour market which has led to a deterioration in job satisfaction, particularly among women with children. This is the result of longer working hours and a lack of flexibility regarding their caring commitments. Women in Britain now work longer and more unsocial hours, travel longer to get to work and are increasingly subject to electronic supervision in the workplace. Women with young children are the most discriminated against, with thousands losing their jobs each year simply for being pregnant (Equalities Review, 2007).

Maria, a 32-year-old single mother of one discusses her situation, which exposes the impact of workplace bullying and being caught in a 'poverty trap':

> 'They started putting pressure on me at work when I was signed off sick ... I was threatened with disciplinary action ... and felt that I was being bullied. The added stress was affecting my health, and eventually I decided to leave. I lost my entitlement to maternity pay and my salary dropped from £27,000 [per annum] to £5.85 an hour. For the first four weeks after my baby was born, I only ate once a day ... that was all I could afford after paying the bills and buying everything for the baby. I would like to go back to work, but I would lose my benefits and would have to pay for childcare ... so overall I would lose £40 a week. If I went back to temping and the work dried up I would have to wait for weeks to get back on to benefits with no income. It's just not a risk I can afford to take.' (Fawcett Society, 2010)

The negative impact of poverty on the lives of women and their families is also reflected in their access to and experience of services such as health, housing and education. For most children, experiences at school are determined by the level of disadvantage they face, with opportunities narrowing for poorer children who have limited access to out of school activities such as music and art (Horgan, 2007). Inequality in education affects future career opportunities, reflected in figures that demonstrate that 'despite only 7% of children being privately educated, 75% of judges, 70% of finance directors, 45% of top civil servants and 32% of MPs were independently schooled' (Hutton, 2010, p 32).

It is also well established that children in disadvantaged families experience higher rates of mortality and morbidity (Ascheson Report, 1998), and lack access to decent housing (Burrows, 2003). For black families the situation worsens. In terms of childhood poverty, 70% of Bangladeshi/Pakistani children live in poverty which is two and a half times the rate of white children (Penketh, 2006, p 88). This leads to even greater levels of inequality when considering health, housing and educational provision. Disadvantaged families are also overrepresented in the criminal justice system, with the majority of poor women being punished or imprisoned for non-violent offences related to debt and shoplifting. High numbers of these women have experienced domestic violence and sexual abuse and 70% have two or more diagnoses of mental health (Prison Reform Trust, 2009).

Poor mothers have also been demonised by policies that link family breakdown with the overall decline of society, with the concerns of politicians increasing in direct proportion to the poverty of the families involved. The wrath of politicians and the media has been particularly directed at single mothers who have been blamed for societal problems, and punished politically and/or financially for their supposed immoral and inappropriate behaviour. Here, single parenthood is viewed as a lifestyle choice and social problems are blamed on the lack of a father figure in families as well as a supposed lack of discipline.

The lives of working-class women have also been negatively affected by attacks on state welfare provision that have been implemented over the past 30 years. Today, many of the social and welfare functions that might once have been provided by local or national government fall back onto individual family members and the family collectively to provide. As dependants are thrown back onto the resources of the family in order to avoid serious deprivation, it is women who carry out the majority of care, which has an impact on their ability to work, their career progression and their financial security, as well as contributing to poor health and overall wellbeing. Poor people have also borne the brunt of the privatisation and marketisation of public utilities. For example, during the cold winter of 2009/10, there were examples of women having to make a choice between buying food and heating their homes. One woman spoke of burning wooden shelving for heat as she could not afford to pay the gas meter charges (Gentleman, 2009).

Women in poorer families who rely on social security benefits or low wages are also susceptible to debt. Although the debt is often used to purchase consumer goods such as clothing and furniture, it is sometimes accessed to pay for utility bills. Levels of debt are also linked to a relentless consumer culture and the commodification of home life that promotes the acquisition of material goods. Here, the pressure to acquire material goods is intense and fuelled by advertising campaigns and magazine articles. However, you need to be financially secure to buy into a particular image of the family that includes having an attractive home, fashionable clothes, holidays abroad, and affording hobbies and interests for children. For poorer women who do not have access to bank accounts and favourable credit terms, the only way to afford some of these goods is to borrow from lenders who charge exorbitant rates of interest.

The outsourcing of welfare delivery has also had an impact on how poor working-class women are treated by 'privatised' agencies. During 2010, I interviewed a group of women from the Speke area of Liverpool. Speke is one of the poorest areas of the city and is subject to a range of local welfare initiatives around 'inclusion' and health improvement. My aim was to revisit some of the issues addressed in the work of Mayer and Timms (1970) by exploring the perspectives of working-class women linked to their relationship with welfare providers. Although the research is ongoing some of the initial feedback from women was particularly shocking. One woman, who had worked for many years, described her experience of having to 'sign on' for the first time. She recalled her experience in the following way:

> 'When I went into the Job Centre with my baby boy in his pram, I was followed by one of the security guards. As it was the first time I had ever 'signed on', I said to him, "I didn't realise I had to go through all this to claim benefits." He turned round and said, "well, you should have kept your legs shut."'

A second woman told of being referred by her doctor to a local leisure centre for health reasons, so that she could use the gym. She spoke of her dismay and embarrassment when, at the induction session, she was verbally called 'the referral' in front of the group, and directed away from the main gym to a small room containing only a few pieces of equipment. Unsurprisngly, she did not return. These experiences reveal the ways in which working-class women are discriminated against, stigmatised and humiliated within the 'privatised' welfare industry, and how this leads to disengagement with welfare provision.

As well as experiencing a harsh economic and welfare agenda, women are subject to rising levels of sexual objectification, and liberation is increasingly interpreted as the right for their bodies to be sold in lap dancing bars and on the front cover of magazines. This has created an atmosphere where female sexuality is seen as something to be bought and sold, reflected in the fact that the global sex industry is now worth an estimated US$97 billion, and that visits to brothels as part of stag parties are seen as par for the course (Banyard and Lewis, 2009). Katherine Rake believes that:

> What the sex industry has done in the past 10 years ...is repackage itself in a way that seems 'innocent, fun and ironic' – and women can be part of it too, so let's throw in a few pole-dancing lessons ... but you hardly need to scratch its surface to discover the same old exchange. How many people know ... that the women who dance in lap-dancing clubs pay the owner to do so? (cited in Cooke, 2008, p 4)

Women, teenagers and young girls are also faced with increasing pressure regarding their appearance, which is exploited on the high streets in relation to fashion and beauty products. As Natasha Walter states, 'It has become increasingly difficult for young women to opt out of this culture, to take any path other than that which leads inexorably to fake nails, fake tan, and finally fake breasts. And if they do, there are serious penalties' (2010, p 8).

Inequality and oppression: a critical analysis

So far, the chapter has discussed historical developments linked to the oppression of women in society, challenges to this oppression during the 1960s and 1970s, and the status of women in Britain today in relation to economic, political and social representation. It will now move on to critically assess why women's lives are still characterised by high levels of inequality and oppression, with a focus on structural inequalities, and the ways in which political ideology continues to reinforce their status as wives and mothers within a nuclear family setting. Such an analysis is of importance for social workers, for without this understanding there is a risk that their intervention will be informed by individualistic and moralistic assumptions about poor women which will reinforce their oppression.

Social workers need an understanding of the levels of poverty and inequality in society and an awareness that poorer women are either in low-paid jobs or are reliant on men or state benefits for financial support. Levels of inequality have widened over the past 30 years under the New Right and New Labour. As Dorling (2010) states: 'In countries like Britain, people last lived lives as unequal as today, as measured by wage inequality, in 1854, when Charles Dickens was writing *Hard times*.'

He adds:

> Politicians in Britain and the other most unequal rich countries ... have accepted and fostered the damaging

idea that inequality is 'unfortunate' but inevitable, rather than seeing it, first and foremost as unjust.... The more progressive end of New Labour's policy spectrum, such as its focus on reducing child poverty, is rendered redundant by an elitist system that permits the 'super-rich' to accumulate record levels of wealth.

The impact of inequality in society is examined in Wilkinson and Pickett's research which points to the socially corrosive impact on populations in unequal societies and the consequences for social mobility and geographical segregations. It states that 'Bigger income differences seem to solidify the social structure and decrease the chance of upward mobility. Where there are greater inequalities of outcome, equal opportunity is a significantly more distant prospect' (2009, p 169).

The situation is likely to worsen under the newly elected Conservative/Liberal Democrat coalition government. An analysis of the emergency budget (April, 2010) is that it is 'the worst for women since the creation of the welfare state.' Yvette Cooper states that:

As women make up more of the public sector workforce they will be more heavily hit by the public sector pay freeze and the projected 600,000 net public sector job losses.... Cameron promised the most family-friendly government ever. Yet, they have just launched the fiercest attack on family support in the history of the welfare state.... They've cut support for children more savagely than anything else so far, with billions of pounds being cut from child benefit, child tax credits, maternity support and child trust funds.... Women are more affected by the cuts in things like housing benefit, public sector pensions or attendance allowances, and they benefit less than men from the increases in the income tax allowances. Even putting children aside, they are hitting women the hardest. (Stratton, 2010)

Yet, despite evidence of the impact of poverty and inequality on the lives of women, and that work is not an escape from poverty, politicians continue to reinforce a return to the labour market as the main way to improve financial wellbeing. Under both New Right and New Labour governments, women have been subject to contradictory political approaches to work and family life. On one hand, they have been under pressure to fulfil family caring obligations as social policy developments have reinforced the role of the informal care sector and the market, while 'rolling back' state welfare provision. On the other hand, mothers in particular have been castigated for their reliance on benefits and have been under increasing pressure to work outside the home. For example, the New Labour government introduced a policy that single parents should return to work once their youngest child reached the age of seven, and the incoming Conservative and Liberal Democrat coalition favour a similar policy to be implemented when the youngest child starts school. These politicians fail to acknowledge or recognise the incompatibility associated with participation in a low-wage working environment characterised by inflexibility and increasingly long and often unsocial hours, and fulfilling caring responsibilities within the family. For most women in work, the ability to balance work and family life is increasingly difficult, particularly as women still carry out the majority of domestic chores within a household. Women within poor families also tend to bear the brunt of poverty, and are more likely to deny themselves rather than any other family member (Graham, 1987).

For single parents, the problem is even more acute, and they have come under particular scrutiny regarding their lives and parenting attributes. Politicians promote the argument that being a single mother is a personal choice, yet work by Robert Rowthorn, a Cambridge economics professor and David Webster, a senior research fellow at Glasgow University, refutes this analysis and suggests that a marked increase in single parent numbers is directly linked to the rise in male unemployment as a result of de-industrialisation (Sunderland, 2010, p 33). In this respect it is economic insecurity rather than immorality that has undermined traditional family structures.

Research carried out by academics at Sheffield Hallam University reveals how increasing numbers of women are dependent on incapacity benefit, with numbers rising from 350,000 claimants in the 1980s to 1.1 million today. However, the research does not support political arguments that portray claimants as fraudulent; instead, it reveals that women in receipt of the benefit are concentrated in areas suffering from high levels of unemployment, and do not have qualifications or have worked in low-grade jobs. Here, the political drive to instigate work-based interviews is seen as a way to reduce claims rather than recognising that there are few jobs available and/or these women require physical and mental rehabilitation (Viney, 2009).

Yet, in contemporary Britain, politicians continue to deride poor families, unmarried couples and single parents. For example, David Cameron speaks of the need for the feckless and immoral poor to be persuaded to marry, and promotes the 'warmth of parenting', and the need for 'strong and secure families, confident and able parents, and an ethic of responsibility instilled from a young age'. Before the election he voiced the opinion that 'the differences in child outcomes between a child born in poverty and a child born in wealth are no longer statistically significant when both have been raised by confident and able parents' (Toynbee, 2010, p 31).

This statement is undermined by research carried out by the Centre for Longitudinal Studies (2007), which highlighted the immense effect of poverty on children and families, and is refuted by research carried out by Leon Feinstein that, in exploring the impact of inequality on young children, found that:

> [A]fter 23 months of age the dim but rich child begins to make faster progress than the bright but poor child – until at the age of six their achievements cross over, the poor child sinking, probably for ever, as the dim but rich rises inexorably. Nurturing, conversation, stimulation, a good nursery and attention from educated parents push one upwards while the other falls prey to adversity. (cited by Toynbee, 2010, p 31)

Social policies also impact on the role of social workers when they reinforce familial ideologies which oppress women in their role as providers and recipients of social care. Of particular importance is the concept of the 'normal' family and 'normal' parenting, which draws on individualistic and moralistic portrayals of family life that tend to pathologise poor women and children. Jen Luxford, a Demos researcher who analysed the figures from the Millennium Cohort Study (Centre for Longitudinal Studies, 2007) regarding children born in 2000, reinforced the impact of poverty on their lives when she said:

> It may not be in the best interests of the child growing up in hostile surroundings to be trusting and full of empathy. It may be rational to be bad, aggressive and impulsive. Expectations of stable employment, affordable housing, decent state education, and safe pensions have been blown apart and this can be laid at the door of the philosophy of economic liberalism promoted by Tories.

Policy developments over the past 30 years that have attacked state welfare provision have been detrimental to women. For example, 'community care' legislation has been criticised as a euphemism for the unpaid work of women within families, as it is mainly care by women

(Finch, 1988). Political developments that have reinforced the role of the informal sector in caring for dependants, also fail to acknowledge that the family can be a dangerous institution for women and children, and that 'the number of women being killed by a current or former partner has remained constant at two a week and the rape conviction rate has been diminishing to the point of near-invisibility' (cited in Cochrane, 2008, p 9).

As well as experiencing a backlash in relation to wages, labour market conditions and access to state welfare provision, the lives of women and young girls are also being negatively affected by increasing levels of sexual objectification. This scrutiny of women's bodies is creating a range of problems for young girls. Jessica Ringrose of the Institute of Education, has carried out research examining the effect of the normalisation of pornography on teenage girls, and its contribution to mental health problems and sexual bullying in schools. She states that 'it's verbal: slut, whore. It's also physical: touching up, coercion … women also harass and pathologise other women. There is so much sexual competition. Even friends call each other "slut" or "whore". But they are caught in a trap. You can't easily shake off these words in everyday society' (cited in Cooke, 2008, p 4). A recent survey by the Children's Society entitled Understanding Children's Well-Being pointed to serious problems associated with body image. It found that what made children most sad was their appearance. It also discovered that by Year 10 (ages 14–15), 28% of girls were miserable about their appearance. A study by the Girl Guides reinforced this concern, when 46% of girls aged 11 to 16 said they would consider cosmetic surgery (Cooke, 2008). The high value placed on looking good and acquiring material possessions also increases the risk of social problems linked to, for example, depression, anxiety and substance abuse.

This backlash has had a worrying effect on public attitudes. For example, an Amnesty International poll carried out in 2005 revealed that 26% of respondents thought that wearing revealing clothing and/or being drunk meant that a woman was partially or totally responsible for being raped, and in 2007, research carried out by the American Psychological Association found that men exposed to images that sexually objectified women were significantly more accepting of sexual harassment and sex role stereotypes (cited in Cochrane, 2008).

In conclusion, the concerns of the Women's Movement that were embedded within the radical social work movement of the 1970s and 1980s are still relevant for social workers today, for despite experiencing a revolution in some aspects of their lives during that period, inequality and oppression are still key features of women's lives. In order to develop anti-oppressive practice, social workers should give gender a high priority in relation to theory and practice. They should have a critical understanding of the impact of poverty and inequality on the lives of women and their families, and should be prepared to challenge stereotypes and assumptions that reinforce discrimination. They should also be prepared to ask questions about the position of women in relation to social policy and social problems, and be critical of political approaches that reinforce the role of women within the family by reducing state welfare provision and promoting the role of the informal care sector. It is also important to recognise the impact of privatisation and marketisation on their lives. Social workers need to be aware of more recent developments linked to the commodification of women, and how they have reinforced sexual divisions and skewed notions of equality and liberation. In order to ensure that gender inequality and oppression are challenged effectively, social workers should listen to women's voices, and be prepared to contest hierarchical forms of organisation. Most important, they should adopt a political understanding that includes strategies for change. It is only by adopting a critical understanding regarding women's oppression and being prepared to challenge policies, practices and procedures that progressive change will come about.

FOUR

The jester's joke

Charlotte Williams

In the opening months of 2010, the Communities Secretary, Lord Denham, launching a review of government policy on 'race', posed racism as somehow unproblematic in the light of the fact that we are all now 'comfortable with diversity' (*The Guardian*, 14 January). Denham suggested 'we must avoid a one-dimensional debate that assumes that all minority ethnic people are disadvantaged' and argued that factors of class probably outweigh racism as the contemporary issue of inequality. Denham sees a Britain that has changed 'immeasurably for the better' and argued that 'sustained action over the last 10 years has promoted racial equality and better 'race' relations, dismantled unfair barriers faced by many and helped to nurture a society more comfortable with diversity than ever before.'

These proclamations chime with an evident and sustained government trend systematically to rework and reposition 'race' in public policy. In three terms of new Labour administration there has been a gradual but consistent retreat from targeting 'race' and racial inequality as a distinct issue. This identifiable shift commenced with a reworking of the public policy discourse in which policy makers and policy papers preferred to use terms such as diversity, communities, cohesion and inclusion as euphemisms for the ubiquitous word 'race' and policy speeches more overtly signalled a distancing from what has now been dubbed old style and outdated multiculturalism (Phillips, 2005). In 2008 the establishment of the new Equalities and Human Rights Commission amalgamated the equality strands into a single enforcement body thus ending some 30 years of the Commission for Racial Equality and effectively ensuring the gradual demise of local 'race' equality councils as originally constituted. The Equality Act adopts a *generic* approach to tackling equalities dismantling the so-called 'silos' approach which has been branded as out of step with contemporary demographic realities. These manifestations ride on the back of a more fundamental and sustained neoliberal assault on the 'black' political constituency in the post 9/11 society in which a number of strategies have ensured the fragmentation and dissipation of any critical or sectional edge in the light of a 'crisis of integration' (Bloch and Solomos, 2010, p 223).

Social work is accordingly and inevitably deployed in this contemporary mission, if perhaps unwittingly. This repositioning echoes with much of the rhetoric that has come from our own ruling body in social work, the General Social Care Council, in its not-so-subtle shift away from what might be called the radical moment in anti-racist social work. The most forthright example of this came with the reformulation of the mandate on racial and cultural diversity under the new requirements for qualifying social workers with the introduction of the new degree in social work in 2004. The impact of this retreat from an explicit 'race' effort is evident and measurable (Tomlinson and Trew, 2002). In a recent survey of social work education providers across Wales for example, a study indicated respondents reporting that 'anti-racism in social work as a discrete approach is now dead ... we are using the generic approach', and suggested that 'other competing priorities' had been foisted on education providers that displaced any focus on 'race'. One respondent in the study concluded that 'race' and racism had been 'reduced to just three letters: BME' as an add-on appearing in various documents (Williams, 2010).

The implication that can be drawn from this repositioning in social work is that the task, as defined, was either wrongheaded and needed to be abandoned or that it is complete: that at best a variant of anti-racist practice is embedded in social work education and state practice and that there is no longer a need for this particular strand of radicalism. The okay/not okay conundrum has even failed to hold the ground as a central debate in social work with the presumption towards the former. Neither has social work come up with any tangible evidence that there has been a substantive shift in thinking and approach to the advantage of 'race' equality (Williams and Soydan, 2005). It is easy to conclude therefore that the 'anti-racist project' is a spent force; a project that has lost its way and cannot reorientate itself appropriately toward the contemporary political mandate.

There is, of course, substantial evidence to suggest this repositioning is somewhat cynical in the light of the deep and entrenched inequalities faced by black and minority ethnic groups and the ongoing and fundamental racisms they face day to day (Walby et al, 2008; Bloch and Solomos, 2010). The reality is that racial disadvantage is pernicious, deep-seated and enduring generation by generation. Racialised minorities are disproportionately represented in prisons, youth custody centres, as children in care, in mental health institutions, in stop and search, and relatively disadvantaged in health outcomes, unemployment, earnings, low pay and pensions (CRE, 2007). They are indeed a substantive sector of Britain's poor but they are also subject to widespread discrimination, personal and institutional within other tiers of society. They are underrepresented in positions of power in public authorities, including social work and social work academia, as elected representatives in local and central government and as within corporate institutions. In addition there is little to suggest that racist sentiments and prejudices within the dominant community have abated (Heath et al, 2010).

There is therefore no small amount of irony involved in the current positioning of social work vis-à-vis 'race' and racialised minorities which deserves examination. In Stan Cohen's essay in the classic *Radical social work* collection he draws on the idea of 'the jester's joke' (1975, p 43) as a means of illustrating the need for the occasional prompt to jolt professional thinking and action. The jester of medieval times had privileged access to the court of the ruling group, s/he was granted insider status for the amusement of the powerful and a guaranteed amount of proximity to the decision makers. The jester uses this positioning to make the uncomfortable joke, the jibe that tickles but is also an irritant, to pose the seemingly innocuous but awkward question that is intended to illustrate a truth either directly or ironically. In this way, says Cohen, it 'can puncture a lie in social work's self awareness' (1975, p 43). In this chapter, the jester opens with a pointed comment:

> *Jester:* 'How radical is radical?'

I will suggest that the radical trajectory of anti-racism in social work has found itself in a cul de sac characterised by a politics of compromise. Social work deployed a particular model of radicalism and a set of strategies that have been exhausted in terms of their usefulness in the current political context such that they cannot be regarded as 'radical' at all. The current impasse is the result of a crisis of ownership of the transformatory mandate which I suggest ultimately lies beyond the reach of social work as it is currently conceived.

The radical trajectory

The value of the Bailey and Brake momentum to the development of what came to be called 'anti-racist social work' is a matter of record (Payne, 2005). Bailey and Brake drew attention to the structural determinants of disadvantage and distress, in a way not previously acknowledged in social work circles and illustrated the pathologising and limited potential of the casework methodology in sustainably meeting the needs of the disadvantaged. The text provided a trenchant critique of the workings of the welfare state and perhaps most significantly charged the profession with an unequivocal responsibility – a moral and political responsibility not to collude in oppressive state practices but to transform them, and a responsibility to critically examine the assumptive world of social work itself. It offered an assault on liberalism, more particularly on the liberal reformism of the social democratic welfare state and its politics of piecemeal adjustments and tokenistic appeasement. It argued that the mend and patch approach of the average social worker did little to change the fabric of society – a fabric woven with deep inequalities. Social workers, for these writers, were caught up in a web of contradictions and irreconcilable imperatives that positioned them as 'dirty workers' (Cohen, 1975, p 77) somehow caught between their duties as functionaries of the state and the claims of those they purport to serve. These writers collectively provided a new paradigm of analysis and a conceptual apparatus that would become the basis for further explorations of the position of disadvantaged constituencies beyond those that had captured their attention and which were purely class based.

The Bailey and Brake departure had implied a significant rethink of the role and identity of social work and the ways in which social workers were being prepared for the world of practice. In many ways the stall that was laid out by the early 'radical' writers provides the prototype 'in and against the state' formulation of radicalism that we evoke to this day. It accepted the inevitability of social work as a state-controlled, state-run profession and sought to propose a number of ways in which the available wriggle room in the bureaucracy could be exploited toward the cause of greater empowerment and equality for the users of services – namely poor and working-class people.

There are things that they missed, of course. It is not that they didn't see the rise of the 'black'/civil rights movement which they mention in passing, nor the mobilisation of alternative forms of welfare and the lobbying of an emerging 'black' constituency against the injustices they were experiencing, but they stopped short of any thoroughgoing analysis of the crafty devices which the British state deploys to manage and control its minority ethnic citizens and those seen as denizens. In this respect, social work practitioners, however benign, were key agents in the distortion of the stories of black and minority lifestyles, in pathologising difference, in categorising, controlling and colluding in the labelling of minority ethnic clients as mad or bad, in the wholesale neglect of their needs (Bryan et al, 1985; Phillips and Phillips, 1998). Yet this was not simply the product of the malfunction of casework as

Bailey and Brake suggested but the product of an as yet largely unnamed and invidious force – that of British racism – that permeated not only the corridors of social service institutions but also the consciousness of the practitioners and policy makers. It would take later writers (for example Charles Husband in a later collection by Brake and Bailey (published in 1980) and Dominelli, 1988) to name and make explicit social work's role in the production and reproduction of racist ideology and practice and to challenge the idea of the benign, well-meaning social work practitioner.

Neither could Bailey and Brake have anticipated the inexorable rise of multiculturalism and the course these struggles would take, beyond the state. Dissatisfaction among black and minority ethnic communities was forcefully expressed in uprisings (riots) and protest on streets across British cities in the 1980s in an effort to capture recognition of unmet needs and draw attention to the discriminatory practices of the state apparatus. A 'Windrush scepticism' based on loss of trust and confidence in state providers (Williams and Johnson, 2010) came to replace the optimism of the early migrants to Britain that the mother country would support them as citizens and a 'race' politics forged along a black/white colour-coded axis became etched more rigidly into the public policy parlance than any of the lines of the class war that preceded it. The early social work response to these minorities did not, as the radical writers might have anticipated, give rise to a coalition with black-led groups, strategies of client cooption or a revisionist politics of welfare but to a politics of assimilationism, appeasement and annexisation onto the faulty machinery of the welfare state.

The variant of radicalism proposed by Bailey and Brake placed too much confidence in the trade unions, while failing to observe the discriminatory practices of trade unionists themselves. It ignored the deep antipathy of the white working class towards those they saw as 'immigrants' and a threat to their already disadvantaged position, an antipathy that would express itself in client against client and client against black worker. It relied on the sensibilities and patronage of a liberal middle class who were inherently committed to big government in resolving public ills. Indeed the proposed allies were not allies at all in the radical project. Radical strategies such as client cooption (1975, p 85) as part of a collective working-class struggle would fail, as would a welfare rights movement aimed at helping clients to get their rights which would not encompass those denied rights at all on the basis of their citizenship status or, should we say, presumed citizenship status. The universalist distributionist policies of the welfare state based on ensuring 'fit' to the one-size-fits-all model of delivery would be a poor armoury in the battle against racial inequality. This paradigm for a radical practice was fundamentally flawed in addressing the needs of Britain's black and minority ethnic population.

Anti-racism and social work's de-radicalising tendencies

The manifestation of these concerns in social work reached a zenith at the end of the 1980s. The origins of the anti-racist 'movement' lay outside the sphere of state-managed multiculturalist policy and rose from the grassroots, most notably through the actions of users and user groups themselves articulating their needs and despair at the welfare framework. It was a politics of the streets as a response to state intransigence in addressing racial inequality. It was, however, quickly embraced by radical professionals and left-wing academics well positioned to direct state policy and practice during the early 1980s. Reliance on the powerful force of the state took anti-racism off the streets, wrenched it out of the hands of the grassroots movement and put it in the classroom, overcrowded offices of social services departments, the local bureaucracy and under the pen of academics. It became proceduralised, institutionalised, shaped, reconfigured, stripped of its passion and emotional context, fragmented and regularised and ultimately subject to the exigencies of the neoliberal agenda. An emerging 'black' caucus within social work struggled hard to hold onto the reins of a Trojan horse that some momentarily thought might just be capable of bringing down the edifice (see Patel, 1995) but it was to no avail. In terms of popularity and government funding and support this approach was short lived and its failings were roundly rehearsed in the academic literature.

The anti-racist project within social work experienced a rocky ride ultimately finding itself not only the subject of vociferous critique – academic, political and populist – but somehow increasingly hampered by its own inner logic. This somewhat painful story has been recounted by a number of writers (Patel, 1995; Penketh, 2000; Sakamoto and Pinter, 2005; McLaughlin, 2005; Laird, 2008) with varying explanations for its demise. The range of critiques available graphically illustrate that this was an ideologically-driven movement which failed to find easy applications in the realm of practice. Some went as far as to argue that such politics is not the business of social work at all and that the movement was an oppressive, dogmatic, top–down academic-led white evangelism (Melanie Phillips, 1993). Clearly the movement engaged an intellectual acknowledgement within the profession but overall it lacked moral and critical engagement, largely because of its distancing from the grassroots groups who spawned it. The approach came under sustained attack because of its failure to provide flexible and usable messages for practice. In a trenchant analysis, Gilroy, as one example, announced the 'end of anti-racism' (1987) denouncing among other things the way in which the movement had been de-radicalised by its incorporation into the bureaucracy and had effectively lost touch with its grassroots ambitions.

There were other faultlines, however. The early tendency of social work to be preoccupied with 'culture', in what Charles Husband wonderfully called then a 'travelogue anthropology' (1980, p 72), later vied with a special brand of municipal anti-racism based on political correctness quirkery. This was a twin track trajectory in which what became known as the 'politics of recognition' (or politics of difference), with its focus on the particulars of culture and identities, ultimately won out over the 'politics of redistribution' based on material inequalities. If the 1980s version of multiculturalist policies was marked by the emergence of the radical moment of anti-racist welfare politics based on a power-based analysis of society, the 1990s would see the rise to ascendency of identity politics. The politics of recognition has privileged issues of culture over issues of material redistribution – a focus that has been deployed to good effect to mask a consideration of structural inequalities.

Atkin and Chattoo (2007) argue that a preoccupation with 'culture' and 'cultural attributes' has hampered the development of more sophisticated responses to diversity. A preoccupation with 'culture' has led to a failure to challenge mainstream services and to what they call 'the ethnicization of practice' whereby the user's ethnicity becomes the primary and defining feature determining their needs (2007, p 45). Atkin and Chattoo discuss the way in which the emergence of the politics of difference has acted to engage those responsible for the delivery of services and for resource allocation in accommodating the complexity of identities but at the same time substituted for a discussion of power, privilege, oppression and processes of discrimination. By focusing, for example, on religious or cultural attributes as responsible for the disadvantage of Bangladeshi groups, it obscures the real source of the issues affecting their lives such as poverty, poor housing, or exclusion from the labour market. Focusing on minority cultures is to foster the idea that the people themselves are somehow the problem, that their cultural attributes, their language, their lack of skills in the labour market, their lack of network, their failure to adapt and/or their desire to self segregate is responsible for their distress. Accordingly 'culturalist' solutions to these issues will be ineffective as the real root of the problems lies elsewhere. Yet this has perhaps always provided an easier focus for social work intervention; it is a more tangible and manageable arena in which to be responsive to need on an individualised and experiential basis, and therefore necessarily stands hostage to its deradicalising potential.

The anti-racist strategy of the 1980s also allowed itself to be wooed by the notion that increased representation among its ranks of 'black' social workers might resolve the issue of poor service delivery. This cooption of black workers into the state machinery has been described by writers such as Paul Stubbs (1985) and Gail Lewis (2000) as itself a major strand in the deradicalising armoury of the state. Indeed, even in the 1980s, the trajectory of positive action strategies aimed at identified 'minority needs' and policies of incorporation of a new cadre of 'black' social workers into the ranks of 'dirty workers', however seemingly radical, were effectively marginal and ill-conceived responses to issues of racial and cultural diversity, albeit well intentioned. This debate is underdeveloped in social work but this politics of jobs and appointments may be more about patronage and tokenism – a politics of appeasement – than about the revolutionary potential of these workers to transform institutions from within or service their respective heritage communities more sensitively. Nevertheless, the representation issue is an important one, even if not as a mechanism for service responsiveness. More black and minority ethnic faces, more diverse workplaces, more experiential diversity should be the profile of a profession which seeks to disturb the power structures of society. Within the profession – whether it be in senior management in practice, on editorial boards, in terms of research grants, or in academic and professorial appointments – we have seen little shift in the power base and, effectively, the attrition of the black-led lobby in social work. All the while a quietly complacent profession has acquiesced with little attempt to nurture the potential that such recruitment offered.

The notion that state social work was somehow in the 'right' place as a liberal profession to effect change was also a prevalent component of this trajectory: the idea that if we could just cleanse the thinking of the average social worker, teach them a new language and get their heads around cultural differences – all would be okay (Sivanandan, 1985). The assumption that social work could change institutions ('in but against the state') from within meant that they struggled in the context of complacent, lethargic and resistant institutions to put some 'style' into their work, to make changes at the margins for the benefit of black and minority ethnic service users and to very occasionally speak out, albeit with a very weak voice, in the lobbying rooms – all while Rome burned. The state remained unchallenged. It was not social work but some of its high-profile tragedies that prompted reform in the law (for example, that of Victoria Climbié), not social work but legislative concessions prompted by a litany of deaths, including that of Stephen Lawrence, which ultimately brought institutions to heel.

The struggles in practice to interpret the mandate on anti-racism led to a retreat into the comfort of easy formulas, defensive practices, fear and political correctness all-too familiar to this day. There was a notable retreat from institutional commitments to anti-racist ambitions from the mid-1990s onward (Tomlinson and Trew, 2002) when policies on issues such as transracial adoption were dismantled and depoliticised. McLaughlin (2005) has argued that this retreat from the anti-racist movement is not so much attributable to a political backlash as it is to the fact that by the late 1990s events such as the Stephen Lawrence inquiry quickly led to widespread institutional acknowledgement of the issues of racism, such that 'radical theories and practices are now embraced by most sections of the British establishment' (2005, p 297). To a certain extent, McLaughlin may be right, but perhaps the word 'acknowledgement' is more accurate than 'embrace' as the available evidence from the CRE in its valedictory publication (2007) *A lot done, a lot to do* suggests. Far from embracing the 'race equality' mandate public sector organisations have been characteristically recalcitrant. That this 'mission' should so easily lose ground reflects the wider ambivalences of the state and the public to the presence of minorities and perhaps a wider sense of ineptitude on the part of social work in facing what are complex challenges of a multi-ethnic, multi-faith, multicultural society.

Social work as a profession has, however, shown itself to be accommodating to the principles and values of 'race equality' at least, even if it has not been capable of translating these into progressive practices. Social work practitioners and educators have failed to advance the radical mission into anything like workable alliances with black and minority ethnic constituencies or indeed with individual client cooption on any significant scale. Was it too great an expectation that local state institutions and a weak profession could lead to substantive change? Or was it always going to be the small things that would count – those social relationships and the experiential encounters at the interface of worker and client that would produce the most rewarding potential for change? Whether we have we touched the lives of minority ethnic groups experientially in terms of the quality of welfare relations or acted to protect rights and shifts in the distribution of societal resources, are claims difficult to establish in the absence of systematic research evidence and documented testimonies and narratives of black and minority ethnic users of social services. The research dearth in social work is arguably one of the biggest shortfalls of the whole radical trajectory, for without tangible hard evidence to support the moral ambition it was always going to be easy to brush it aside in the world of shifting public policy priorities. Evaluation of the claims was always one part of the story that was missing.

Several writers suggest the greatest impacts or gains have been for the profession itself, in terms of providing an identity hook on which to locate the distinctiveness of social work in the mêlée of new and old professions (Millar, 2008). Anti-oppressive practice (and anti-racist practice), it is argued, provided a distinctive feature of the value base of the profession, something of an ideological device to enhance the reputation of the profession and the moral authority of its practitioners. Social work is certainly more adept at talking the talk than some of the sister professions in health care, such as nursing, medicine and allied health professions and the principles of equality practice are firmly endorsed in their professional codes of practice. This is undoubtedly a gain of the radical moment. It would be disappointing, however, to conclude that the gains have been largely transient, self interested and tokenistic and demonstrated merely the limits of liberal tolerance. While there are now undoubtedly stronger levers in terms of equality law, as key implementers, the profession remains sadly deficient in responding to issues of cultural diversity and sadly deficient in contributing to redressing what are sustained and widespread inequalities of outcome. As a professional grouping social work has not engaged sufficiently in robust partnerships with the black voluntary sector which overall continues to be underfunded, unsupported and marginalised in the welfare framework. As a profession, social work has not had a sufficiently strong voice to counter political discourses that pose black and minority ethnic communities as a drain of welfare services and/or as undermining the cohesiveness necessary for a risk-sharing welfare state. We have henceforth plunged into a period of navel gazing and fallen back onto the technocratic securities of the cultural competency approach (Laird, 2008).

That is not to say that there is no lasting legacy of the radical moment in social work. We have undoubtedly gained as a profession from this 'radical' legacy in terms of our analytical eye, our social science (sociological) perspective, in terms of advancing the theory of anti-racist/anti-oppressive practice, and hopefully in terms of our mistakes in practice. But the frustration of how to take forward transformatory change, progressive practices and radical intent to the benefit of those whom we serve has not mutated into new and refreshed strategies for action beyond looking back to the past. The movement that gives rise to the project of this text is itself an exemplar of the search for a refreshed radicalism in social work (SWAN). The challenge therefore is to re-theorise, debate and discuss the contemporary 'radical' paradigm in the light of a modernised politics of welfare. Is it once again time for an irony check?

The jester comments:

> 'In an era when we don't need to talk about 'race' as we can more easily talk about diversity or communities; when identities are fluid, uncertain and defy political category that might become the basis of a collective; when inequalities are not viewed as systemised but measured in terms of individual capabilities or propensities; when 'race' is but one dimension in the multiple matrix of a variety of claims of inequality all somehow the same, equal yet different; when we can all have a voice if we choose and we can all participate in the democratic mêlée of welfare and the state will leave it largely to us; when users are not just users anymore but themselves the apparatus of governance... as the us become them and the them become us; when our grassroots groups sign up to extend the arm of the state into the heart of civil society and the private sphere to listen and care... or listen and watch, and when all the state institutions are busy doing equalities – who needs to question anything at all?'

The contemporary compromise

Questions arise therefore about the nature and focus of radicalism within the contemporary welfare framework: how to take forward the anti-racist ('race equality') ambitions of social work, given the different political, social and economic circumstances to the situation that prevailed when Bailey and Brake penned their manifesto for change.

A lot has, of course, changed since the 1970s when Bailey and Brake and colleagues formulated a strategy for a refreshed practice. Multiculturalism is now acknowledged as dynamic, subject to change and internal differentiation beyond the black/white divide of the traditional 'race' politics (Vertovec, 2007; Fanshawe and Sriskandarajah, 2010). Multiculturalist policy and practice has adapted to the realities of the complexities of identity formations, acknowledged new and emerging forms of racism based more broadly on factors of culture and religion than simply colour and, as Denham (Lord Denham, 2010) pointed out, Joe and Jill Bloggs have now become at least more accustomed to the fact that Britain is indeed a multicultural society, albeit ambivalently. Alongside this evident and increased cosmopolitanism, the anxieties of a post 9/11 society continue to manifest themselves in the so-called 'war on terror' and in these more stringent economic times anxieties are fuelled about the presumed link between immigration and the drain of welfare services. Powerful discourses fanned by media hype communicate these ideas about minorities irrespective of their citizenship status.

The neoliberal approach to 'race' has gained ground and been cemented on the twin strategy of strong assimilationism for those at 'home' – evident in strategies such as community cohesion policies and a variety of Britishness projects and ever-increasingly stringent policies in relation to immigration and asylum for 'outsiders'. Under pressure from 'black' radical grassroots groups and individuals, successive governments have responded to this changed demographic and a gradual strengthening of the legislative framework for advancing 'race' equality has developed, including the acknowledgment of 'institutional racism'. The welfare system that is emerging as a result of modernisation no longer assumes that one size fits all (Williams and Johnson, 2010). 'Race' has effectively been incorporated into considerations at the heart of public service delivery by statutory mandate if not into the spirit of implementation. However, there is little reason to suggest that the legislative push has led to effective, sensitive and responsive service delivery for the UK's black and minority ethnic peoples. The CRE in its final assessment of public sector bodies noted that even within Whitehall departments, a large number had not complied with the existing 'race equality' duty (*The Guardian*, 18 September, 2007) and its report *A lot done, a lot to do* noted that in a recent monitoring round of 47 local authorities sampled, 30 were not compliant with the duty to promote 'race equality' and all of the district councils targeted in the project were non compliant (CRE, 2007, p 53). Social workers remain key gatekeepers in access to services and key implementers of policy. They are uniquely placed at the interface of the public and private spheres to bring about tangible changes on behalf of minority ethnic individuals, groups and communities and to lobby for real changes to their social circumstances.

Within the neoliberal state the incorporation of 'race' has been a most effective ploy in muting dissent, critique and dissatisfaction. 'Race equality' has become subject to the technocratic culture of the bureaucracy, stripped of its moral and emotive content and subject to standardisation and quantification through mechanisms such as 'impact assessments'. The tick box culture of modernized service delivery fosters a focus on procedural compliance and minimal statutory obligations rather than providing any substantive challenge to prevailing norms and cultural practices within organisations. The assumption underpinning the new legislation is of willingness on the part of public authorities to engage with and implement the duties. This clearly requires conditions in civil society that cannot be created through legislation alone, such as capacity building for wholesome engagement and higher levels of public participation. Yet the very nature of this participation is itself a double-edged sword for minority ethnic groups.

Under the semblance of care, involvement and participation the radical potential of the anti-racist lobby has been carefully stripped out, for who could speak out against concepts such as user engagement, partnerships, empowerment, community engagement and cohesion and yet it is these very notions, so central to the modernised welfare framework that are serving to de-radicalise any radical intent. The participative paradigm operates as a powerful silencing mechanism, giving the appearance of significant power shifts, suggesting itself as more democratic but masking deep seated unequal power relations between groups and vis a vis the central state. It is effectively *responsibility* that has been devolved while power remains firmly consolidated at the centre and the methodologies of participation are by design constrained, limited and selective. The participatory initiative should be the forum on which people have the opportunity to influence policy and learn as political actors but this has come with certain conditions for black and minority ethnic people such that the rules of the game include:

- Assimilation into shared values – and the acceptance of the rules of engagement. New and invasive forms of assimilationism related to dress, lifestyles, community association now condition the nature of black and minority ethnic engagement with public services
- Minority ethnic groups must not use the platform of their ethnically distinct grouping to engage in the political process as this is seen as segregationalist and they are deterred by levers such as funding streams from lobbing their specific cause or their specific constituency. The current culture of engagement with the 'black' voluntary sector by state bodies manipulates and colonises their functions, aims and ambitions in the pursuit of the state agenda to deconstruct multiculturalism.

- They are subject to ever closer surveillance of their lifestyles by this closer to home governance as the voluntary sector organisations are increasingly coopted into the state machinery or treated with suspicion.

To this end a social work harnessed to the neoliberal mandate is, as McLaughlin (2005) has pointed out, well placed for extending the state's arm of surveillance and control into black and minority ethnic community life. McLaughlin says, 'in the sense that it is about fostering individual personal change and enforcing a new moral consensus *from above*, the anti-oppressive social worker is well placed for personally policing, not politically empowering the disadvantaged' (2005:300). Ironically, therefore, the democratic relationships suggested by the participatory paradigm may themselves be dangerous for democracy and in reality subject to compromise by mechanisms such as gatekeeping, quick fix consultations and incorporation, while all the while portraying the state as somehow the neutral and benign arbiter adjudicating the variety of claims.

There is accordingly a major challenge to the public service ethos suggested by this idea of the state as a neutral rational arbiter with which social work must engage toward progressive change. The Parekh Report on the *Future of multiculturalism* (2000) some 10 years ago critiqued of the idea of public services based on common and shared values and suggested that state institutions far from being impartial are based on essentially liberal values that are non negotiable. This has been well illustrated in social work in relation, for example, to the cultural universalism of services organised around White norms (Atkin and Chattoo 2007). In this respect Newman (2007) calls for a *rethinking* of the liberal public sphere. She argues, that the state is far from the transparent, neutral arbiter of competing claims and has proved itself to be out of step and unable to respond to competing claims for recognition and justice, utilising liberal values as its default positioning. Accordingly reworking the structures of the welfare state but leaving untouched its assumptive world (its values) can only produce a never ending cycle of ineffectiveness in response to multiculturalism. Social workers are well placed to engage in this crafting of a refreshed notion of the public service ethos.

In this diffuse, multi-level, multi-tiered and more open mixed economy of welfare, new welfare arrangements are emerging at local and sub national level. Governance has replaced big government and there are more opportunities for directly influencing policy and practices across the welfare sectors. There are evident implications here for equality practices that must straddle multi-disciplinary, interagency and devolved policy circuits. Minority ethnic communities, their groups and associations are generally weak actors in the new collaborative politics of welfare as the 'black' voluntary sector continues to be underfunded, unsupported and largely marginal to mainstream welfare delivery (Syed et al, 2002). There are evidently new opportunities for re-engagement with the issues of achieving parity, wholesome engagement and participation in this radical restructuring of welfare provisioning (Williams and Johnson 2010).

Social work as key actors in this welfare framework are subject to the contemporary compromise on 'race', to the concepts, language, values underpinning the new rules of engagement in this modern welfare framework. Contemporary practice has accommodated the repositioning of the state as neutral in the arbitrations of competing identity claims, it has been accommodative of the refashioning of the discourses on 'race' and it continues to co-operate in the naming of the problems that face 'black' and minority ethnic communities as 'cultural' at best or part of their moral failings or lifestyle choices at worst.

This is the contemporary compromise. Social work needs to be deeply suspicious of state-led initiatives for change on 'race equality' given that the state is contradictory and ambivalent about its minorities. The state has been neglectful and at times downright hostile to the nation's minorities (Craig 2007), which raises the question: can this be the locus of change?

In the light of this what might therefore be the contemporary interpretation of the 'in and against the state' model of radicalism proposed by Bailey and Brake in relation to the anti-racist project?

The jester comments: 'What state? Or should I ask: whose state?'

Unfinished business: the way forward

Social workers are on the front line of the neoliberal deception both by being *acted on* by the neoliberal modernising project but also as *agents of it*. The professional agenda has been ideologically controlled and its critique muted, its politics have been managed and its progressive discourses have been usurped and incorporated in numerous ways including transformations to the language in use (Harris, 2003). It is largely a 'white' institution based on liberal norms and values and largely based within state organisations. It might be useful to reflect, therefore, if social work, as it is currently conceived, is capable of carrying the torch for 'race equality', for effecting beneficial changes on behalf of black and minority ethnic communities. It could be argued that the demands of the modern bureaucracy leave little scope, time or energy to commit to a radical cause and that practitioners retreat in the face of the enormity of the tasks involved in realising change. They could be said to have *satisficed*: accepted their weak positioning as a profession and are just 'getting on with the job at hand' as anti-discriminatory practitioners.

It is worth returning to the tension the radical writers recognised as the lever or change in their early formulations – that of being 'in and against the state'. In Stan Cohen's interpretation of this mission he drew on the idea of 'unfinished business' (1975, p 92). The 'unfinished' refers to a programme which does not exist indicating the need to engage with long-term strategic change as well as expedient short-term goals. Cohen refers to grasping the contradictions presented by the positioning within the state (the jester's position) and exploiting it, utilising it as a creative space to create change.

> As every social worker well knows, absorption eventually takes place through all sorts of subtle ways of incorporation, initiation into the agency's secrets, compromising for too long. On the other hand there are some very effective short term possibilities, not just through humanitarian work but in conscious policies of raiding the establishment for resources, contributing to its crises, unmasking and embarrassing its ideologies and pretentions. Any such effectiveness can be lost by finishing. (1975, p 92)

In his suggestions for a radical social work programme he includes the note:

> In practice and in theory, stay 'unfinished'. Don't be ashamed of working for short-term humanitarian or libertarian goals, but always keep in mind the long-term political prospects. This might mean living with the uncomfortable ambiguity that your most radical work will be outside of your day-to-day job. (1975, p 96)

These writers were of course building formulations in the context of a highly centralised universalist state of big government. The locus of change was to be reform from within and largely in the hands of the beleaguered social work practitioner. What is implied today is more far reaching and multilayered. It involves a detailed facing up to the contemporary political challenges and possibilities, the development of new strategies for engagement and alliance building, it involves utilising and deploying all the potentials of the new technologies – (the sit-at-home activist?) – and above all facilitating and being led by (not leading) black and minority ethnic groups in their ambitions for change. This is not a call for any universalistic formula but for rigorous principles of engagement, it's about listening, knowing, negotiating and exploiting the spaces available in particular political contexts at particular moments. It requires skills in working in a collaborative politics of welfare. Minority ethnic communities are not a threat but an asset to welfare delivery, they are not a drain on the resources of welfare but major contributors to it. As such, social workers can contribute to a reworking of the prevailing discourses that cast them as 'problematic' to, or a drain on, services.

All the tinkering in the world with the available structures and with the mechanisms of engagement will be to no avail if the social relations of welfare remain largely monocultural and monodimensional. Where welfare interventions are characterized by misrecognition of the issues facing minority communities and where they represent an affront to the values and beliefs of others, they will clearly be limited in their impact. While welfare assimilationism prevails services will continue to fail the needs of diverse groups. It will be important to continually hold up for inspection not only the agenda in these new collaborative arrangements but the very 'rules of engagement' and to subject to critical scrutiny the underpinning values and potential conflicts of those values. The public service ethos needs scrutiny and can be transformed by key implementers such as social workers. In this arena the state is not neutral, not benign and impartial but reflective of liberal values, full of contradictions and ambivalences towards minority peoples, swayed by its need to retain populist appeal and has proven itself to be riven with racisms (Craig, 2007).

In this respect it is important to recognise that locus of change lies well beyond the state and will be realised not through top-down social engineering but through real and significant shifts in power within the organs of civil society, voluntary associations, citizen collaborations and in particular welfare arrangements secured between multiple actors at local level. In these encounters state social workers have a role in facilitating genuine engagement, holding fast and ensuring equality principles are maintained, advocating for the weaker voices, maximising the interventions of co-producers, ensuring adequate resources to support collaborative ventures and keeping a rein on the interventionist state. The contemporary shift to more inclusive governance, far from reducing social work 'radical' potential, can provide opportunities for more direct work in policy making and shaping as it implies greater proximity to decision makers. It also brings into focus the inevitable tension between professionalism and equality in the social relations of welfare, an issue worthy of critical introspection within contemporary social work. There is a crisis of ownership of the mandate for change that needs resolution, a moment has been reached to return and consider the locale for advancing progressive change. I believe this to be at the level of the *social practices* of welfare, the emergent methodologies that arise from practice engagements in the private sphere and at the level of civil society. It is timely to capture these narratives, these workings out, these negotiations and their outcomes and their theoretical import. This process of reclaiming is under way.

The advance made by the anti-racist project of the 1980s should not be underestimated or discredited in our desire to find new operational methodologies fit for the 21st-century welfare framework. With the benefit of hindsight it is easy to identify the way in which the theoretical trajectory and the political advocacy got disassociated from the front line of practice and from the grassroots actors. Academics were woefully deficient in matching their admonitions about 'race equality' with hard research evidence and the research dearth needs filling to provide demonstrable evidence for practice and for advocacy. Old debates need revisiting and researching such as the relevance of ethnic matching in care giving, assessing the nature and quality of 'race equality' training, localised mapping and needs-based studies, building narratives from practice of care and caring experiences, assessing the competencies of street level implementers in responding to diversity among many others. The potential impacts on minority ethnic groups of new directions in welfare delivery, such as personalisation of care and the privatisation of care, are areas that are under-researched despite the statutory requirement for 'equality impact assessments' in all new areas of public policy, as is the role of faith-based and other third sector organisations in the development of the mixed economy of welfare. Up-to-date ethnicity mapping is long overdue, given age shifts, new migrations and other changes to the profile of ethnic demography. Challenges also need to be made to ideas such as 'self segregation', co-ethnic and co-faith exclusion (or inclusion) through the development of demonstrable evidence. Research is a critical tool for political advocacy and for advancing radical change.

In addition more critical leadership on issues of 'race' needs to come from within the profession, from the Association of Professors of Social Work, from the British Association of Social Workers and from the General Care Council itself. A re-endorsement of the profession's commitment to 'race equality' should be part of the current deliberations of the emerging Social Work College in England and embedded in the newly qualified training year. Academic leadership is needed in freeing up the curriculum to allow spaces for learning and skills development in political advocacy and strategy in the new welfare framework and more detailed skill on working alongside diverse communities.

As a profession we have let things slip, we have become complacent and fallen into easy ways, hidden behind the familiar language of anti-oppressive, anti-discriminatory practice and we have lost our outrage. Social workers are moral agents, making moral and political choices daily. 'Race equality' is a moral issue as well as an issue requiring technical skill and competency in responding to diversity and advocating for change. As a profession we need to reclaim our anger and outrage at the immorality of racism in contemporary society if we are not to become mere functionaries of the state.

> *Jester:* 'May I be so radical as to ask who needs social workers?'

FIVE

LGBT oppression, sexualities and radical social work today

Laura Miles

Introduction

The year 2009 marked the fortieth anniversary of the Stonewall riots in New York and the subsequent birth of the Gay Liberation Front. It is difficult to underestimate the significance of the Stonewall Rebellion of 27 June 1969 which was initiated by the lesbians and gays, drag queens, transvestites and transsexual people in the Stonewall bar in New York who had grown sick of police harassment and who therefore said, 'Enough is enough'. The resistance at a seedy New York club ended up with a group of brutal, racist, homophobic cops being penned up inside the Stonewall bar. It was a moment of celebration and inspiration which ignited a movement.

For many lesbian, gay, bisexual and transgender (LGBT)[1] people at the time it was a crowning moment, a decisive and defiant shift away from guilt about oneself to pride in who you are, explicitly modelled on the civil rights and Black power movements in the US. That pride, protest and defiance carried over into the early Pride marches. The mood of the times is summed up by the recollections of one of the participants in the rebellion, Sylvia Rivera, who went on in 1970 to co-found Street Transvestites Action Revolutionaries (STAR) with the black drag queen Marsha P. Johnson. A few years before her death in 2002 Sylvia gave an interview to Leslie Feinberg (1998) recalling the atmosphere of those days:

> We were not taking any more of this shit. We had done so much for other movements. It was time. ... All of us were working for so many movements at that time. Everyone was involved with the women's movement, the peace movement, the civil rights movement. We were all radicals. I believe that's what brought it around. ... I was a radical, a

> revolutionist. I am still a revolutionist. … If I had lost that
> moment, I would have been kind of hurt because that's
> when I saw the world change for me and my people. Of
> course, we still got a long way ahead of us. (1998, p 107)

LGBT oppression is an issue with which social workers and social
work educators need to concern themselves. LGBT oppression needs
to be resisted actively and promotion of LGBT liberation should be
integral to the development of any effective radical social work theory
and practice which seeks to challenge oppression in modern capitalist
societies.

In 1975 Don Milligan wrote a groundbreaking chapter in the Bailey
and Brake collection entitled 'Homosexuality: sexual needs and social
problems'. Although it is undeniable that progress has occurred since
the mid-1970s, in terms of formal equality rights and legislation and
the general liberalisation in social attitudes with regard to sexual
orientation and gender expression, there is still a long way to go both
more broadly within society and within social work itself in fighting
oppression, promoting equality and struggling for liberation. So what
has changed since Milligan wrote his chapter?

Changes to the LGBT experience since 1975

For LGBT people in 1975 the situation was beginning to improve from
the dire circumstances of post-war austerity and the lived reality of the
closet, guilt and fear of arrest and imprisonment. The social and political
turmoil of the 1960s had begun to thaw the punitive and oppressive
legislative framework in the UK and elsewhere which previously had
driven LGBT people underground and set up gay men in particular
as prey for police *agents provocateurs*. This was accompanied by greater
visibility of lesbians and gay men, not least in sections of the socialist
and trade union movements at the time, and the beginnings of some
liberalisation of social attitudes.

Don Milligan's chapter can therefore be read partly as an historical
document, a snapshot from the time which very effectively described
the impact on confidence, self-esteem and self-image for gay people
who had been brought up in a 'straight' society largely lacking any
role models and subject to expectations and assumptions which both
denied and denigrated their sexual orientation.

Being gay in 1975 was generally perceived as an affliction or an
inadequacy or even as pathological. As Milligan describes:

> All homosexuals are brought up as heterosexuals in a
> heterosexual world. The 'rightness' of heterosexuality is
> confirmed in every classroom, game, street, park, pub,
> cinema, dance hall, daily paper, and on every juke-box, radio,
> television and advertising poster. (1975, p 97)

At this time homosexuality (and transsexuality) were still regarded by many, not least mental health professionals and GPs, as forms of mental illness for which cures were often attempted sometimes through psychoanalysis but also along behaviourist lines using aversion therapy.

The American Psychiatric Association regarded homosexuality as an illness until 1973, when the Diagnostic and Statistical Manual of Mental Disorders (DSM) definition was changed. In the UK the British International Classification of Disease list included homosexuality as a mental illness until 1994. Similarly it was not until 1994 that psychological orthodoxy in the UK (represented by the British Psychological Society) even sanctioned the formation of a Lesbian and Gay Section after several previously unsuccessful attempts by members to initiate one. It is worth pointing out the continuing application of the medical model today with regard to transgender people. Those who want to 'transition', to access state medical intervention and help in the process of gender affirmation (formerly called 'gender reassignment' or the commonly used misnomer 'sex change'), still have to submit themselves to psychiatric assessment and seek to be diagnosed as suffering from 'gender dysphoria', a form of mental disorder listed in the current edition of the DSM (APA, 2002).

Milligan highlights the huge impact for gay men in the UK who emerged from the 1960s no longer criminalised (at least not in private between consenting adults) after the adoption of the Sexual Offences (Homosexual Reform) Act of 1967 following the Wolfenden report of 1957. Lesbian relationships, of course, were not directly part of this since lesbianism had not suffered criminalisation in the UK in the late 19th century through the notorious Labouchere Amendment – Section 11 of the Criminal Law Amendment Act of 1885 – which had made 'gross indecency' between men an offence.

The 1967 decriminalisation was a huge step forward, fondly remembered by many older gay people to this day. The previous situation, in which it has been estimated that one in six men in prison had fallen foul of the legislation and often of entrapment by a homophobic police force, was a major source of fear, stress and suicide and served to keep most gay people in the closet. By allowing sexual relations between two men who are willing and over 21 (the age of consent was only lowered to 16 in 2000) the Act removed much of the fear of arrest and imprisonment which gay men had suffered for decades. But Milligan rightly highlights the partial nature of this decriminalisation. It did not make such sexual relations lawful, since one man making a suggestion or a request to another constituted 'importuning'. It did not apply to men in the Armed Forces or on board British merchant ships. It did not apply in Scotland or Northern Ireland.

Thus a great deal has changed for LGBT people since the mid-1970s. One well-known writer in this area (Weeks, 2009), has summarised the LGBT journey from the 1950s to today as 'a great transition – with some way to go'. In the 1950s the UK had one of the most reactionary sexual regimes in the world. Today that situation is very different. In the 1950s marriage was perceived of as the only gateway to respectable sexuality, there were powerful taboos against premarital sex, pregnancy out of wedlock and divorce. Backstreet abortion was widespread and homosexuality existed in the shadows with male homosexuality being totally illegal. Now there is a new framework of legislation which confers social and human rights and rights at work for LGBT people, male homosexuality is largely decriminalised, the legal age of consent has been reduced, gay adoption and civil partnerships are legal, and social attitudes especially among the young tend to be more liberal and tolerant.

Not that the process of liberalisation has been continuous and uni-linear. In 1988 Margaret Thatcher's Tory government tacked a vicious piece of homophobic legislation onto the Local Government Act which sought a prohibition on 'promoting homosexuality' such that a local authority could not:

(a) intentionally promote homosexuality or publish material with the intention of promoting homosexuality;
(b) promote the teaching in any maintained school of the acceptability of homosexuality as a pretended family relationship.

Section 28 emerged in the aftermath of what has been termed the Tories 'watershed election' of 1987 (Lavalette and Mooney, 2000). At the time HIV and AIDS were being used as a political stick with which to beat an already frightened and angry LGBT community. Section 28 was not repealed until New Labour's second term of office in November 2003.

In practice Section 28 meant that young people in care (and in schools, of course) were denied the space to discuss their sexuality and the support and acceptance of their sexual identity. In some cases this meant active discrimination. In others it opened the way to bullying

(Equality Challenge Unit, 2009). In fact no one was ever prosecuted under Section 28 but its existence was enough to create a climate of fear, denial and ignorance in schools and other institutions, a climate which continues to have repercussions today.

Surveys by Schools Out have consistently demonstrated the worrying extent of homophobia and transphobia in schools today and the lack of confidence that many teachers have in challenging this. For example a recent survey by Salford National Union of Teachers (2010) found that 52% of members had witnessed or observed homophobic abuse on a daily or weekly basis, and 74% on a termly basis. Among teachers, 13% had themselves been subject to homophobic abuse on a termly basis, and 23% during the school year. Although 80% of NUT members thought that homophobia was a serious issue demanding action, only 33% thought that their school was vigorously addressing the issue.

The impact of Section 28 went much wider than just schools. As the Care Leavers' Association (2010) note:

> One of the main areas in which Section 28 impacted on the lives of LGBT young people in the care system was through the lack of information and support regarding their sexual health needs. Through entering into discussions regarding the sexual health needs of their young people, social workers, foster carers, RSWs etc. could have been seen to be 'promoting homosexuality'. Many therefore avoided the subject completely.

Nonetheless, in many ways over the past 35 years the picture has been one of general overall improvement. In a review of the changing state of LGBT equality in Britain, Sue Botcherby of the Equality and Human Rights Commission (EHRC) quoted research showing that, for example, while the 1987 British Social Attitudes Survey found that 75% of people thought homosexuality was 'always or mostly wrong', by 2008 this had fallen to 32%. These figures may need some caution as 1987 was when the HIV/AIDS epidemic among gay men was raging in the West and thus they could reflect the heightened homophobia of the time. However later surveys have found continuing liberalisation of social attitudes.

Interestingly though, in respect of gender identity and transsexualism, even in 2006 the Scottish Social Attitudes survey found that 50% of respondents would be unhappy if a close relative entered a relationship with a transsexual person and 30% thought a transsexual person would be unsuitable as a primary school teacher (Bromley et al, 200).

Milligan also takes a very progressive view (for the time) of 'cottaging' (when men seek out other men for sex, traditionally in public toilets), explaining how this involves the search for sexual relations 'without emotional entanglements and how it can arise from the social situations of gay men. It is one response to oppression and homophobia and even today much liberal tut-tutting about the practices of cottaging and cruising is patronising and misses the point. He also makes very prescient comments about the gay scene and the gay community, explaining and defending its existence but writing for example that: 'The gay community is not a true community.' He continues: 'Composed simply of bars and clubs, the gay scene is a social ghetto with specific limitations. It is not residentially concentrated and it has no class, racial, occupational or sexual homogeneity' (1975, p 102).

Given the subsequent development over the past three decades of the Pink Pound and the gay scene these comments seem to have been well-founded. One only has to look at the way in which many Prides, most notably London Pride, have become lifestyle celebrations dominated by commercial interests and corporate sponsorship. They are devoid of genuine political protest and one can see how far they have been incorporated into the norms of market capitalism and the primacy of the market and how far they have migrated from the ideals of the post-Stonewall Gay Liberation Front.

Milligan's chapter is therefore a demand that social workers and associated professionals need not just be aware of homophobia but are involved in actively combating it, that LGBT social workers need to organise in order to define themselves and engage in political struggle, and that social workers need to work closely with enlightened anti-oppressive counsellors in combating the collective and individual effects of homophobia such as emotional distress, isolation and the potential for self-harm and abuse.

Yet groundbreaking as Milligan's chapter was in 1975, unsurprisingly it has some rather dated aspects to it when reread nearly 35 years later. For example, there are some comments in the chapter which would be contested today. In discussing bisexuality he argues that bisexual people who present to GPs or counsellors are effectively in the same position as lesbians or gay men. On page 107 he writes, 'bisexuality is often a defensive description used by people who are afraid of the label homosexual' (1975, p 107). This is a highly debatable comment. Today bisexuality has acquired a much greater specificity than formerly.

Similarly, there are passages in which Milligan appears to conflate issues of sexual orientation with gender variance or with masculinity/femininity, all of which ought to be considered as conceptually distinct.

The increasing visibility since the 1970s of gender variant people, from crossdressers and transvestites to transsexual people who seek gender reassignment (or gender confirmation) has hopefully begun to raise awareness that being gender variant is quite distinct from being gay or straight (although gender transition clearly raises some interesting potential redefinitions or realignments of a trans person's perceived sexual orientation).

At the time Milligan was writing gender variance and transgender issues, even now a minority of the LGBT acronym, were barely a blip on the general social and political horizon. In the UK the case of April Ashley (1970) and the annulment of her marriage due to her transsexuality (a legal adjudication which hindered trans legal rights for decades) was the famous lone example of a trans person of whom many people were aware in that period.

Milligan's chapter is notable also for its lack of reference to studies of LGBT social workers' experiences or the needs of LGBT service users. That is not a fault: there was little in the way of research evidence or a research literature at the time. Even now if we compare the UK with, for example, the US, studies in the UK of the needs of LGBT workers and service users are limited. Yet crucially, as we shall see given current estimates of the numbers of LGBT people and the problems they face, large numbers are to be found in looked-after situations, and/ or suffering from the effects of drug and alcohol misuse, emotional distress and mental illness, self-harm, and increasingly, as a proportion of older people seeking shelter and support.

A MIND survey in 2002 indicated that LGB people seem to be overrepresented in terms of anxiety, depression, self-harm and suicidal behaviour as well as drug and alcohol misuse. Another study found that 40% of young LGB people had self harmed at least once (Rivers, 2000). There is anecdotal evidence that young transgender people are at particularly high risk (Social Perspectives Network, 2006). Evidence from the US (Reardon, 2009) provides support for the view that young LGBT people who suffer familial rejection are at risk of several health problems as adults. LGBT youth were up to three times more likely to attempt suicide than their straight peers.

The Department of Health's Sexual Orientation and Gender Identity Group (SOSIAG) suggests that action to tackle these mental health inequalities in relation to LGBT people has been missing or under-resourced. Partly these shortcomings relate to lack of or minimal monitoring, very few national surveys or national data collection agencies have monitored for LGB, and none for transgender. This means the evidence base which could relate to policy formation, allocation of resources, training and so on is often simply not there or is small scale or ad hoc.

In a study of the housing and community support needs of older lesbians and gay men for the Polari Housing Association in London, Hubbard and Rossington (2005) presented a range of concerns and shortcomings that were identified by older LGBT people themselves about housing and community care provision, the lack of training for service providers about sexuality and LGBT people and their relationships, and the need for networking between individuals and relevant organisations and user groups.

Similar issues have been identified by Age Concern, who organised the first UK conference in 2002 to examine social policy issues affecting older lesbians and gays. Age Concern has pointed out how most health professionals and social workers automatically assume patients or service users are heterosexual (Age Concern, 2002). Concannon (2009) draws attention to the need to consult and involve LGBT elders and how this can help to avoid examples of such poor practice as the use of inappropriate language or insensitive questions and assumptions.

Most professional guidelines in respect of awareness of oppression and human rights have shown considerable improvement since the mid-1970s. The General Social Care Council published codes of practice for social care workers and for employers of social care workers in 2002, the first clause of which is:

> 1. As a social care worker, you must protect the rights and promote the interests of service users and carers.

This includes:

> 1.5 Promoting equal opportunities for service users and carers; and
> 1.6 Respecting diversity and different cultures and values.

The Gender Identity Research and Education Society who advocate for trans people, point out on their website (www.gires.org.uk) that 'there appear to be no recent data obtained from robust research that assesses the extent to which local authorities are meeting their legal obligations specifically with regard to trans people'.

A Scottish 2006 survey relating to LGBT people showed that while all 32 councils had an equality policy, only nine referred to sexual orientation, just one had a separate LGBT policy, and none had a specific transgender policy.

Certainly any social worker concerned to be part of developing an engaged, committed and empowering approach to social work practice needs a critical awareness of homophobic and transphobic oppression. They need to be equipped with an understanding which generates confidence to challenge these oppressions in the workplace and beyond and in so doing to ally themselves, whether LGBT or straight themselves, with LGBT service users. That necessitates an understanding of the roots of LGBT oppression in modern capitalist society (Halifax, 1988; Carlin, 1989; Wilson, 2007).

Social workers will be dealing with LGBT service users in a range of circumstances right across the age, gender and ethnicity spectrum whether this be the assessment of needs and the procurement of services for older LGBT service users, looked-after children, asylum seekers being expected to 'prove' their sexual orientation by the immigration and asylum authorities, the adoption of children by gay couples, domestic violence, mental health, drug and substance abuse. In short, whatever it is that social workers do in their practice should require an awareness, empathy and non-judgemental sensitivity towards the impacts that LGBT oppression causes.

More than that, current legislation requires that social workers be trained to *combat* homophobia and transphobia and *promote* LGBT equality. Recent equality legislation provides the legal framework for this. The new Equality Act (2010) requires public sector organisations and organisations contracted to or funded by the public sector to develop single equality schemes covering all seven equality strands ('race', gender, disability, age, sexual orientation, gender identity, and religion and belief) in order to abide by the duties to be determined under the act.

Many organisations have made headway in developing single equality schemes but many have a long way to go. Unions during the past four decades have been influential drivers for equality in the workplace and for progressive equality legislation. The trade union movement in the UK pushed for the Equal Pay Act, the Race Relations Act, for abortion rights (mobilising again and again against attempts to restrict abortion), for the DDA and for LGBT rights in the workplace. The unions supported civil partnerships and the Gender Recognition Act.

In a way this strand of trade union engagement has marked a rebirth of the drive towards LGBT equality, justice and liberation (and gender and racial equality and liberation) which had been part of the earlier socialist and trade union movements in Britain (Engels, 1884; Carpenter, 1908).

Questions of 'prevalence'

It is not simply a matter of demanding more funding for more training, important as this is. Some argue that before being able to address issues of homophobia and transphobia in society, and in social work practice, it is necessary to gauge the extent of the problems and the nature of the shortcomings involved. There is some truth in this, but the research base remains weak. This partly reflects the generally poor database in UK official statistics – the national census and criminal statistics do not monitor LGBT factors, for example, and few institutions carry out staff or service user monitoring on this basis. This can make it hard even to estimate the numbers of lesbian, gay, bisexual or transgender people that are in society let alone find out the extent to which they may be over- or underrepresented in various social arenas.

What do we know about the prevalence of sexual orientation and gender variance in society? The estimate of the number of gay and lesbian people in the UK used by Stonewall is 3.6 million, around 6% of the population. This figure derives from Treasury estimates in 2005 carried out to examine the possible actuarial impact of the Civil Partnerships Act of that year. The national census in its ten-yearly survey does not include an item relating to a person's sexuality although advocacy organisations have been pressing for this for some time.

A large National Survey of Sexual Attitudes and Lifestyles (NATSAL) carried out in the UK in 1989/90 and again in 2000 surveyed around 19,000 people in 1989/90 and 11,000 in 1999/2000. A comparison of the findings over this 10-year period suggests interesting trends towards more people being prepared to disclose same-sex sexual behaviour and attitudes, no doubt a reflection of the generally more positive attitudes to homosexuality expressed in general surveys in the UK in recent decades, especially among young people.

The figures suggested (in 2000) that 9.7% of women reported having had a same-sex sexual experience, not necessarily involving genital contact (up from 2.8% in 1990) and 8.4% of men reported the same thing (up from 5.3% in 1990). By 2000 8.1% of men and 11.7% of women reported having felt sexual attraction towards a same-sex person at least once in their lives. Of course this does not mean that these men and women necessarily identify as lesbians, gay men or bisexual. It does suggest that people are more prepared to disclose the information and that there is no clear division between exclusive homosexuality and exclusive heterosexuality. This in turn reflects the much earlier results of Alfred Kinsey's research in the 1940s and 1950s in the US (www. kinseyinstitute.org/research/).

US figures on the composition of households, derived from the 2000 10-year national survey, indicated that there were 595,000 households consisting of same-sex partners out of a total number of 105.5 million households (www.avert.org). Thus about 1.2 million gay people in the US were living with a same-sex partner, a very considerable increase in the number from the previous census in 1990 which reported only 145,000 such households. These figures are bound to be a huge underestimate of the number of single gay people in the US. The Human Rights Commission, analysing voter polls and other surveys, concluded that 5% of the US population over 18 are gay, a figure similar to findings in the UK.

Stonewall deals only with lesbian, gay and bisexual people and does not advocate for trans people at all. Figures from GIRES suggest some parallels with the figures discussed above for lesbian and gay people. Reed et al (2009) drawing on three recent surveys of transpeople in the UK and Europe suggest that in 2009 there were approximately 10,000 people with 'gender dysphoria' of whom about 6,000 have undergone gender transition. About 80% of them had been assigned boys at birth, only 20% girls. However, the number of female to male transsexual people seems to be increasing disproportionately and it seems likely that the proportions of ftm (female to male) and mtf (male to female) trans people in the population are much more equal.

Add to this the figures available from gender identity clinics which report increases of around 15% per annum of gender dysphoric people presenting and this suggests the numbers are currently doubling every five years. It would seem likely that the greater exposure of role models, more support groups and more awareness of social and medical provision as well as recent positive legislative changes are factors encouraging more trans people to come out and seek help and advice.

It should be pointed out here that people who seek help with transition are perhaps the tip of a substantial iceberg of gender variant people in society. The term 'trans' is generally applied not only to transsexual people but to cross-dressers, drag queens and kings and others who subvert gender normative assumptions and expectations. Reed et al estimate that a more realistic number of gender variant people in the UK is around 500,000 if it is assumed that the gender balance is likely to be equal.

We can conclude, therefore, that 'service providers and employers need to be aware of this large group who, whether or not they present for medical treatment, may still experience discrimination and be vulnerable to bullying and hate crime' (Reed et al, 2009, p 4).

Despite a similar doubling in numbers every five years relatively few young trans people present for help and there is only one specialised gender identity service in the UK dealing with young people. When to start treatment is currently a contentious issue and UK policy is out of line with the more client-centred best-practice international approaches.

The median age at which transsexual people present is 42, even though they describe having experienced gender variance from an early age. Coming out to family, friends, school and work remains a difficult, stressful and risky prospect for many people whether LGB or T.

The improvement of data collection in order to make reliable estimates of need and user demand has been slow. LGBT advocacy organisations have not been unanimous in their support for the inclusion of monitoring at national or institutional levels, particularly in relation to trans people for reasons which may include concerns about confidentiality and anonymity, the potential for discrimination, the impact of homophobia and transphobia, data security, and so on.

This is despite the fact that gay people are now more visible as public figures, that there are prominent and established Pride parades, that there are 'safe' spaces such as pubs and clubs, and that civil partnerships are legal. Trans people and transgender issues have certainly made some progress out of the closets and into public consciousness over the last decade or so from being exclusively the subject of titillating press outings to sometimes more considered publicity. The fact that LGBT oppression, discrimination and hate crimes remain common means that people's concerns are hardly unreasonable.

So, on the one hand we have more 'out' LGBT people and greater formal rights and protections, but at the same time the incidence of reported homophobic crime in the UK actually rose during 2009. In London the figure jumped by about 20% compared with 2008, in Glasgow by 32%, Liverpool 40% and Manchester a staggering 63%. Stonewall reported figures in 2008 suggesting that 20% of lesbian and gay people had experienced homophobic aggression during the last three years. The increase does not seem to be a reflection of greater confidence to report to the police.

On the night of 25 September 2009 a gay man, Ian Baynham, was viciously attacked in Trafalgar Square, London. Eighteen days later doctors switched off his life support machine. Around the same time there were attacks in Liverpool which left other gay men seriously injured. Shortly afterwards there were protest vigils in London and Liverpool and later a sizeable demonstration in Liverpool which reflected not only the shock that LGBT people felt but also the determination that they and many straight people have to resist homophobic and transphobic hate crimes and oppression.

Another example was when the gay Boyzone star, Stephen Gately, died in late 2009. One newspaper carried a piece by a columnist, Jan Moir, attacking Gateley's 'unnatural' lifestyle, implying that this was implicated in his tragic death. It provoked over 25,000 people to complain to the Press Complaints Commission. Subsequently the PCC decided that while her comments may have been offensive to many they did not breach the guidelines. Many LGBT people will have seen this as the PCC pandering to homophobia in the guise of 'press freedom' and free speech.

Such attacks, sadly often carried out by young people, are, of course, not restricted to people perceived as gay. The website Transgender Day of Remembrance compiles international information about those murdered because of their perceived gender transgression. Brandon Teena is relatively well known because his life has featured in two movies (*Boys don't cry* and *The Brandon Teena story*). Brandon was a young trans man who was raped and beaten to death in the US after being outed by local police. In fact, you don't have to be a Trans person to be attacked. One man was attacked and killed in a Tennessee department store because he was guiding a blind man by the hand to the toilets and also carrying his wife's bag while she was trying on clothes. Sometimes the perception of gender transgression is enough.

Keeping body and soul together for trans people can be tough enough, but in virtually all countries insurance companies and health services will not pay, or are very reluctant to pay, for sex reassignment surgery, electrolysis to remove beard growth for transwomen, or hormonal intervention. Clearly there is a class element here in that for working-class people the options are much more limited.

There is also a perception among some trans people of a 'hierarchy of oppressions', a sense that LGBT rights, and especially trans rights, are low down the equality pecking order. Hence the outcry in the UK in 2008 from many activists in the trade union movement and beyond over the appointment of Joel Edwards, an evangelical Christian (to whom homophobic remarks had reportedly been attributed), as a Commissioner of the new Equality and Human Rights Commission (EHRC). Perhaps understandably this was regarded as an example of religious rights trumping LGBT rights.

The EHRC is the unitary body which, as a result of the Equality Act 2006, replaced the Disability Commission, the Equal Rights Commission and the Race Relations Commission. It is charged with opposing hate crime and promoting equality. Many people have been critical of the levels of funding afforded the EHRC by the Labour government, the provenance of various commissioners who have been appointed, and its underlying ethos of 'fairness' which is, arguably, a meaningless equality concept.

Social work teaching

It is only in recent years that unions like the National Union of Teachers (NUT), the University and College Union (UCU), and the local government union, Unison, have been able to negotiate model national policies covering lesbian and gay staff, and trans staff, in educational institutions.

Those of us who teach on social work courses know that many of our students may reflect some of the less liberated assumptions and attitudes of the society in which we live. Any student cohort would be unlikely to be otherwise. Thankfully some students, of course, are fully on board with LGBT rights and the class nature of our society. But good social work training and the development of ethical, empowering practice necessitate that all views antithetical to LGBT equality need to be explicitly challenged. The new Equality Act similarly includes the notion of *promoting* equality and resisting hate crime rather than merely responding to discrimination. This clearly requires that trainers, lecturers and practitioners need to take seriously the need to challenge LGBT oppression.

Resisting LGBT oppression and fighting to promote equality in social work practice is not simply a matter for explicitly LGBT staff or service users. No one would argue that resisting racism should only be down to black or minority ethnic people, or resisting disability oppression is only down to disabled people, yet sometimes educators and trainers will come across the notion that LGBT rights 'are fine, but I'm not gay so it doesn't really involve me'.

This is clearly a misapprehension of which colleagues and students need to be disabused. Any oppressed group must have the right to self-organise but the resistance to that oppression can only be ultimately effective if it seeks to unite with those not oppressed in these ways, and with other oppressed groups (Dee, 2010). Resistance to LGBT oppression has historically been most effective and successful when it has combined straight and gay people in a common struggle for gay rights.

Conclusion

If we are to seek to develop a radical social work which is empowering and liberatory then social workers need to be encouraged to identify with the demand for LGBT liberation, in other words to identify with the drive to create a society within which people are able to express their sexuality and their gender identity freely and without fear and intimidation.

A number of suggestions can be made in regard to social work training and practice:

1. Awareness of LGBT oppression and its effects needs to be embedded within social work training courses and practice. This needs to involve not just knowledge and understanding of policies, legislation and good practice but also an understanding of the roots of this oppression within the structure of the capitalist system and the role of the family within it. Training materials on LGBT issues are available and should be widely used (for example see the Learning and Skills Improvement Service, LSIS, www.lsis.org.uk).
2. Staff and service users need to be encouraged to get involved in forums, networks and conferences (such as the SWAN network in Scotland) which can examine shared experiences and good practice in respect of challenging LGBT oppression.
3. If we want to know what people feel and what they need and want, we could do worse than ask them. Social workers in every appropriate field need to develop genuinely reciprocal relationships with service users and advocacy groups. This has already been happening with disability and mental health user organisations; it needs to be developed with sexual orientation and gender identity groups.
4. Appropriate LGBT monitoring and evaluation mechanisms need to be introduced across the board. Again, this will need to be carried through in a positive and supportive way in cooperation with user and advocacy groups.
5. Social work institutions, workplaces and training environments need to consciously develop as LGBT friendly environments for staff, students and service users.

Over the next few years the impact of the global crisis means that social workers are unlikely to find social work practice easier. We are told that financial stringencies must result from the insistence that workers and the poor should pay for the crisis created by the rich. That means that the drive towards further privatisation and managerialism is almost certain to increase significantly. However there is never a right or wrong time to address the issues aired in this chapter. The hope is that the development of collective forms of resistance to the impact of the cuts which are bound to attack frontline services and benefits as well as increase poverty generally can be fought through growing networks of anti-oppressive social work practitioners and service users who actively rediscover a truly radical social work ethic which puts sexual orientation and gender expression front and centre.

Note

[1] In this chapter I will normally use the acronym LGBT but where authors or organisations restrict their remit to matters of sexuality only it may be more accurate to use the acronym LGB (lesbian, gay, bisexual).

SIX

Radical social work and service users: a crucial connection

Peter Beresford

Introduction

Social work is an activity that is essentially about relationships. A wide range of such relationships are involved between social work, the social worker and the state, society, communities, the family, the individual, collectivities, difference and equality. It is the nature of such relationships which signifies the form and purpose of social work. This is why historically social work has been conceived as both a liberatory and regulatory force – and indeed why it may sometimes be identified as both at the same time. It may not only serve to support or restrict human and civil rights. It may also privilege the state and its service system, or seek to prioritise the rights, needs and interests of the service user. All depends on the nature and purpose of its relationships. The relationship that has most often been considered is that between social work and the state. But the relationship of ultimate importance for social work, which defines its role, process and raison d'être, is that between it and service users.

This chapter focuses particularly on the relationship between radical social work and service users. It explores how this relationship has developed and changed since the inception of radical social work a generation ago, in the 1970s, and how it might need to be explored and further developed, if radical social work is to be sustained and best support the rights and needs of service users for the future. While much if not all of the original writing about radical social work was by people involved in the production of social work – as academics, practitioners, educators and so on, this chapter has a somewhat different origin. It comes primarily from a service user perspective. That is to say that I write primarily from my direct experience of using mental health services, including social work and my resulting involvement in service user organisations and movements. However, I also write as someone with an academic involvement in social work as a social work educator and researcher in a British university. It is helpful to be clear about our affiliations and perspectives because these undoubtedly affect our understandings of these issues.

The emergence of service user movements

Radical social work can be seen as a development that was increasingly influenced by women's, black people's, civil rights and lesbian, gay men and bisexual movements, as well as growing out of more traditional leftist and trade union campaigning and organising (Langan and Lee, 1989; Williams, 1989). But it is also the emergence of other movements that concerns us here. One far-reaching development which has taken place largely since the creation of radical social work, has been the emergence of service user movements (Lent, 2002). This has profound implications for social work generally and radical social work in particular, extending to both their understandings of and relationships with service users.

By such service user movements I mean those of people who identify as having been on the receiving end, particularly long term, of heavy end social policy practices and provisions and where this has played a central role in shaping their identity and/or their understandings of themselves and the policies and services they have experienced. Members of such movements are particularly associated with long term use of health and social care services. In developing their own ideas and discussions, they have highlighted the differences between their perspectives – where direct and explicit experience of such social policies is centrally involved – and those dominant discussions where this has not been the case. They have highlighted that people's status and role in relation to the use of such services are both relevant and important in understanding the values, beliefs and ideas that they have developed.

These movements include those of disabled people, psychiatric system survivors, people with learning difficulties, older people, looked-after young people in state care, people living with HIV/AIDS and other recipients and users of health, social care and income maintenance services. They have become increasingly powerful and influential, with their own democratically constituted local, national and international organisations and groupings. These movements and the organisations operating within them, have developed their own cultures, arts, ways of organising, knowledges, theories, values, strategies and demands (Campbell, 1996; Campbell and Oliver, 1996; Morris, 1996; Oliver and Barnes, 1998; Barnes et al, 1999; Beresford, 1999; Lindow, 2001). It is also important to note that, as with radical social work, Marxist analysis and leftist critiques played a significant part in the development of the thinking of these movements (see, for example, Oliver, 1990; Shakespeare, 1998).

Radical social work and service users

While these movements mainly came to prominence in the 1980s, the disabled people's movement had earlier origins, which can be traced to the 1960s and the efforts of disabled people segregated in institutions to live equal lives in mainstream society (Oliver, 1990 and 1996). They were the pioneers of such movements. Disabled people drew a distinction between organisations *for* disabled people, controlled by non-disabled people – notably large traditional disability charities – and organisations *of* disabled people (Oliver, 1990). These were the new organisations that they were developing. These were subject to the control of disabled people themselves and formed the basis of the disabled people's movement.

Key initial publications, of radical social work and the UK disabled people's movement, were almost contemporaneous, even though they were probably entirely separate developments. A founding document of the UK disabled people's movement, *The fundamental principles of disability* (UPIAS/Disability Alliance, 1976), was not published until a year after Bailey and Brake's (1975) *Radical social work*. There was little overlap or linkage between nascent service user developments and moves to radicalise social work, even though the latter have always concerned themselves with changed relationships between practitioners and service users or clients. Mary Langan's and Phil Lee's *Radical social work today* published in 1989 charted progress on this issue in one of its chapters (Beresford and Croft , 1989), highlighting how much work still needed to be done. By this time, radical social work had achieved only a limited degree of user involvement, despite its commitment to service users and the fact that the issue had been raised from service users' perspectives for some time (Beresford and Croft, 1980; Oliver, 1983).

The emergence of service user movements has significantly changed how service users have been understood by social work, including radical social work. The supporters of radical social work have always placed an emphasis on service users or clients and the need to align with them. Langan and Lee, writing in 1989, for example, argued that one of the major achievements of the original radical social work movement was that it 'pushed the interests of the client to the fore' (p 7). There was talk of 'clients' as 'political allies' (Taylor, 1972). Roy Bailey, one of the founding parents of radical social work emphasised its role in supporting 'those who seek to oppose the stigma and stereotyping of the recipients of social work, and who resist authoritarian attempts by the state to undermine their dignity' (Langan and Lee, 1989, foreword, pxviii).

However, the role of service users in the early days of radical social work seems to have been more symbolic than as active partners in its construction.

What seems to have shifted over time in radical social work is how service users have been understood and how this has been expressed. It is interesting to see the different ways in which different groups have been conceived in social work and radical social work literature. Some groups, for example, unemployed, homeless and poor people and people in prison and the criminal justice system, for example, seemed to be seen as the outcomes and symbols of the oppressive nature of the state and capitalist economy and therefore natural allies of and focus for radical social work seeking to counter this (Bailey and Brake, 1975; Brake and Bailey, 1980). On the other hand, Mary Langan and Phil Lee in their 1989 book revisiting radical social work, talked of social work's role in relation to other groups that they described as 'supposedly perennial social casualties such as the disabled, neglected children, the psychologically disturbed and older people' (p 7). They saw radical social work as having a real role to play in 'empowering' such service users (p 9). This was consistent with the views of mainstream social work commentators like Olive Stevenson and Phyllida Parsloe, who wrote about social work's role as an empowering profession (Stevenson and Parsloe, 1993). Service users, in contrast have repeatedly rejected this view, arguing that only they can empower themselves and each other and that what social work can helpfully do is support this essentially user-led and collective activity.

Thus to begin with, social work clients or service users tended to be framed in terms of claimants' and tenants' organisations and homeless people. This can be seen to be related to how people were organised (as far as they were at that time) and what were seen as key issues. Inequality, poverty and homelessness were seen by radical social workers as burning and worsening issues under Thatcherism. While it is difficult to be exact about this, radical social work of the 1970s and 1980s seemed to focus more on families and children than on social work with adults. Since then it could be argued that discussions about user involvement in social work and social care have done the opposite and that both the needs of families and children and the complexities of involving them have been paid less attention.

More recently in the UK, the focus has been on adult groups of disabled people (generally taken to mean people with physical and sensory impairments), older people, people with learning difficulties and mental health service users/survivors. This can clearly be linked with the emergence of movements and organisations of such service users, which have themselves pressed for such involvement in social policy, social care and social work. Although social work with these adult groups can certainly include the controlling functions of state social work, this has sometimes been glossed over and the controversies associated with child protection and some other areas of social work more readily sidestepped.

Interestingly, when I was involved in a recent national Swedish project to evaluate and advance user involvement in social work education, different groups of service users seemed to be involved. There was more emphasis on the involvement of people with experience of illegal drug use, alcohol dependence and the criminal justice system, as well as mental health service users, with less involvement, for example, from people with learning difficulties and physical and sensory impairments. Students were also, helpfully, more actively involved in the process (Bergsten et al, 2009).

Service user values, social work values

There are local, regional, national, European and international service user organisations (Beresford, 1999). While service user movements vary in nature and purpose, they tend to be based on formally democratically constituted organisations. Such movements have developed in the majority world as well as in Western societies (Charlton, 1998; Stone, 1999). While for example, the disabled people's and mental health service user/survivor movements can be seen to have a number of significant differences, all service user movements seem to have important values and goals in common. They all highlight the importance they attach to:

- service users speaking and acting for themselves;
- working together to achieve change;
- having more say over their lives and the support that they receive;
- challenging stigma and discrimination;
- having access to alternatives to prevailing medicalised interventions and understandings;
- the value of user-controlled organisations, support and services;

- a focus on people's human and civil rights and their citizenship. This has emerged later, but is increasingly evident of the survivors' movement;
- being part of mainstream life and communities, able to take on responsibilities as well as securing entitlements (Beresford and Harding, 1993; Campbell, 1996).

The first clear expression of a service user movement's principles were included in the set of 'fundamental principles of disability' referred to earlier, which were identified in 1976 by the Union of the Physically Impaired Against Segregation (UPIAS) to explore how disabled people 'could become more active in the disability field' and consider a 'long-term programme of action' to make that possible (UPIAS/ Disability Alliance, 1976, p 3). UPIAS, which was founded in 1972, has been described by disabled people as 'an important organisation in the development of the [UK] disabled people's movement [which] firmly placed "disability" within a social context... [It] became the first disability liberation group in the UK, and one of the first in the world' (www.gmcdp.com/UPIAS.html).

Its 'fundamental principles' were that 'disability is a situation, caused by social conditions, which requires for its elimination':

(a) that no one aspect such as incomes, mobility or institutions is treated in isolation;

(b) that disabled people should, with the advice and help of others, assume control over their own lives;

(c) that professionals, experts and others who seek to help must be committed to promoting such control by disabled people. (UPIAS/Disability Alliance, 1976, p 3)

Underpinning the 'fundamental principles' and UPIAS's values were two ideas which have been key for the future of disabled people's campaigning and self-organisation and which have also had significant impact on other user movements as well as public policy. These are first the social model of disability, which rejects a medicalised individual understanding of disability and highlights the discrimination and oppression which disabled people experience in society. Second, following from this is the philosophy of independent living, which argues that disabled people should have the access and support they need to live their lives on as equal terms to non-disabled people as possible, rather than seeing the need for support as following from the deficits, deficiencies and pathology of disabled people (Oliver, 1996; Thomas, 2007).

The failure to meet the challenge

Writing in 2009, Mike Oliver, the disability activist and academic reported on his efforts to influence social work and his conclusions about social work's response. The aim of his 1983 book, *Social work with disabled people* was to 'switch social work intervention away from impaired individuals and target the disabling society' (Oliver, 1983). In 1986 the British Association of Social Workers adopted this social model approach, but Oliver concludes that the individual model still dominates in social work as in other professions and that disability issues are still poorly dealt with in social work education. (Oliver and Sapey, 2006):

> Social work has failed to meet disabled people's self-articulated needs. Twenty years ago, I predicted that if social work was not prepared to change in terms of its practice relating to disabled people it would eventually disappear altogether (Oliver, 1983) … It seems likely that the forecast is about to come true. We can probably now announce the death of social work at least in relation to its involvement in the lives of disabled people. (Oliver, 2009, p 51)

Some might feel that Oliver is unduly pessimistic and his conclusions are too sweeping. Certainly, in Shaping Our Lives, the national service user organisation and network, we have found strong support for social work among many service users because they value the social approach which they associate with good practitioners who work with them, which takes account of both them as individuals and their broader circumstances and the relation between the two (Beresford et al, 2005; Branfield et al, 2005). But at the same time, adult service users now have much less contact with social workers; the approved social worker role, for example, has been replaced by the approved mental health professional, who may come from a range of disciplines, the move to care management has meant that much social work with adults is concerned with rationing and restricting, rather than providing support and the move to 'personalisation' and 'self-directed support' has been associated with the loss of professional social work jobs and their replacement with unqualified staff to make assessments and provide 'care packages'.

Roy Bailey wrote in 1988 that social work education and training must be 'practice-led' otherwise, he feared, it would be 'employer-led' and that will 'be to the detriment of educator, student, practitioner and "client" alike' (Langan and Lee, 1989, foreword, p xviii). This same point might be made about social work generally as well as its education. The reality is that social work has been far from being practice or practitioner-led, let alone user-led. As a result it has increasingly been shaped by other external forces, notably ideological, political (including both local and central state), managerialist, technical and hierarchical forces. This is reflected in the conclusions even of the government-established Social Work Reform Board in its final report where the adverse consequences of over-reliance on inappropriate information technology and bureaucratisation are noted (DCSF/DH, 2009).

Social work's weak leadership

Social work's leadership has long suffered from chronic weakness. This has been typified by social work's professional organisation, the British Association of Social Workers (BASW). In early 2010 it was again in the news for balloting its members over establishing its own college of social work in direct competition to the independent college to which the government had made both political and financial commitments. Many of BASW's problems might be seen as social work's problems too; the problems of a profession lacking the status or security of medicine or the law; which is associated with difficult and politically sensitive practice and often unpopular groups of service users.

However, BASW's difficulties have been long term, as a reading of back numbers of the magazine *Community Care* makes clear (Editorial, 1978a, 1978b and 1981; Bessell, 1978). They seem to have begun early in its life. So in 1978, a *Community Care* editorial was headlined 'Time to resolve BASW's crises' (Editorial, 1978b, p 1). By 1981, another editorial said that BASW has been suffering 'some of the worst turmoils in its history' (Editorial, 1981, p 1). Over the years BASW has been faced with repeated financial problems, internal disagreements and the making of difficult decisions. At different times, it decided both to include and exclude unqualified social workers; not to be and to be a trade union, as well as a professional association. As long ago as 1981, *Community Care* reported that 'a strong, self-confident professional organisation willing and able to examine the sometimes complex issues of care and control involved in the provision of personal social services is becoming more necessary than ever' (Editorial, 1981, p 1). It would be difficult to disagree. These were exactly the same conclusions that the Social Work Task Force reached nearly 30 years later (DCSF/DH, 2009).

In 1978 *Community Care* was expressing concern over the 'waning membership' of BASW (Bessell, 1978). Then it was under 10,000. The key issue here, however, is that then represented *30%* of qualified social workers. Its situation now is far worse, with 80,000 qualified social workers and *less than 13,000 BASW members*. When we look to other professions, like occupational therapy, which faces many of the same difficulties as social work, it has nonetheless established its own national college, which has a far higher proportion of the profession as members and is a trade union as well as being a professional association.

Such weakness in social work leadership and collectivity, as well as independence, extends beyond BASW. Less than half of all qualified social workers are believed to be members of any kind of collective organisation. Associated bodies like the General Social Care Council, Social Care Institute for Excellence and Skills for Care, have been variously tied in with government funding and agendas and branded in social care terms, which carry little public understanding or support rather than focusing specifically on social work, like past bodies, along the lines of the National Institute for Social Work. It is so far not clear how the proposed Social Work College will avoid the problems of being top-down and over-bureaucratic that have damaged other bodies.

Radical social work and service users now

This is why the role for radical social work is so important. It is difficult to see how a positive role for social work will be secured and sustained for the future without the existence of a determined and effective radical social work movement. This is a time of great change and uncertainty generally and for social work specifically. In 2004, Suzy Croft, a long-term qualified social work practitioner, and I wrote that since the publication of an early pamphlet of ours in 1980, *Community control of social services departments* (Beresford and Croft, 1980):

> the situation of service users and their organisations has in some ways been transformed. That of social work practitioners, has if anything, been further weakened and that of other local people [in social services] continues to be marginal. But now there is, at least, a force to make 'community control' possible, in the form of service users' movements and organizations. (Beresford and Croft, 2004, p 65)

Judging from the Social Work Task Force's work, the negative pressures on face-to-face social work practitioners have not diminished since then (DCSF/DH, 2009). Little seems to have been achieved in the mainstream to strengthen social workers' solidarity in the intervening years (Beresford, 2010). But there have been major developments in social work radicalism. A shift in atmosphere can be sensed if not evidenced. There are clear signs of a fight-back with some positive things happening.

Two major national events in 2006 and 2008 and a smaller planning one between them, with more to come, focused on social work's value base. They brought together, as speakers, some of the key spokespersons of radical and progressive social work. They first launched a Community Care magazine campaign: 'Affirming our value base in social work and social care'. Organised by Jim Wild and his then colleagues of Nottingham Trent University, these massive and hugely popular events brought together thousands of social work practitioners, social work students, educators and service users and were followed by a number of high-profile publications (Beresford, 2006a, 2006b; Barnard et al, 2008). Attendance highlighted the youth and diversity of participants. Students came to the events in coachloads, some taking part in the conference as a formal part of their curriculum. Service users were involved in planning and as key contributors as well as being participants.

The second key development is the establishment of the Social Work Action Network (SWAN), one of whose initiatives is this book. The development of SWAN followed the publication of the *Social work manifesto* in 2004 (Jones, et al, 2004). SWAN describes itself as: 'a loose network of social work practitioners, academics, students and social welfare service users united in their concern that social work activity is being undermined by managerialism and marketisation, by the stigmatisation of service users and by welfare cuts and restrictions' (SWAN, 2010).

Led by a steering group, SWAN works through organising events, establishing regional groups and activities, developing an international presence and voice, responding to mainstream events and developments like the Baby P Inquiry and England Social Work Task Force, as well as producing its own initiatives, discussions and publications and building links with workers, community, service user and other progressive organisations. In its process, focus and goals, from its early days, SWAN has sought to involve service users and service user organisations actively and on equal terms. A service user is chair of its steering group.

Both these developments, the Nottingham events and SWAN, have prioritised user involvement and the equal engagement of service users in an effective and meaningful way. There seems to have been a genuine commitment to such involvement in both their process and purpose. In my view, this has reflected a step change in radical social work's relation with service users from its earlier manifestations. While a strong allegiance to the struggles and interests of service users was firmly expressed in the earlier days of radical social work, this was not routinely linked with meaningful partnerships in developing its strategy, or in its day-to-day working. While this may reflect the fact that the development of service user organisations was then at an earlier stage, radical social work and service user activism were essentially unconnected developments.

The two radical social work developments detailed above, as well as others at local and national level, provide a benchmark for taking forward radical social work that is based on and fosters equal relations with service users. They also highlight, from a service user perspective, two key areas of concern for the future if such radical social work is to be sustained, and exert a strong influence on social work and social policy more generally. These relate to:

- the form such radical social work may need to take
- how it is to extend and maintain user involvement and equal relations with service users and their movements.

It is with these two areas of focus that I will end this chapter. Two points should be made about this. First, these are my thoughts, intended to provide a basis for discussion rather than to close off debate. Second, both areas of focus might most helpfully be seen as the basis for *all* social work, not just a specific species of 'radical' social work. All social work should be committed to anti-discrimination, rights-based social change, independent living and empowerment. However, the valuable role that radical social work is still called on to play is to help make it possible for social work more generally to come closer in its day-to-day reality to supporting such values and principles.

The form of radical social work

While this list is not intended to be exhausted, here are some of the qualities and components that we might expect to be essential if radical social work is to be participatory, inclusive and sustainable as a force for change in social work. Certainly, these are elements that service users and their organisations highlight.

The essentially political nature of social work

Ultimately social work is a *political* profession unlike most others. This is its defining characteristic and doubtless the reason it encounters such opposition from state and other dominant institutions. It is inherently and essentially concerned with supporting people's empowerment, with challenging existing inequalities and disadvantage, ensuring people receive their entitlements, enabling them to undertake their responsibilities and securing and safeguarding their civil and human rights. Acknowledgement of its essentially political nature is crucial; it cannot merely be seen as offering technical assistance or functioning in a consensual way as a 'helping profession'. If social work is functioning effectively with and on behalf of the individuals, families, groups and communities with whom it works, then it is likely to be challenging the market, both local and central state, and other powerful interests that may disempower them.

Recognising the micro politics of social work

Radical social work commentators have written helpfully about the importance of 'micro politics' for social work (Statham, 1978). They have highlighted the importance of addressing 'how broader political processes operate at the level of the individual and personal relationships, among social workers and at the interface between social workers and [service users]' (Langan and Lee, 1989, p 8). This also includes supporting service users' access to benefits and developing welfare rights work and take-up campaigns alongside them (Langan and Lee, 1989, p 8). As has long been argued, some social workers have failed adequately to acknowledge the importance of material issues and poverty for the people with whom they work or to incorporate this adequately into their practice (Wootton, 1978; Jones and Novak, 1999).

The primacy of the relationship and human qualities in social work

Repeatedly, when they are asked, service users highlight that they see the relationship that they have with the social worker as key to the support (s)he can offer. This relationship is the precondition for building trust and understanding and for the social worker to be able to offer the service user meaningful and appropriate support. Despite this, such relationships have often been restricted in modern statutory social work. Alongside this relationship, service users prioritise the human qualities of social workers as important to them. These include qualities of empathy, listening, being non-judgemental and accepting, being warm, well-informed, supportive and committed to anti-discrimination and equality. These are seen as key to positive practice (Beresford et al, 2007; Glynn et al, 2008).

Social work based on a social model approach

What distinguishes social work is the social. Yet social work, as Mike Oliver has observed, is often still tied to medicalised models and understandings. The particular strength of social work is that it focuses on the person, their social setting and the relation between the two. However, social work needs to be based on a social model, not only in the sense that it recognises 'environmental' issues and sees service users in their broader socio-political context. It needs to be based on a social model approach inspired by the social model of disability developed by the disabled people's movement. This has since been developed more generally by service users as a barriers-based model that takes account of the discrimination and oppression they experience. Following from this, social work should also be based on the philosophy of independent living, an emancipatory model of practice and service user values and ideas more generally.

Supportive not controlling social work

Social work has long been concerned with restricting as well as supporting people's rights. Sometimes ostensibly to safeguard one person's rights, it may be involved in limiting someone else's. Recent government statements which have discussed social work 'reserved tasks', that is, tasks which it sees that only social workers are qualified to do, have tended to place an emphasis on social work's control role (Beresford, 2007a and 2007b). This is as unhelpful as the emphasis on social work as a rationing system in care management. Social work primarily needs to be seen as a source of support. Where, for example, a social worker has to prioritise the rights of a child over its parent, then another social worker or other advocate should be involved to safeguard the latter's rights, which may be at risk. A single social worker should not be expected to be concerned with both the rights of children and parents suspected of abusing them. This equivocal allegiance has been the starting point for many of the child protection problems we have seen in recent years. The primary role of social work should be seen to offer support. Where it retains control roles, it must be clear that these are to safeguard another person's interests, rather than merely serving as an agent of the state.

Participatory social work education

All qualifying and post-qualifying social work education and training is now required to have user and carer involvement in all its aspects and stages. This is greatly valued by students and service users. However, such practice and policy continue to be patchy, with very positive developments in some colleges and areas and less progress in others. The Social Work Education Participation project (www. socialworkeducation.org.uk) a joint initiative between service users, carers and the Social Care Institute for Excellence, works to develop a user-led strategic approach to such involvement to provide information and guidance nationally.

Participatory social work

If social work is to be a truly emancipatory activity rather than a paternalistic or regulatory one, then it must be fully participatory, involving practitioners, local people and, crucially, service users on equal terms (Beresford and Croft, 1980). The nature and value-base of such involvement must also be clear. As Suzy Croft and I wrote in 1989 in *Radical social work today*, 'democratisation should not be confused with the new welfare pluralist consumerism. ...the consumerist model imposed a passivity on service users that ideas of democratisation based on citizenship seek to challenge' (p 117). Social work, as is further discussed below must be participatory in its process and goals, fully and equally involving service users and their organisations in the development and decision-making of both.

Practice-led social work

It is essential that social work also prioritises the perspectives and experiential knowledge of face-to-face practitioners. They have frequently been marginalised in the mainstream development of social work, particularly statutory social work, where political, economic, managerialist and top-down criteria have tended to predominate to the detriment of social workers and service users. Social work needs to be practice-led, and if it is to be so, then practitioners will require much more support – in the workplace and beyond. The final report of the Social Work Task Force included key recommendations consistent with this, encouraging workers to stay in face-to-face practice as a career, rather than having to go into management and emphasising the importance of a supportive and 'healthy' workplace environment, ensuring workers adequate and appropriate support, supervision and resources (DCSF/DH, 2009).

Practice as co-production

There is a tendency for user involvement to be abstracted and treated as a distinct entity on its own, based on meetings, committees and information seeking. Occupational practice, however, is a key, if often neglected area for involvement. What this means is that understanding and construction of social work practice comes to be seen as a joint activity or project between service user and worker, in which the former can play an active role in structuring and shaping in accordance with their rights and needs. The service user is thus able to feed into and influence such practice through its whole course, as long as they are able and wish to. This is probably what good practice has always been.

Social work for all

Modern social work has mainly been focused on individuals and groups seen as particularly disadvantaged and disempowered. It unquestionably has a valuable role to play with people in such circumstances, helping them to gain a voice and secure their entitlements. But there is no reason why it should be restricted to such a narrow and residual role. This reflects policymakers' preoccupation with social work as a marginal activity. It is important that social work is reconceived and its value as a source of support for *all* and not only marginalised people facing particular material barriers is acknowledged and recognised. This has been the case with specialist palliative care social work, which reaches a very wide range of people and is greatly valued by service users (Beresford et al, 2007).

Addressing equality and diversity

A growing concern first of radical social work and then of social work more generally over the years has been the need to address issues of diversity and equality. This has been reflected in the development of concepts of anti-discriminatory (ADP) and anti-oppressive social work practice (AOP), with much discussion on the subject. AOP has been presented as a key approach to, and theory of, social work. Yet while AOP has been a guiding theme in social work teaching and practice for at least two decades, the picture of social work practice emerging from service users is still generally far from positive (for example, Harding and Beresford, 1996; Oliver and Sapey, 2006). So far there has been a noticeable failure to include service users and their organisations in the development of anti-oppressive practice. As a result it can be seen more as an 'expert' appropriation of service user knowledge and experience than a genuinely liberatory development (Wilson and Beresford, 2000). This must be challenged if issues of equality and diversity are to be effectively advanced in radical social work.

Ensuring equal involvement in radical social work

Ensuring effective user involvement in radical social work will mean extending the co-production of social work between practitioners and service users that defines good practice, to social work's production as a policy and practice overall. This means the effective involvement of service users and their organisations in shaping social work policy and practice. 'Nothing about us without us' has become a rallying cry of the international disabled people's movement (Charlton, 1998). This phrase has increasingly come to be used by policymakers and in the service system. In the process, it has become somewhat devalued and clichéd. Its true meaning, however, remains powerful for service users and it is a valuable way of highlighting what the relationship between radical social work and service users needs to be – one in which service users and their organisations are constantly involved and ever-present.

If radical social work is to maintain and extend its commitment to advancing the rights and interests of service users, then user involvement has to be built in systematically to its organisations, structures and activities. This has long been the message from service users and their organisations, if such involvement is to be effective rather than tokenistic and subversive (Beresford and Croft, 1993; Campbell and Oliver, 1996). Such involvement needs to be ongoing, put in place as early from the start of any initiative as possible and constantly monitored and evaluated. It also needs to be based on a democratic rather than a managerialist/ consumerist approach to participation, if it is to increase the say and control of service users and equalise power relations, rather than merely serve as a form of consultation, market research or information gathering (Beresford and Croft, 1992).

While we should not under-estimate the difficulties of supporting such involvement, the lesson from the substantial body of experience that now exists is that it is feasible and achievable. This is true so long as the commitment to involvement is there and to new learning to achieve it. It may not always be possible to ensure ideal involvement, but this should never become an obstacle in the way of working for the best possible outcome. A number of key elements to ensure effective involvement are repeatedly identified and these need to be addressed in taking it forward in radical social work.

Ensuring diverse and inclusive involvement

It is crucial to work to involve the wide range of social work service users, otherwise participation will merely mirror broader exclusions. Thus efforts to involve people as service users should include:

- challenging exclusions and discriminations on grounds of gender, sexuality, 'race', belief, disability, age, class, culture, and so on;
- involving all groups of service users, from children and young people to older people, people with chronic and life-limiting illnesses and including service users subject to control as well as receiving support, for example, mental health service users under section and in forensic services, parents in child protection situations, illegal drug users, or people in the criminal justice system;
- involving service users regardless of where they live, including people living in residential institutions, in prison, who are homeless, travellers, or living in rural as well as urban areas; involving service users facing additional barriers, for example asylum seekers, those who communicate differently, including non-verbally, who use British Sign Language, or for whom English is not their first language, disabled parents, and so on;
- service users with complex and multiple impairments.

Access and support to enable diverse involvement

A key lesson learned about user involvement is that for it to work for everyone, to enable diverse involvement and to embrace 'seldom heard voices', there are two essentials which need to be in place. These can be simply headlined as: access and support. Access means that there are structured, on-going ways of being involved; of engaging with services and agencies, of getting in and connecting with structures of organisation, management, control and decision-making. Access needs to include:

- physical and environmental access
- communication access
- cultural access

Support means that people can expect to have whatever help, support, encouragement, information and skill development they may each need to contribute what they want to, how they want to. Support can mean gaining new skills and confidence as well as having practical resources to participate, like expenses, payment, child and respite care and accessible meeting places. If there isn't access, trying to be involved can feel like banging on a closed door. But if there isn't support, only the most confident, experienced and assertive people tend to get involved – and then they can expect to be criticised for not being 'representative'.

Both components: access and support, are crucial if the aim is to move to more equal and broad-based user involvement; ensuring the availability of both means that organisations will have to work differently (Beresford and Croft, 1993). My personal experience from years of involvement in Shaping Our Lives, the national disabled people's and service user organisation and network, is that seeking to work in more inclusive and accessible ways is actually to everybody's benefit. However, it does mean recognising the need for significant change in how individuals and groups work together.

Over time, we have also learned that enabling user involvement in particular areas is especially helpful. This includes developing user involvement in:

- professional practice
- professional education and training
- developing user-controlled services and support

We have looked at each of these earlier. But user involvement is also important in the areas of:

- developing standards and outcome measures, so that these are user-led rather than professional or bureaucratic in origin;
- research and evaluation (Beresford, 2005; Lowes and Hulatt, 2005).

Ultimately effective and inclusive user involvement in radical social work will also mean:

- building such involvement routinely into the structures, processes, activities and organisations of radical social work. SWAN, for

example, has so far shown a real commitment to do this;building alliances with service users and their organisations and movements;
- ensuring involvement in all stages and levels of decision-making;
- supporting the development of local, regional, national and international user-controlled organisations, services and support. Radical social work needs to be seen as an international movement and user involvement will need to develop internationally consistent with that.

Conclusion

In early 2010 a group of social work students from London South Bank University, some of whom are involved in SWAN, organised their own conference, Neoliberalism versus Social Justice.They asked two key questions for social work and social workers:

- Can I practise the social work I *believe* in within the statutory sector?
- Is social work ready for the ethical challenges of the future?

Underpinning the event was their concern with practising value-based social work, consistent with the rights and needs of service users in the face of managerial, ideological and political pressures pulling them in different directions.This is the crucial issue for the future of social work. Participants included practitioners, service users and educators as well as social work students. Significantly, in addition to major figures like the Chair of the Social Work Reform Board, Moira Gibbs, unlike most social work conferences, current social work practitioners and service users featured centrally in the speaker line-up.The conference gained high visibility, featuring in an online thread of *Community Care* magazine and then being reported in the magazine (Morton and Angel, 2010).

It is perhaps with social work students that the future of sustainable radical social work truly lies. Significantly they have featured strongly in both the events organised by SWAN and Nottingham Trent University. Social work students now include a growing number with their own experience as service users, for whom user involvement is becoming routine in their social work education. Each year as new social work students are recruited, educators again hear the positive reasons why people come into social work – to support people, to overcome disempowerment to help secure their rights.Too often such commitments have been ground down or subverted by the opposing forces working on social work and social policy more generally. Radical social work – co-produced with service users and alongside service users has a key role to play in keeping that flame burning for all of us.

SEVEN

Why class (still) matters

Iain Ferguson

Introduction

Politics in the UK took an unexpected detour towards the end of 2009. Following 12 years during which the notion of class was effectively banished from official political discourse and poverty was presented as an issue of social exclusion rather than of income inequality, New Labour rediscovered class.

The rediscovery began in November of that year with Chancellor Alistair Darling's imposition of a windfall tax on bankers' bonuses. It continued with a well-prepared, and much publicised, jibe by Gordon Brown during Prime Minister's Question Time about the Conservatives' economic policies having been 'dreamed up on the playing fields of Eton'. And it culminated in Equalities Minister Harriet Harman's response to the publication in January 2010 of a major government-commissioned report on equality when she declared that 'persistent inequality of socio-economic status – of class – overarches the discrimination or disadvantage that can come from your gender, race or disability' (*The Guardian*, 20 January, 2010).

Despite the predictable outrage of the Conservative front bench and right-wing tabloid press at what they portrayed as a return to 'class war' politics, those who hoped that this development might presage a rejection of the neoliberal principles which had informed the social and economic policies of New Labour governments since 1997 were to be disappointed. Within weeks of his attack on the class background of the Tory leadership, Prime Minister Gordon Brown had gone out of his way to counter the attack from the Right by emphasising New Labour's mission as a party not of the working class but of the middle class, committed above all to social mobility and the encouragement of social aspiration.

In truth, few were surprised by this rapid retreat to conventional Third Way politics. As most people recognised, the Party's rediscovery of class owed less to some change of heart on the part of the leadership and more to the imminence of a general election and the perceived need to address two very different sorts of electoral considerations.

First, there was the enormous public anger generated by two events in the preceding year: one, the extraordinary greed of bankers who continued to receive huge bonuses, despite having brought the global financial system close to meltdown in 2008; the other, the revelation that more than half of all British Members of Parliament had fraudulently claimed expenses, in a scandal that led to the resignation of the Speaker of the House of Commons and saw popular confidence in Parliament plummet to new levels. Failing to express that widespread anger in some form would have risked further electoral damage for a party which, despite its record in government, was still seen by many as being in some sense a representative of working-class interests.

There was, however, a second, more disturbing, reason for New Labour's use of class rhetoric. For 2009 also saw the promotion of a new discourse by politicians and sections of the liberal media concerning the plight of the 'white working class', the implication being that material and educational advances by black and Asian people had been at their expense. The evidence for this argument will be considered later in this chapter but a key factor underpinning it was a none-too-subtle attempt to undercut the electoral appeal of the fascist British National Party by shifting the debate onto their terrain (Sveinsson, 2009).

That said, a positive outcome of New Labour's flirtation with class politics has been to let the genie of class out of the bottle, putting issues of poverty and inequality back onto the agenda of political discussion and debate. In relation to the themes of this collection, then, it provides a useful point of connection with the radical social work debates of the 1970s. For if there was one issue on which the editors of the collection *Radical social work* were clear, it was the centrality of class in shaping the lives of the people who used social work services. As they wrote in the introduction, 'radical social work ... is essentially understanding the position of the oppressed in the context of the social and economic structures in which they live. A socialist perspective is, for us, the most human approach for social workers' (Bailey and Brake, 1975, p 9).

In this chapter, I want to explore the extent to which class continues to matter for social work 35 years on in what are, in some ways, the very different conditions of the 21st century. This exploration will involve addressing three distinct but related aspects of class:

- class as social division and determinant of life chances;

- class as an explanatory framework, a way of making sense both of the experience of people who use social work services and those who work in them;
- class as agent of social change – the politics of class.

Class as social division and determinant of life chances

A curious paradox surrounds contemporary discussions of class. On the one hand, class as a *theoretical* concept has never been less fashionable and to all intents and purposes has been excised from political and academic discourse (Westergaard, 1995; Mooney, 2000). On the other hand, as a body of evidence compiled by health epidemiologists, geographers and economists over the last three decades convincingly demonstrates, class as a social division has seldom been more significant, with income inequality currently standing at its highest level for more than half a century (Dorling, 2010; Wilkinson and Pickett, 2010). If we wish to talk about an evidence base for practice, then it would be difficult to find a more robust and consistent body of empirical data in any area of social science than that concerning the extent and impact of such inequality.

Much of the existing data, alongside new data, was brought together in early 2010 by the social policy academic John Hills and his colleagues in a 456-page government-commissioned report entitled *An anatomy of economic inequality in the UK* (Hills et al, 2010, hereafter referred to as the 'Hills Report'). This report might with justification be seen as the 21st-century equivalent of the landmark 1979 Black Report on health inequalities (Whitehead et al, 1988). The Hills Report contains a wealth of valuable information but here I shall focus on two of its key findings which relate to the themes of this chapter.

Inequality in household wealth

The Report found that inequalities in income in the UK, as measured by the widely-used Gini coefficient, are higher now than they have been at any time since shortly after the Second World War (Hills et al, 2010, p39). The household wealth of the top 10% of the population stands at £853,000 and more – over 100 times higher than the wealth of the poorest 10%, which is £8,800 or below (a sum including cars and other possessions). When the highest-paid workers, such as bankers and chief executives, are put into the equation, the division in wealth is even more stark, with individuals in the top 1% of the population each possessing total household wealth of £2.6m or more.

In the 1990s, it was fashionable among Third Way theorists to refer to a 'two thirds, one third' society in which the majority of people were reasonably well-off, while another third constituted an underclass who had somehow failed to benefit from the general rise in prosperity. As Hills and his colleagues demonstrate, the reality, both then and now, is very different. Instead, we are talking about a society where, according to the Report, more than 50% of the British population have a weekly income of less than £223.

As Hills shows, most of this increase in inequality occurred during the 1980s and 1990s under the Conservative governments of Margaret Thatcher and John Major. This is a finding which needs to be emphasised. It has become fashionable in recent years for politicians of different political persuasions to seek to pin the blame for contemporary social problems on the values of the 'permissive society' of the 1960s, notably in the 'Broken Society' rhetoric of David Cameron and Iain Duncan Smith and their ideological supporters in the Centre for Social Justice (www.centreforsocialjustice.org.uk/). By contrast, what the Hills Report suggests is that to the extent that British society *is* broken (and the thesis is a contentious one), the origins of that fracture should be sought in the 1980s, not the 1960s.

That said, while the greatest growth in inequality took place under the Conservatives, the Report is also clear that 13 years of New Labour governments have done little to reverse that trend:

> Over the most recent decade, earnings inequality has narrowed a little and income inequality has stabilised on some measures, but the large inequality growth of the 1980s has not been reversed. (Hills et al, 2010, p 1)

The finding is not perhaps a surprising one, given the New Labour leadership's rejection of redistributionist tax policies since 1997, and their unwillingness to countenance measures to address poverty and inequality which would have involved challenging the vested interests of British capitalism.

Class, gender and 'race'

A second finding of the Report which I wish to address concerns the levels of inequality *between* different social groups (such as women and minority ethnic communities) as well as the degree of inequality *within* them. According to Hills:

Differences in outcomes between the more and less advantaged *within* each social group, however the population is classified, are much greater than differences *between* social groups. Even if all differences between groups were removed, overall inequalities would remain wide. The inequality growth of the last forty years is mostly attributable to growing gaps within groups rather than between them. (Hills et al, 2010a, p 1)

The finding is a significant one. As noted earlier, some politicians and media commentators have seized on the evidence of educational progress among BME communities in particular to argue that the struggle against racism has now been won, and that the focus of concern should now shift to the 'white working class'. Thus, in a statement in early 2010, New Labour Communities Minister John Denham argued that the significant improvements in 'race relations' over the previous decade required a shift on the part of government from 'race' to class strategies (J. Denham, 2010). As Hills makes clear, however, this is a spurious conclusion to draw, for two reasons.

First, while

some of the widest gaps in outcomes between social groups have narrowed in the last decade, particularly between the earnings of women and men, and in the educational qualifications of different ethnic groups...deep-seated and systematic differences in economic outcomes remain between social groups across all of the dimensions we examine. Despite the elimination and even reversal of the qualification differences that often explain them, significant differences remain in employment rates and relative pay between men and women and between ethnic groups. (Hills et al, 2010, p 385)

As an example, research published by the Institute for Race Relations in 2010 showed that, after two years of recession, almost half of young black people were unemployed, and that the unemployment rate of black people aged 16–24 was well over twice the 20% rate of their white counterparts (cited in Bourne, 2010).

Second, as these figures suggest, while the past few decades have seen the emergence of a black middle class in the UK, and while a minority of women have also managed to break through 'the glass ceiling' into well-paid positions in industry, finance, public services and the professions, in each case, we are talking about a minority – the experience of the great majority of women and of black people has been very different. As in the US, the rise of both of these groups is in part a product of the great social struggles of the late 1960s and early 1970s against racism and women's oppression, in part a product of a dominant neoliberal worldview in which, where necessary, market considerations can trump the barriers of oppression and inequality. (The election of Barak Obama as President of the US is a perfect example of the confluence of these two factors; Michaels, 2009.)

Denham's argument, however, is also wrong for another reason. As Bourne argues, it presupposes that the nature of racism is a constant, and that an increase in occupational mobility for the BME middle classes equates to a decline in racism. But as she points out:

> racism changes all the time with changes in the economic and social systems – and globalisation and the market have thrown up new racisms. Where that racism is raw and unremitting today is in the treatment of asylum seekers and their children who have been unashamedly viewed as a class apart with no rights, no sustenance, no refuge. An equally virulent racism that has risen in the last ten years, compounded by the 'war on terror' and the politics of fear, is that meted out to the Muslim community. And both these are underlined by government policies which constitute the type of state racism that fuels popular racism and provides a breeding ground for the BNP. (Bourne, 2010)

Inequality: does it matter?

One obvious explanation for income inequality in the UK reaching its current levels is that until very recently its growth was not seen as a problem by the New Labour leadership (and even less so by the leadership of the Conservative Party). In part, that lack of concern reflected an acceptance of the neoliberal dogma that, sooner or later, all would benefit from the general rise in prosperity that free-market policies would produce, but it also reflected a view that as long as residual poverty was addressed (primarily through welfare to work policies), then preventing people from becoming rich should not be a government priority. Even before the onset of the most serious crisis of capitalism for 60 years, however, the suggestion that inequality didn't matter was a false one. As Wilkinson and Pickett have argued convincingly in *The spirit level: Why more equal societies almost always do better*, the level of income inequality is in fact a key determinant not only of health and mortality rates but of a host of other social problems, including mental illness, obesity and homicides (Wilkinson and Pickett, 2010). It is what provides us, they argue, with a measure, or 'spirit level', against which we can assess the overall health of any given society. The mechanism, they suggest, that implicates economic inequality in the production of these social problems is the way in which inequality affects people's sense of their own worth:

> Individual psychology and societal inequality relate to each other like lock and key. One reason why the effects of inequality have not been properly understood before is because of a failure to understand the relationship between them. (Wilkinson and Pickett, 2009, p 33)

Their conclusion is one which should give both social workers and also advocates of cognitive-behavioural approaches as a solution for unprecedented levels of mental ill-health, pause for thought:

> We are not suggesting that the problem is a matter of individual psychology, or that it is really people's sensitivity, rather than the scale of inequality, that should be changed. The solution to problems caused by inequality is not mass psychotherapy aimed at making everyone less vulnerable. The best way of responding to the harm done by high levels of inequality would be to reduce inequality itself. (Wilkinson and Pickett, 2009, pp 32–3; see also Ferguson, 2008b)

The spirit level has been – deservedly – well received and its arguments have undoubtedly changed the terms of reference of the debate around inequality. Despite its many strengths, however, its central contention – that all members of society suffer from the effects of inequality and that therefore all have an interest in reducing inequality – needs some qualification.

First, as some critics have noted (Runciman, 2009) – and, to be fair, as Wilkinson and Pickett themselves acknowledge – not all suffer equally. The fact, for example, that in a highly unequal society like the US, far more people are likely to go to prison than in the Scandinavian social democracies, does not alter the fact that very few rich white people in the US will end up in prison.

Second, Wilkinson and Pickett's emphasis on the *psychosocial* impact of inequality leads to an underestimation of the extent of *material* poverty in Britain today and of the ways in which it continues to have an impact on every aspect of people's lives (to the extent that one chapter in *The spirit level* is entitled 'Poverty or Inequality?'). Psychosocial factors *are* important in terms of people's health and well-being, but so, too, is the material impact of poor diet, damp housing, lack of play spaces, unemployment, and access to well-resourced health and social care services. According to a report in early 2010 produced for the charity Save the Children by the New Policy Institute:

> 1.7 million children were living in severe poverty in 2007/08 across the UK. That means that around two-fifths of all children living in poverty in the UK were living in severe poverty. The proportion of children living in severe poverty increased from 11% of all UK children in 2004/05 to 13% in 2007/08. This increase has occurred against a backdrop of rising levels of child poverty. (Save the Children, 2010)

Third, while Wilkinson and Pickett convincingly demonstrate that all are affected to different degrees by the effects of inequality, some caution needs to be exercised in relation to the political conclusions we draw from this. To return to an example given above, not only is it the case that far fewer rich white people will go to prison in the US than young black males, but neither are they likely to be persuaded of the need to reduce inequality in order to keep young black males out of prison; they are in fact more likely to retreat even further into their gated communities and demand greater spending on law and order. As Marx noted some time ago, under capitalism the bourgeoisie are also alienated but unlike the proletariat, they are happy in their alienation!

Finally, there is their construction of the problem. Wilkinson and Pickett see the central problem as being inequality and the solution lying in the redistribution of wealth. As Mike Haynes has argued, however, inequality itself is a symptom or a product of a society whose central dynamic is the overriding need to accumulate profit and therefore both the roots of the problem and the potential solution lie not in the sphere of distribution but rather in the sphere of production (Haynes, 2010). Class, in other words, is more than simply a way of *describing* an unequal society. It is also an analytical tool which helps us to understand that society's underlying dynamic. It is the notion of class as an explanatory framework to which we shall now turn.

Class as an explanatory framework

The evidence of the Hills Report, alongside the work of health epidemiologists like Wilkinson and Pickett, Michael Marmot and others suggests that class divisions, in the broad sense of income inequalities, have an impact on the lives and relationships of many of those who seek help from social workers today no less than they did 30 years ago, and that developing meaningful ways of responding to the effects of such divisions is just as urgent a task now as it appeared to Bailey and Brake in the 1970s. Pointing to the existence of such divisions, however, or even analysing their impact, is not the same thing as explaining why such divisions exist or how they are sustained. One response to the publication of the Hills Report on some right-wing blog sites, for example, was that its findings simply demonstrated the genetic deficiencies of poor people! Similarly, in the past, 'cycle of deprivation' or 'underclass' theories have been deployed to blame poor people for their own poverty, while in more recent times, the 'Broken Society' thesis mentioned above has been advanced to account for what in the late 19th century was known as the 'problem of the poor'. Despite their crudity, in the absence of an alternative theoretical explanation, such pathologising explanations can quickly take hold. So to what extent can class-based analyses provide a convincing explanatory framework for the poverty and inequality discussed above?

Individual-attributes approach

In a recent paper, the American Marxist sociologist Erik Olin Wright has considered the three main contemporary contenders for the role of such a framework. First, there is the *social stratification* or *individual-attributes* approach to class (Wright, 2009). This approach, he argues, conceives of class in terms of individual attributes (gender, 'race', health, education, and so on), life conditions (living in a good area, being well-connected, having an adequate income, and so on), and the relationship between these two categories. Where these attributes or life conditions cluster together, then we can talk about 'classes'. Thus, he suggests:

> The 'middle class' here denotes people who have enough education and money to participate fully in some vaguely defined 'mainstream' way of life (which might include particular consumption patterns, for example). The 'upper class' designates people whose wealth, high income and social connections enable them to live their lives apart from

'ordinary' people, while the 'lower class' refers to those who lack the necessary educational and cultural resources to live securely above the poverty line. Finally, the 'underclass' are those who live in extreme poverty, marginalised from the mainstream of society by a lack of basic education and skills needed for stable employment. (Wright, 2009, p 103)

As Wright notes, within this approach the central concern of researchers has been to understand how people acquire the characteristics that place them in one class or another, leading to a focus on 'class background' – the family settings in which these key attributes are acquired.

This is essentially a commonsense approach to class, focusing on how people are filtered into positions and occupations, and is arguably the most frequently used approach within the mainstream social work literature, albeit usually in an implicit rather than a consciously articulated manner. It is often underpinned by a normative, 'equal opportunities' dimension, concerned with how we can improve people's chances of greater educational mobility, give children a 'better start' in life, or reduce social exclusion. As an example, during the 2010 UK General Election campaign, all of the major parties vied to claim the mantle of 'fairness' for their policies. What this approach seldom does, however, is to question the *roots* of inequalities within society, why it is that some people might possess much more power and wealth than others, and specifically, what might be the relationship between that power and wealth enjoyed by some and the lack of it enjoyed by others.

Within anti-oppressive social work literature, it is reflected in the tendency to see class principally through the categories of oppression and discrimination – 'classism' – akin to ageism, disablism and heterosexism (see, for example, Thompson, 1998). Examples of classism might include working-class people being mocked in the media for the way they dress, for their eating preferences, or for the way they speak. Arguably, popular television programmes such as *Shameless* or *The Royle family*, enjoyable as they often are, have helped to legitimise such attitudes.

Such stereotypes can be highly damaging, not least in relation to the current demonisation of working-class youth (as 'hoodies' or 'chavs', for example) and they should indeed be challenged. However, as Walter Benn Michaels has observed in connection with recent debates around the 'white working class', portraying class primarily in cultural terms, or viewing the injuries of class through the lens of discrimination and oppression, can also trivialise and obscure the structural realities of class:

The great virtue of this debate is that on both sides inequality gets turned into a stigma. That is, once you start redefining the problem of class difference as the problem of class prejudice – once you complete the transformation of race, gender and class into racism, sexism and classism – you no longer have to worry about the redistribution of wealth. You can just fight over whether poor people should be treated with contempt or respect. And while, in human terms, respect seems the right way to go, politically it's just as empty as contempt. (Michaels, 2009)

Weberian approaches

As Wright notes, such an individual-attributes approach to class divisions lacks both a relational dimension and also a theory of power. By contrast, he argues, the second main approach to class, deriving from the writings of Max Weber, possesses both of these attributes. Here, the central concept is 'opportunity hoarding' (sometimes also referred to as 'social closure'): 'In order for certain jobs to confer high income and special advantages, it is important for their incumbents to have various means of excluding others from access to them' (Wright, 2009, p 104).

Within this framework, he argues, three broad categories exist within advanced capitalist societies (Wright's model being the US): a capitalist class, defined by private-property rights in the ownership of the means of production; a middle class, defined by mechanisms of exclusion over the acquisition of education and skills; and a working class, excluded from both (although that section of the working class protected by trade unions is sometimes seen as a privileged layer, or even part of the middle class) (p 106).

While within the individual-attributes model, Wright argues, the conditions of poor people are seen as capable of improvement without damaging the interests of other classes, by contrast with an opportunity-hoarding model, there is a clear relational dimension in the sense that 'the rich are rich in part because the poor are poor, and the things the rich do to maintain their wealth contribute to the disadvantages faced by poor people' (Wright, 2009, p 107).

In similar fashion, Callinicos argues that 'Weber's view of capitalism is in many ways very similar to Marx's. He does not see it, as Adam Smith and his laissez-faire successors did, as an economically efficient means of realising individual freedom. It is, on the contrary, a system of domination' (Callinicos, 1999, p 171).

While this model therefore offers a much richer explanatory framework than the first model, it does nevertheless suffer from a number of limitations.

First, as Kieran Allen argues in his critical study of Weber, Weber's explanation of power struggles is an essentially ahistorical one. Unlike Marx, he locates such struggles not in the origins of class society nor in social movements responding to the inequality and oppression that class society generates, but rather in 'a metaphysical view, drawn from Nietzsche, that the struggle for power is at the heart of human life. Class and status are therefore just one expression of this general distribution of power' (Allen, 2004, p 82–3; see also Callinicos, 1999, p 154). Given such a timeless view, it is perhaps not surprising then to find that in this model, as in the previous model, the existence of classes and class inequality is taken as a given, with little interest or consideration as to how they came into existence in the first place, or how they might be transcended. Nor, Allen argues, given Weber's 'top-down' view of power (defined as 'the chance to realise one's will against the resistance of others') is much credence given to the possibility of popular movements from below successfully challenging the dominant powers.

Second, while both Weber himself and subsequent generations of his followers acknowledged the existence of classes and class conflict, he saw them as simply one form of social conflict among many others, with conflicts over status at least as important, or more important, than class conflicts:

> His fundamental argument is that 'classes are not communities' and so the basis for collective class action is fairly minimal. Classes are riven by divisions created by the market, and contrary to Marx's notion of two polar classes at either end of the modes of production, there are many different classes. Conflicts occur but they are not built around fundamental contradictions or exploitation. Crisscrossed onto this fragmented class struggle is a conflict between status groups. (Allen, 2004, p 91)

While status differences and intra-class conflicts can be important, to prioritise these dimensions can lead to a superficial view of class which places too much importance on factors such as dress, lifestyle and consumption choices and neglects the way in which both long-term processes (above all, what Braverman called 'the degradation of work in the twentieth century' (Braverman, 1976)) and the new public management or 'managerial' policies of the past two decades are changing both the working conditions and the consciousness of groups of workers previously seen as 'middle class', especially in the public sector (Harris, 2003; Ferguson, 2008a; Harris and White, 2009).

So, for example, among the groups of workers most frequently involved in strike action in recent years have been several often thought of as being 'middle class', such as civil servants, teachers, university lecturers and air stewardesses. The growing convergence of their experience in the core areas of wages, job security and promotion, coupled with other pressures such as work intensification and the subordination of professional skills to the demands of IT-based systems suggests that the potential for class unity and solidarity between different groups of workers, both white-collar and manual, as opposed to the 'opportunity-hoarding' and 'social closure' which Weber saw as inevitable, may in fact be increasing.

Finally, there is the relationship between class conflict and the economy. While, as noted above, Weber saw capitalism as a system of domination, that domination was an aspect of a wider process of bureaucratisation, not, as Marx argued, the product of economic exploitation. Rather, his economic views, Allen argues, like his wider sociological views, were underpinned instead by a methodological individualism derived from the Austrian School of marginalist economics. He wrote that:

> If I have become a sociologist (according to my letter of accreditation), it is mainly to exorcise the spectre of collective conceptions which still lingers among us. In other words, sociology itself can only proceed from the action of one or more separate individuals and must therefore adopt strictly individualist methods. (Cited in Allen, 2004, p 71)

That view of the relationship between individuals, classes and the economy was also reflected in Weber's emphasis on the key role of ideas (as opposed to Marx's emphasis on economic contradictions) in the process of social change, above all in his classic text *The Protestant ethic and the spirit of capitalism*. It is a feature of the richness of Weber's thought that that emphasis can still provide the basis for powerful critique, in this case of contemporary neoliberal ideology, by two of his French disciples Boltanski and Chiapello in their massive study (and homage to Weber) *The new spirit of capitalism* (2007). That said, as Callinicos notes in his discussion of Boltanski and Chiapello, '[they] make little attempt to develop an account of capitalism as an economic system that goes beyond its minimalist definition as "the unlimited accumulation of capital by formally peaceful means". Indeed they seem to argue that capitalism's main problems are not economic' (Callinicos, 2006, p 71).

To be fair to these writers, they were far from being alone in seeing neoliberalism as a system of ideas and practice that had somehow risen above the vulgar workings of the capitalist economy. That illusion, however, was one of several which was abruptly brought down to earth by the return of crisis to the global economic system in 2008 (Callinicos, 2010a).

Marxist approaches

The third model of class discussed by Wright draws on Marx's analysis of capitalism and differs from the previous two in two key respects. First, its primary focus is not on the market and distribution, fair or otherwise, but rather on the ownership and control of the means of production; second, the relationship between the main classes in society is not simply one of domination but rather of exploitation, in the sense of the extraction of surplus value. Thus, classes for Marx, according to one recent definition, depend on 'the real social relations of production in which people find themselves. They are aggregates of people whose relationship to material production forces them to act collectively against other such aggregates' (Harman, 2009, p 113).

It is this *dynamic* relationship, based on the need of one group of people – under capitalism, those who own the businesses, the banks and so on – to continually seek to maximise their profits by increasing the exploitation of another group – those who have to sell their labour power in order to live – that drives the system forward, creates classes and creates class struggle, as those at the receiving end of the exploitation seek to resist.

Such exploitation, driven by competition between capitalists, has succeeded in creating a system which is both the most dynamic and also the most destructive that humanity has ever seen. Harman describes the process in graphic terms:

> Capitalism has been a totalising ... system, in a way which no previous mode of production had been, compelling the whole world to dance to its frenzied rhythms of competition and accumulation. ...It forces each capital to force down the price of labour power to the minimum that will keep its workers willing and able to work. The clash of capitals compels each to accumulate in a way that will produce downward pressure on profit rates for all of them ... It is

a system that creates periodic havoc for all those who live within it, a horrific hybrid of Frankenstein's monster and Dracula, a human creation that has escaped control and lives by devouring the lifeblood of its creators. (2009, p 85)

From the perspective of developing a radical social work theory and practice, this approach to class enjoys two main advantages. On the one hand, it provides a coherent and convincing explanation for the development of the unprecedented levels of inequality discussed in the first part of this chapter. Far from being contingent or secondary, as David Harvey has argued, the central concern of the neoliberal project from the outset has been with 'the restoration of class power' (Harvey, 2005), following the emergence of the global crisis in the early 1970s. It was – and remains – an ideology whose primary concern has been with restoring profitability, through removing all barriers to increased profits, through privatising public utilities, creating new markets in areas like sub-prime mortgages, and weakening trade unions.

Second, this approach provides a framework for understanding the specific ways in which the neoliberal agenda has reshaped social work and social welfare, primarily through the ideas of managerialism, or new public management. There is now a substantial literature exploring different aspects of managerialism within social work and social care, but at its heart is the idea of 'getting more for less' through the intensification of work, bigger caseloads, less resources in the statutory sector, and the 'race to the bottom' in the voluntary sector. Understanding managerialism in this way as essentially a class-based project, involving the application of neoliberal ideas and practices to the public sector, allows for the development of responses which address the source of the problem (the application of market values and priorities to social work and social care) and make it less likely that workers will be persuaded to settle for partial solutions (such as more user-friendly IT systems for assessment) which focus only on the symptoms.

Class as agent of change: the politics of class

The final aspect of class I wish to consider is that of class as an agent of social change and societal transformation. Famously for Marx, socialism was 'the *self*-emancipation of the working class' (my emphasis). In concluding her chapter on the radical potential of community development in Bailey and Brake's collection, Marjorie Mayo approvingly cites the view of the socialist writer Ken Coates that

> [A] specifically socialist view of community action should 'support anything which increased the solidarity and self-confidence of working people and their dependants'. But 'what consciousness can be aroused in such struggles will remain *sectional*, unless it is keyed into an embracing political strategy involving all the poor, all the ill-housed, all the deprived. (Mayo, 1975, p 143)

The belief that the collective struggles of working-class people, whether in the community or in the workplace, should be central to community work and radical social work practice is one which has by and large disappeared from professional literature and practice in the UK over the past two decades. The reasons for that disappearance are not hard to see. *Radical social work* was written against the background of an exceptionally high level of class struggle, which included a wave of occupations against redundancies (most notably at Upper Clyde Shipbuilders in 1972) and successful national miners' strikes in 1972 and 1974. In the year before the book appeared, the then Prime Minister, Edward Heath, called a general election around the slogan 'Who runs the country – the government or the trade unions?' Heath lost. Far from being an abstract theoretical concept, evidence of working-class power was all around (Harman, 1988; Sherry, 2010).

By contrast, when a wave of strikes in early 2010 involving British Airways cabin staff, civil servants and railway workers led to comparisons with the 1970s 'Winter of Discontent', *The Guardian*'s Labour correspondent Larry Elliot pointed out that in that year of 1979, almost 30 million working days were 'lost' to strike action, or 0.45% of the total. During 2009, the comparable figures were 456,000 and 0.006%. 'Industrial action would have to rise 75 times this year to get back to the levels seen in 1979' (Elliott, 29 March 2010).

That fall in the level of industrial struggle, coupled with the decline in trade union membership by approximately one half over that same period, is one of three main arguments frequently advanced in support of the view that the working class has effectively 'disappeared' or at the very least, no longer has any role to play as an agent in the creation of a more equal society. A second argument is that the restructuring of the working class during this period, primarily as a consequence of deindustrialisation and globalisation, means that it is no longer capable of playing the emancipatory role which socialists previously envisaged. Finally, there is the view that 'we are all middle class now', that the growth of white-collar employment, coupled with the spread of home ownership, easier foreign travel and so on, has led to a growth of individualism and a collapse in collective attitudes and class identity. How should we respond to these arguments?

'We're all middle class now'

It is undoubtedly the case that there has been a long-term decline in manufacturing employment in the UK during the second-half of the 20th century and a parallel growth in white-collar employment, to the extent that white-collar and service sector workers now make up a majority of the workforce. No doubt some of these workers will see themselves as 'middle class' and have 'middle-class aspirations' for themselves and their children (though this should not be exaggerated: in a MORI poll conducted in 1994, 51% of those surveyed described themselves as working class; in a similar poll in 2002, that figure had risen to 68%). In contrast to the period in which Weber was writing, however, most white-collar workers today are not employed in privileged positions as senior managers, bankers or highly-paid civil servants. Instead, many will work as low-paid administrative staff in central and local government departments while a growing number will work in call centres (850,000 in 2007 (Smith, 2007)). In terms of wages, the overwhelming majority will be among the 90% of the population whom the Hills Report found earned less than £42, 000, while many are likely to be on much less than that, hovering around the median income of £21,000. (More than 70% of the BA cabin staff involved in industrial action in 2010, for example, were earning less than £20,000 a year (*The Independent*, 26 January, 2010). In terms of their conditions of work, many are likely to be involved in monotonous, repetitive work, with little control over the process and content of what they do. According to one council housing worker interviewed by Martin Smith:

> We don't have to clock in and out like my dad did when he worked in a factory. We now have a computer – I call it the hidden foreman. It is used by management to record and monitor how much work we do. It knows what time I start work, what time I finish, how long it takes me to have a piss. It monitors the number of telephone calls I answer and at a flick of a switch a supervisor can increase the pace of our work. (cited in Smith, 2007, p 55)

As is shown both by White's research into the use of computerised assessment systems in children and families' teams (White et al, 2009) and also by Coleman's work on the spread of 'e-social work' in contact (or call) centres (Coleman, 2009), social work practice has similarly been transformed by the introduction of IT systems over the past decade.

More generally, the dominance of managerialist ideas and practices in the public sector means that groups such as social workers or lecturers in further and higher education typically now enjoy much less control over the content of their work than they did previously, while the job security which they previously took for granted will be threatened by the deep cuts in public sector spending which will be a feature of the next decade

The fact, however, that at 51%, union density is higher in the public sector than in any other industry (and that groups such as further education lecturers and civil servants have regularly been involved in industrial action in recent years) shows just how superficial and misleading it is to assume that simply because people employ mental or interpersonal skills rather than manual skills in their work activities, they will inevitably therefore adopt individualist attitudes and values.

Deindustrialisation and globalisation

The argument that deindustrialisation and globalisation have destroyed workers' capacity to resist the power of capital is similarly flawed. Without underestimating the ways in which the industrial landscape of the UK has been transformed over the past three decades, it is still the case that one in seven workers in the UK are employed in the manufacturing sector. While these numbers are considerably less than they were three decades ago, it is also true that those who are still employed are usually more productive and potentially more powerful. For example, one of the most successful industrial disputes of 2009 was the Lindsey Oil Refinery dispute which saw swift unofficial (and illegal) action by a relatively small number of workers across the country secure a stunning victory against some of the most powerful oil companies in the world (Basketter, 2009b). Meanwhile, on a world scale, the spread of globalisation has led to a huge *expansion* of the international working class to an estimated 700 million workers, 60% of whom live outside the OECD countries, with approximately 25% in China, 7% in India and a further 7% in Latin America (cited in Harman, 2009, pp 331, 337) – hardly a vanishing working class. And while space does not permit a detailed examination of the thesis that globalisation means that workers can no longer resist employers' demands since to do so means that they will simply uproot and move to another part of the globe, in reality the picture is much more uneven and complex than this (Doogan, 2009; Dunn, 2009). A recent review of the some of the 'myths of globalisation' concluded that that:

> In short, the evidence of capitalism's globalisation is patchy at best, and its association with workers' experience even weaker. Capital can flee – and has fled – high wages and labour militancy, but to a much lesser extent than its supporters suggest. The implication is that the potential for resistance 'in situ' remains considerable. (Dunn, 2009)

None of the above is intended to suggest that the working class both in Britain and globally has not changed significantly since the advent of neoliberal globalisation in the early 1980s. What it does suggest, however, is that the issue is less the disappearance of the working class but rather, in a process that has gone on since the dawn of capitalism, its restructuring (with each of these new phases leading to revived theories of the 'disappearing working class', most famously in the 'affluent worker' thesis of the 1960s: Goldthorpe and Lockwood, 1968).

Conclusion

'The party's over'

Much of the above discussion has centred on the differences between the period in which the text *Radical social work* first appeared and the present period. I wish to end, however, on a note of similarity. In 1975, Anthony Crosland, a leading Minister in the Labour Government of Harold Wilson which was then facing a financial crisis due to a run on the pound engineered by international financiers, announced to the Local Government Association Conference of that year that 'The party's over' (cited in Timmins, 1995, p 313). The parlous state of the economy, in other words, meant that previous levels of public spending could no longer be sustained – there would have to be cuts. Almost 40 years on, in the wake of another global crisis of capitalism, history is repeating itself, with the Con–Dem coalition introducing savage welfare cuts in their first post-election budget. Now, as in the mid-1970s, people who rely on public services and those who provide them are being told that they will have to pay the price for an economic crisis not of their making.

In the face of this attack, groups of workers and service users throughout the UK are starting to organise themselves. In Edinburgh in late 2009, for example, demonstrations by hundreds of service users and their allies were successful in preventing a tendering process which would have seen vital services for 800 people with physical disabilities, mental health conditions and learning disabilities transferred to new, cheaper providers, pending an independent inquiry (Edinburgh Support Workers' Action Network, 2010). Still in Scotland, in early 2010 demonstrations were called by both UNISON and also by the Scottish teachers union, the EIS, in defence of public services. The EIS demonstration, called under the slogan 'Why should our children pay?' was the largest trade union demonstration in Scotland for many years.

That resistance is still at a low level. Nevertheless, these sparks of resistance continue to offer the best hope of defending the services on which so many depend. For all its limitations and its loss of confidence following too many defeats over three decades, the trade union movement with almost 7 million members, many of them working in health and social care, remains by far the largest social movement in the country. Building alliances between that movement and organisations of service users, alliances of the sort which Bailey and Brake wrote about more than 30 years ago, continues to offer the best hope both of protecting services and also of forging a new kind of social work, very different from the neoliberal, managerial model which has suffocated workers and oppressed people who use services for far too long.

EIGHT

International social work or social work internationalism? Radical social work in global perspective

Michael Lavalette and Vasilios Ioakimidis

Introduction

Bailey and Brake's collection aimed to provide a series of arguments for, and about, radical social work in Britain. It did not look at social work engagement beyond Britain's shores. This is no great surprise; in 1975 international and comparative social work was still some considerable distance off! Nevertheless, in the second decade of the 21st century it would look odd for any radical social work book to restrict itself to debates about social work within a single nation-state and ignore developments and arguments that are drawn from the international stage. More than this, it is now clear that many of the questions posed in the Bailey and Brake collection, such as the meaning of 'professional' social work, the relationship between social work and the state and the elements of social control within social work practices, are posed sharply and in different ways when we look at social work in various global locations, with different traditions and methods of work, alternative relationships with and to the local and national state and competing perspectives on the role and task of social work.

There is another important reason for including a discussion on international social work in the present volume: internationally, social work is expanding at a rapid pace. In the 'Tiger economies' like China and India and in the former Soviet Republics, for example, exploitation, oppression, poverty and inequality have created social problems which these states have looked to social work to 'solve' and control. But how should social work 'solve' such problems?

International social work attempts to look at a range of social problems that social work can address, at local 'indigenous' practices and the way(s) in which they can be incorporated into professional and regulated modes of social work delivery (Healy, 2001). The expansion of social work has opened up discussion about what the appropriate forms of social work should look like – but increasingly discussion is framed in terms of how close 'new social work models' will match existing Anglo-American conceptions of social work practice. In part such conceptualisations reflect an arrogance within British and American social work – an assumption that they provide the bench-mark against which all others should be judged. In part this reflects a view of social work history that is 'developmentalist' in origin. We want to challenge the euro-centric (or Anglo-American) view of social work and its history. Malcolm Payne (2005, p 9) has suggested that social work histories are problematic because they tend to draw a narrow 'single historical narrative': a 'whiggish' interpretation of a single, 'official' social work, based on a simple story of historical progress towards today's dominant models and interpretations of social work practice – and those models are overwhelmingly portrayed as British and American ones!

As Payne points out, however, social work is different in contrasting welfare regimes, where there are different traditions, different relationships between social work and the state and different perspectives on what counts as 'social work' (2005, pp 5–9).

By way of an example, on a recent trip to the Palestinian West Bank we met practitioners with a quite different perspective on what counted as social work. We were in Palestine as part of a field trip with some of our social work/social pedagogy students. We visited the village of Bil'in that has featured in many Western newspaper headlines over the last three years because it is central to the campaign of non-violent resistance to the Israeli occupation (see BBC, 2010). Every Friday, local Palestinians, alongside international and Israeli activists, demonstrate against the Separation Barrier that the Israeli government has constructed as part of their 'land-grab' expansion into the West Bank.

Rateb, one of the local community leaders, explained that the Friday demonstration is one of the various activities in which the community and international activists engage. They are also involved with cultural events, community assemblies, support for victim's families, international campaigns to boycott Israeli goods and provision of material and psychological support for the people of the village who have found themselves in the frontline of the struggle.

A visit to Bil'in exposes the violent response of the Israeli state to the non-violent resistance of the locals. Hundreds of sound grenade canisters and rubber bullets are scattered on the ground close to the separation fence. But despite the brutal Israeli response the resistance has delayed the expansion of the Separation Wall in the area and attracted international attention and support.

As we left Bil'in, Rateb, enthusiastically turned to our students and informed them that he was also a social work academic. He went on:

> 'What we are doing here is social work. Remember that social work consists of three methods: casework, groupwork and community work. This is community engagement and community work. It is about understanding our situation. It is about fighting for our rights. And in the process we generate feelings of support and solidarity that keep our community together, that keep it strong in the face of our troubles.'

Rateb's comments stimulated a long discussion with the students on the nature, boundaries and function of international social work.

Rateb's comments also pose questions about the 'singular narrative' about what counts as social work – and it poses interesting questions about internationalism within radical social work. We live in a shrinking globalised world dominated by economic crisis, war, climate change, inequality, poverty and various forms of oppression. Social workers around the world increasingly face broadly common problems and issues. Crudely, we are a profession that claims to be committed to meeting human need, we live in a world that has never been richer – how do we meet the needs of the many rather than the interests of the few? In this shrinking world what can radical social workers learn from each other?

In this chapter we want to broaden the debate about international social work in two ways. First, we want to suggest that international social work has an ambiguous history – one that is not necessarily progressive, despite the (often 'social democratic') language that it has attempted to utilise to justify its 'humanitarian' and 'reform' interventions. For example, the definition of social work of the present International Federation of Social Workers (IFSW, 2000) defines the profession by reference to its commitment to human rights, its struggle against inequality and oppression, its political engagement to change the world and its emphasis on social justice. Yet however important such statements of principle are, it would be foolhardy to assume that this is what most professional social workers in Britain, for example, are doing on a daily basis. Indeed, if the IFSW definition of social work was taken literally and applied to the British situation, it is not clear how many registered workers would actually meet the international definition of a social worker. Further, despite the international definition there are social workers who are engaged in activities that breach the human rights and social justice imperatives of those with whom they work (such as those involved in age assessments of refugee and asylum seeking children (Mynott, 2005).

The IFSW statement could almost be accused of 'painting social work red', when the reality is that, both historically and today, an awful lot of social work is steeped in pathologising accounts of service users and invokes various 'social control' themes in its practice.

For example the Bailey and Brake collection is highly critical of the then dominant forms of casework because they tended to individualise social problems and pathologise service users. This form of casework had its roots in the Charity Organisation Society and their attempt to 'control' charitable giving. The 'science' of casework was reified and became central to social work's claim for professional status in Britain and the US (see Jones, 1999). In Portugal, social work traces its origins to 1937. It was born within the authoritarian regime of the time and was used as a vehicle to impose control and 'Catholic family values' onto working-class communities – though interestingly, in the Portuguese revolution of 1974, social workers who had trained in the 1960s and been influenced by Latin American models of emancipatory social work were involved in the rebellion against fascism. In Germany, social work existed right through the Nazi period (see Lorenz, 1994). In Spain it developed during the Franco regime (Martínez-Brawley and Vázquez Aguado, 2007) and, as we will see later in the chapter, in Greece it was developed by the authoritarian regime to address the 'problem' of 'red children' in the aftermath of the civil war (see Ioakimidis, 2009). The conclusion is clear: there is nothing inevitably progressive about social work; official social work regimes have contradictory and ambiguous histories – and sometimes histories which involve collusion with fascist and authoritarian regimes.

Here we want to look at another aspect of social work's less savoury history: the intersection of post-Second World War international social work, the Marshall Plan and US imperial interests in post-war Greece.

We also, however, want to draw on our on-going research with those involved in social work in a variety of global settings to suggest that alternatives are possible. We have constructed this last sentence carefully. Over the last four years we have interviewed people involved in social work in Palestine, Lebanon, Greece, India and Cyprus – but not all of them were 'qualified' social workers, or taking part in a 'recognised' profession. Does this matter? We want to suggest that it doesn't and that social work globally could fruitfully learn from a range of activities that are conducted under the rubric of what we call 'popular social work' where communities and activists come together to deal with the social, political and economic traumas that their communities face (see Lavalette and Ioakimidis, 2011).

'Official social work' and 'popular social work'

'International social work' represents an attempt to promote a relatively narrow range of activities as 'legitimate', professional forms of practice. This, however, suggests a homogeneity to social work about which we are sceptical. We want to suggest that social work can be analysed along two intersecting axes. The first is what we call 'official' social work. This *may* be any combination of regulated, qualified, state recognised social work. We have to qualify 'official social work' in this way because it is different in different countries. For example, in Britain, social work is a protected title and there are some jobs that only qualified and registered social workers can undertake. But in India, for example, social workers undertake recognised BSW and MSW courses (which are very similar in content to British BA and MA social work courses), but those with social work qualifications are not formally recognised by the state as being qualified in a distinct profession, are not registered by the state as 'social workers' and compete on an open market for a range of jobs for which other graduates can equally apply (Bhanti, 2001).

'Official' social work, however, is not only distinguished by the varying relationships between social work trained graduates and state registration processes. There are also variations in the tasks social workers undertake in different countries, its dominant methods and its relationship with the state and the voluntary sector. To take India as an example once again, each student on an MSW course in India will have to undertake one of four specialisms: community social work, children and families, medical-psychological and, by far and away the most popular, human resources (HR). The community social work specialism is dominated by collective social action models that train workers to go out and live and work among the poorest communities and look at a variety of advocacy, political and development goals for social work practice (though, as Banks shows elsewhere in this volume, community social work is not always or necessarily 'progressive'). The HR specialism trains people to work in the offices of HR departments in large Indian and global multinational corporations. The HR specialism social work models are based on 'solving and smoothing out' employees' problems – in other words, individualising the collective problems associated with the operationalisation of the labour process within capitalist corporations. The job is relatively well paid and is dominated by male students.

Both these examples are of qualified social work in India. But they reflect quite different conceptions about the role, location and priorities of social work – they reject any simple notion of a single, uniform profession. But if we think about these examples in comparative terms then we would have to conclude that few social work courses in Britain today engage in *either* of these types of social work models. So there is a considerable variation in what 'official social work' might include.

But there is a third reason why there is no single homogeneous official social work identity: politics. Social work is divided by a range of political positions: those who engage in conservative, individualising and pathologising practices; those who look to help service users change their behaviours, access services and reform the local environment in which they live, and those whose practice is much more radical in political orientation and look to link their practice to more fundamental challenges to the structures of inequality that shape the lives of service users and workers – and despite the fact that more radical forms of practice have often been written out of social work histories, social work has always had a 'radical kernel' and some social workers who are committed to more engaged and transformatory practices (Lavalette and Ferguson, 2007).

So 'official social work' is not homogeneous. It is an arena within which there are a range of positions and perspectives over the nature, tasks and methods of practice.

We want to add a second axis, however, that of 'popular social work'. Historically the drive to 'professionalise' social work was part of the attempt to inoculate workers from the perceived danger of them 'going native': to stop the danger of 'contamination'. Professionalisation aims to bring 'distance' between worker and service user and stop workers interpreting service users' problems as a reflection of the nature of society and its iniquities (Jones, 1983; Ferguson, 2008a; Lavalette, 2011). But the history of professionalisation has meant writing various forms of 'popular social work' out of social work's history – of downplaying and/or disregarding examples where social workers stood with service users to provide services which were part of a broader movement for social change.

'Popular social work' covers a range of campaigning, political social work and welfare initiatives. They tend to be linked to broader social movement activity, and undertaken by a range of people (some with official training, some without) who are focused on producing, providing and developing services for their community within the context of unequal, oppressive and hierarchical societies.

Examples of such popular social work are sprinkled throughout the history of the 20th and early 21st centuries. It was present in the work of individuals like Sylvia Pankhurst and George Lansbury in Britain. They combined political campaigning (for women's rights, political representation for working-class communities, trade unionism and against world war) with case-based advocacy work, representation of 'clients' to the Poor Law Guardians, provision of community cafés and meals for poor schoolchildren and fighting for housing and jobs in the face of poverty and mass unemployment (Lavalette, 2006b; Lavalette and Ferguson, 2007).

Visions of popular social work can also be seen in the community and campaigning work of Jaynne Adams and Bertha Reynolds in the US in the first half of the century (Reisch and Andrews, 2002). Or in the work of Mentona Moser, the Swiss social work pioneer, Communist Party member and leader of, and practitioner within, *Red Aid* in the 1930s. Red Aid was an international social services organisation that provided support to political refugees in the 1930s and active support for revolutionary Spain (Hering, 2003). 'Popular social work' was also part of the US welfare rights movement of the 1960s. A number of social workers, like Bill Pastreich, Rhoda Linton, Richard Cloward and others from the Community Action Training Centre, played leading roles in the movement. These workers organised and campaigned alongside black women's groups against poverty, for welfare payments and for a range of political and social rights (Nadasen, 2005).

Examples of popular social work are not restricted to the past, however. In Britain during the great miners' strike of 1984/85 the mining communities organised soup and food kitchens, pantomimes at Christmas, children's parties and entertainment on occasional weekends. The intention was above all to survive, both physically and mentally; to keep up spirits and morale; to stop people feeling isolated; to help counter individual trauma, frustration and depression, and to meet basic needs – an example of the kind of popular social work that we are discussing. Similar examples can be found in many parts of the world today. It is visible in the community-oriented youth and disability programmes, run by 'non-professional' social workers, in the Palestinian refugee camps across the West Bank. These provide grass-roots services to their community that embody a deep understanding of the political and historical situation that the refugees find themselves in – and recognise the importance of understanding and confronting the 'public causes' (the occupation) of the private pains of so many of those in the camps (Jones and Lavalette, 2011).

The welfare and social work activities undertaken by the members of the campaigning group Samidoun during the 2006 Israeli attack on Beirut provide another example. Samidoun members organised to provide shelter, food and medical and psychological support for the war refugees as the Israeli assault was in full flow (Lavalette and Levine, 2011).

Similarly much asylum and refugee work across Europe is community-oriented, rights-based work that brings together community activists and a range of unqualified 'helpers' (often from a range of political and religious organisations) to provide support, help and a campaigning network as part of the struggle for refugee rights (Ferguson and Barclay, 2002; Mynott, 2005; Teloni, 2011).

The narrowing of social work's history to the development of one version of a regulated, qualified professional activity has meant that many exciting, engaged initiatives − with deep connections to their communities and their struggles against inequality and oppression − have been excised from the social work canon. The development of international social work has been part of the narrative of excluding radical alternatives. But its own history has been one of compromise with the powerful at the expense of the powerless.

The formative years of international social work

Before the Second World War, 'official' social work activity was restricted to a small number of countries and was mainly influenced by Christian philanthropy (see Lorenz, 1994, p 44). The main international activities of this period can be seen as an effort on the part of the social work elite to form a common professional identity that could help them defend and promote their status within their countries. This was clear in the First International Conference of Social Work in 1928 when more than 5,000 delegates congregated in Paris in order to 'establish personal relationships, to contribute to the distribution of information to render possible exchange of information between social workers and organisations for social work throughout the world' (Paris Conference 1928, in Eilers, 2003).

Despite the ambitions of the organisers the content of the conference was dominated by European and North American discourses (Eilers, 2003, p 120); while the sessions amounted to a series of country reports. Women from upper-class or aristocratic backgrounds dominated the event − a reflection of the class and gendered dynamics of early 'professional' social work (see also Jones's description of British social workers arriving in America in the 1960s, this volume) (Eilers, 2003; IFSW, 2006;). This first conference was nothing more than a 'congregation' of social work elites seeking professional legitimacy in their own countries. The second conference took place in Germany in 1932, and again the dominant themes were professional identity, the science of social work and 'appropriate' professional training. The tension between the developing official profession and the struggle for more radical collective welfare provision was reflected in the words of Mentona Mosser who despaired at the role of aristocratic women doing good works'. She put it bluntly: 'the bourgeoisie is never so repulsive as in these cases when they are doing charity work, "stinking" charity work' (cited in Hering, 2003, p 90).

These international meetings were extremely important for the development of the profession but marginal to the struggles for social justice at the time. The Wall Street crash of 1929 ushered in a crisis that lasted until the outbreak of the Second World War. It unleashed mass unemployment, desperate poverty and the rise of fascism. The period also witnessed major struggles for worker rights, against fascism and (for example in Spain) a revolutionary struggle for a different world. The conferences had nothing significant to say on these matters.

Imperialism and social work

In a sense social work's identity on the international stage was enhanced by the Second World War. Dealing with large numbers of displaced peoples, orphans, homeless people – indeed the full range of social problems created by the conflagration – created a space where international agencies, employing social work models, became part of the political and social landscape. But in the West European and Asian theatres it also meant that social work became embroiled in the plans for post-war construction, shaped by the ideas, values and politics of the Marshall Plan. The Marshall Plan (which began in 1947) was a programme undertaken by the US government to reconstruct and rebuild the shattered economic and political systems of those countries that had faced the full devastation of world war. But the Marshall Plan operated within an overarching political framework the goal of which was to make the countries 'safe' for Western capitalism and establish a social and political bulwark against Communist expansion. The Marshall Plan was not, therefore, a primarily humanitarian project on the part of the US state, but a political project, tied to the Truman Doctrine, concerned with marginalising and isolating the revolutionary social movements of the post-war era (see Hogan, 1991). The expansion of international social work must be located within this broader context.

The first large-scale international relief programmes started during the war. In 1943, the United Nations Reconstruction and Rehabilitation Agency was initiated by the US, with the support of 44 other countries. Even though this organisation is described as a United Nations agency it was created before the official establishment of the United Nations. The headquarters were in Washington DC and the US government offered more than half of the budget. UNRRA was described by academic and political analysts at the time as 'the most extensive welfare programme in history and as an experiment in international planning with a view to the establishment of a permanent international welfare organisation' (Weintraub, 1945, p 4).

One of UNRRA's main objectives was the creation, or redesign, of welfare systems in aid-recipient countries. As part of this process social work academics and practitioners, mostly from North America, found themselves working on the development of social work education, training and practice in different parts of the world. In 1943, Europe was still in the midst of war, so most of UNRRA's social work operations were targeted on countries like China, Iran and India. But with the conclusion of the war there was a rapid expansion in the areas and regions where UNRRA operated and greater call was made on their social work activities. Kendal, an American international social work academic, reflecting on her experiences in the period suggests why social work was involved:

> Death, destruction, broken homes, loss of parents, loss of children, divided loyalties, and much more can be listed in any inventory of the havoc wrought by war. Much more than social work has to offer is needed to heal such wounds, but it was recognized within the UN that social welfare services and qualified personnel were essential elements in long-term planning for what they called the social field. (Kendal, 1994, p 6)

Even though the need for rehabilitation was unquestionable and obvious to many social work scholars, what was less obvious was the specific political agenda that was tied up with this process. US geopolitical interests (in the developing cold war era) saw the rehabilitation and reconstruction of Europe as a high priority. The end of the war saw an explosion of social struggles in Italy and Greece (where Communist and partisan forces had led the liberation process), France (where the key role in the resistance movement was played by the Communist Party), Japan, across the Balkans and even in Germany (where embryonic anti-Nazi forces appeared as the Nazi regime collapsed) (Birchall, 1974, 1986; Halliday, 1975; Gluckstein, 1999; Behan, 2009). The developing Marshall Plan was about supporting the socioeconomic systems of these countries and bolstering pro-US political formations. As internal documents from the Department of State indicated:

> The emergency needs of certain key countries of western Europe cannot be met without immediate action of the part of the US…. . From the viewpoint of the vital interest of the US, the principal issue in Europe today is whether or not it will be totalitarian [i.e. fall to Communist influence]. If the virus of totalitarianism spreads much further it will be almost impossible to prevent its engulfing all of Western Europe. (Department of State, 1947)

In this atmosphere UNRRA was increasingly viewed as a rather ineffective organisation. Gradually UNRRA agencies were replaced by American Rehabilitation Missions (ARMs). The role of the ARMs was to take part in the construction (or reconstruction) of social welfare regimes in 'key countries' (that is, 'key' in terms of US political and military interests) (Salomon, 1990).

Social work historians recognise this period as a great time for international social work (for example see Healy, 2001). Schools of social work funded by the US and supervised by American academics emerged globally. Even in countries where social work existed before the war the profession enjoyed a period of revival and development. What is important to highlight, however, is that most of the countries that received the attention of international social work were included in AMRs list of 'key countries'. These included Greece, Italy, Turkey, Korea, Latin America and later on Vietnam (see Healy, 1987). In each of these countries open military intervention was followed by a period of 'reconstruction and rehabilitation'. In this process organisations and individuals (including the USC, IFSW, IASSW and other social work 'pioneers') operated as social work consultants whose job was to redesign welfare and social services in the regions in which they intervened. They offered technical expertise in the design of social welfare; development and supervision of social work education and training, curriculum design, translation of American social work texts, scholarships and bursaries to selected social work students to study in the US (mostly funded by the Fulbright fund), development of national social work associations and advice and consultation on the design and development of relevant legislation and regulatory bodies for social work (see Healy, 1987; Lally, 1987; Ioakimidis, 2009)

In order to create these new social work and welfare systems well-trained personnel were needed. As Ernest Witte put it, reflecting on the humanitarian missions of the late 1940s:

> The insistent demand in less advanced areas of the world for improved living standards is dependent on effecting social changes in the habits and living patterns of the people in these areas. ... It is generally agreed that professional education in a school of social work provides the best preparation for many of the functions in developing social programmes. (Witte, 1960, p 123)

There is some evidence which suggests that these operations were centrally funded by the US and closely supervised by the Department of State (see Ioakimidis, 2009). These processes witnessed the development of a new social work profession in recipient countries. But, as part of this process, the knowledgebase, legal context and technical expertise were transplanted from the US. As a result, the newly-developed professions adopted the Anglo-American model of social work theory and practice, which, in many cases, was alien and irrelevant to local cultures and needs. Indeed the 'new' profession often supplanted and over-rode pre-existing grassroots and informal welfare networks – in no small measure because they were linked to more radical political agendas for a reshaped post-war world.

Greece: along with the soldiers came the social workers

The example of Greece clearly indicates strong links between the post-war interests of the US in the region, the anti-communist witch-hunt and the Greek state's intention to develop social work as a tool of social control. The Greek case social constitutes the first example of a social work development model that embodies the dynamics of cold war as declared in the Truman Doctrine in 1947.

In the early 1940s, during the Nazi occupation, a vibrant liberation movement developed in Greece. EAM, the National Liberation Front is estimated to have had up to two million supporters by 1944, out of a population of seven million (Birchall, 1986, p 44). This movement, which was led by the Communist Party, combined a commitment to national liberation and the creation of a post-war society based on equality and social justice. By 1944 the Liberation Army had liberated most of the country, and had held national elections and created a system of 'people's administration' and 'people's justice'. The governmental forms adopted had included the creation of popular forms of education, health and social welfare (where aspects of social trauma, for example, were addressed via lively and engaged cultural and theatre experiments).

However, British interests in the region meant that they were not prepared to allow Greece to turn to socialism (Woodhouse, 1976). In December 1944, the British Army intervened to keep the liberation army out of Athens and repatriate the monarch and members of the old political establishment (see Mazower, 1993). The eventual involvement of the US led to a vicious civil war that ended in 1949 with the victory of the royalist and right-wing parties (Hadjis, 1981). The country entered a period of authoritarianism that lasted for almost 25 years; in the aftermath of the civil war thousands of activists were imprisoned or assassinated.

Interestingly, social work in Greece appeared in 1946, in the middle of the civil war. Official Greek social work historiographies note this as a great and significant event, but they are less sanguine about the role social work performed in its early days. Social work developed in opposition to the radical grassroots welfare developed by the liberation movement, it grew out of the suppression of forms of popular social work in the liberated zones and was, in part, a project to 'rehabilitate' the 'red' children of those involved in the liberation movement.

Initially the Greek state started designing its welfare and rehabilitation services through UNRRA. Almost one tenth of the overall UNRRA funding was allocated to Greece from 1945–47, during the height of the Civil War; 1,200,000 tons of food and commodities worth US$350,000,000 were channelled into the country (Hekimoglou, 2005, p 7). This was an amount equivalent to one year of the Greek national budget. Alongside UNRRA, many minor charity organisations (such us YWCA and the Unitarian–Universalists Association) were also operating under the supervision of the US Department of State (Ioakimidis, 2009). Additionally, hundreds of British and American professionals were employed in Greece and had unprecedented authority over national issues. At its peak in March 1947, UNRRA employed 3,137 people covering the professional spectrum from social work and nursing to technocrats and agents (Close, 2004).

The sidelining of UNRRA and its replacement by AMR led to the creation of the American Mission for Aid to Greece (AMAG). AMAG had absolute control of civil and military affairs in the country and social work fell under its direct jurisdiction. In parallel with official Greek Ministries, shadow divisions, created by AMAG, had strict control over the policies being developed (see Witner, 1982; Kofas, 1989). The main divisions of the AMAG administration were situated in the departments of civil government, labour, law, public finance, public works, military operations, agriculture, and health and welfare. This structure ensured that the funding received by the Greek authorities was utilised to serve American interests in the region:

> As cold war tensions heightened Greece was increasingly seen as a bulwark against Communist expansion, and its administrative, military, economic and political institutions were shaped to serve that purpose. Efficiency and modernisation favoured politicians eager to cooperate,... General Van Fleet, expressed his preference for an authoritarian government. Representatives of the American Missions for Aid to Greece (AMAG) sat on the most important committees and boards while Americans were employed in top administrative positions within Greek ministries and other government agencies. Members of the AMAG were granted extra-territoriality, inviolability of property and exemption from taxes, customs duties and currency controls. (Koliopoulos and Veremis, 2004, p 296)

Dedoulis and Caramanis (2007, p 401) suggest that a complex set of agreements limited the Greek government so that its members almost could not make a decision without the prior consent of the US Administration or its representatives in Athens. They suggest that:

> Up to 1951, American personnel had taken the main responsibility, in fact if not always in legal form, for the planning and carrying through of reconstruction and rehabilitation. Advisers had been installed in the ministries, field representatives had been stationed all over the country to check up on actual performance, and when things went wrong or failed to conform to American ideas, vigorous efforts were made to alter the situation through 'advice' that often took on a peremptory tone. (McNeil, 1957, cited in Dedoulis and Caramanis, 2007, p 401)

It was under these circumstances that social work emerged in Greece. In the Ministry of Public Health and Welfare, AMAG reorganised the structure of the services. Top priorities included urgent sanitary engineering construction, the improvement of public hygiene and the protection of children as a result of the war. On the surface 'protecting children' would seem uncontroversial, but it was anything but this. This policy was in fact highly controversial since it was used as a device by the state to intervene into the families of those involved in the liberation movement to 're-educate' the 'spoiled' generation.

AMAG needed trained 'professionals' to carry out these new tasks. The State Department authorised Charity Organisations, operating under its supervision, to assess the possibility of developing a source of local social workers. The Unitarian Service Committee (USC) was the principal organisation at this stage with the peripheral support of YWCA and the League of American Women in Greece. Domestically the initiatives of the Royal family, especially the Queen's welfare foundations, along with the local aristocracy enhanced the idea of the development of the social work profession. Initially the task was supported by AMAG and the Fulbright Foundation – though after the 1950s the cost passed to Greek taxpayers through the funding of the 'Royal Welfare Foundation'.

Research on USC archives suggests that the US maintained a role in the supervision of social work education and practice in Greece until 1967, more than 20 years after their first involvement (Ioakimidis, 2009). For the next three decades social work remained a profession that was loyal to successive authoritarian administrations.

The development of social work in Greece is celebrated by the 'pioneers of social work' and the IFSW as a fine example of international social work development (see Keeley, 1962). As recognition of the Greek 'success' the IFSW elected a Greek social worker, Litsa Alexandraki, as its president for the period 1962–68 (at the height of the dictatorship). But the roots of the profession in the country, its links with US geopolitical interests, its role in the suppression of the radical grassroots practices in the liberated zones and its links with a succession of Greek authoritarian regimes is glossed over. And it's worth emphasising that, despite the profession's 'loyalty' to the state and the willingness of social work elites to collude with the US authorities, social work remained a marginalised profession within the Greek state (and it remains so today).

Conclusion: social work internationalisation versus internationalism

The period 1945–65 has been described as 'extremely important' for international social work (Kendall, 1978). In this period the International Federation of Social Workers was formed (1956), the *Journal of International Social Work* was established (1958) and the IFSW achieved consultative status at the United Nations. However, this process did not take place in a political vacuum; many international social work activities cannot be seen as politically neutral. In fact the pattern that was followed in the development of social work in different countries (most of them 'key countries' for US imperialism) makes use of the term *international social work* rather problematic. What was described above was rather a process of forced *social work internationalisation* – the export of a narrowly defined Anglo-American model of social work. Moreover, in these 'key countries' social work followed the military or political interventions of the US and played an important role in the redesign of the welfare system in these countries – as part of the US's broader political project to 'stabilise' the country in their interests.

What we witnessed was the export of one particular social work model, but this ignored alternative models from within the US or the UK and rode roughshod over radical grassroots forms of welfare delivery in the country involved.

Rather than internationalisation of social work we should look instead to social work internationalism. This means learning from projects, philosophies and perspectives about what social work is and the activities it encapsulates from across the globe. It means offering solidarity to those whose social work activity is steeped in traditions of resistance and rebellion against injustice and inequality. But more than this, internationalism means addressing the problems of social work within one's own country as part of a struggle for a better world.

In a recent article in the *International Social Work* journal, colleagues from Hong Kong (Chu et al, 2009) complained about Western academics who demand that social workers in the global south should prefigure issues of social justice, human rights and equality within their practice while ignoring the managerialist and market-oriented forms of practice that increasingly dominate within the countries of the West. Their point was not to dismiss human rights and social justice based approaches but to question the hypocrisy of Western academic social workers. We share their concerns. As academics and activists in Britain the best support we could offer to social workers across the globe – a true act of social work internationalism – would be to engage with those movements whose ultimate goal is the defeat of neoliberal forms of social work delivery in the West.

NINE

Rediscovering radicalism and humanity in social work

Mary Langan

> How can social work rediscover its humanity as well as its radicalism? (Ferguson, 2008a, p 21)

The question posed by Iain Ferguson in his book *Reclaiming social work: Challenging neoliberalism and promoting social justice* accurately identifies the challenges facing social work today. These challenges arise from a number of familiar factors – the marketisation of social care services, the demoralisation of social workers under the combined pressures of managerialism and the public opprobrium arising from child protection scandals. Radical social work has suffered a particular loss of focus and direction as a consequence of the fragmentation of the left and the new social movements of feminism and anti-racism from which it emerged. Yet the traditions of radical social work, particularly its critique of the theory and practice of casework, provide both ideas and inspiration for rising to the challenges of the new millennium.

Individual autonomy in question

Iain Ferguson's question implicitly recognises the scale of the problem experienced by the Left and progressive forces over the past 20 years. While there has been progress, the setbacks, particularly of the labour movement internationally, mean that the goals of socialism (first raised in the 'bourgeois revolutions' of 1848, transiently triumphant in the Russian Revolution 1917, and, for our generation, revitalised in the revolts of 1968) are now in abeyance. But the problems go even deeper; even the goals of 'liberty, equality and solidarity' proclaimed by the French Revolution of 1789 are now disparaged. The convergence of the gloomy ideologies of neoconservativism and post-modernism reflect a wider loss of confidence in any conception of human advance or social progress. Enlightenment values – respect for scientific rationality, the commitment to universal concepts of freedom and equality (even democracy) – are widely questioned in the prevailing climate of pessimism and despondency (McLennan, 2010).

The demise of the rival solidarities of capital and labour has undermined collective modes of identity and activity in politics and civil society. Just as the rolling back of the state has betrayed neoconservative hopes of unleashing a vibrant spirit of enterprise (confirming only the dependence of decadent private capital on state support), the decline of collectivism has not produced a dynamic individualism (confirming that robust individuals are nurtured in networks of social solidarity). Indeed the emerging post-modern individual is a fragile and vulnerable subject, requiring professional and official protection and support in the face of the endlessly multiplying vicissitudes of modern life (from climate change and pandemic flu to anti-social behaviour, domestic violence and paedophilia) (Alcabes, 2009). Now that the transformation of society through collective activity is off the agenda of history, the mere survival of the individual subject appears to mark the horizon of human aspirations. Hence the defence of individual autonomy and human rights becomes the starting point for the renewal of the radical project.

Anti-human sentiments have become pervasive in contemporary social policy, from the loss of faith in the concept of rehabilitation in the discourse on anti-social behaviour to the notion that therapeutic psychosocial intervention is the solution to every personal, family and community problem. The socialist, anti-racist and feminist dynamics in radical social work have been reworked into the vague rhetoric of 'empowerment' and 'anti-discriminatory practice' which in turn can be used to bolster professional and managerial authority (Langan, 2002).

Critics of the evolution of social policy and social work under New Labour have analysed the neoliberal agenda launched in the Thatcher era and carried forward by Tony Blair (Ferguson, 2008a; Ferguson and Woodward, 2009; Garrett, 2009; Harris and White, 2009). These authors have exposed the processes of privatisation, marketisation and managerialism that continue to exert their influence on social work clients and practitioners alike. Here we draw attention to an equally important aspect of current social policy: the therapeutic dynamic which accelerated in New Labour's second and third terms.

New Labour's therapeutic turn

The advent of the New Labour government in 1997 marked a decisive shift in social policy from the collectivist, redistributive approach of the post-war welfare state to a more individualistic, therapeutic ethos under Tony Blair. For Anthony Giddens, an important academic influence on the new government, welfare was 'not in essence an economic concept, but a psychic one, concerning as it does "well-being"' (Giddens, 1998, p 117). He emphasised that 'welfare institutions must be concerned with fostering psychological as well as economic benefits', arguing that, for example, counselling 'might be more helpful than direct economic support' (Giddens, 1998, p 119). Though this approach was not entirely novel – Margaret Thatcher's government had provided counselling for industrial workers who lost their jobs in the recession of the early 1980s – it was pursued in a much more systematic way after 1997. New Labour's endorsement of psychosocial interventions extends from 'emotional literacy' courses in schools, to the Connexions programme for young adults, to the mass provision of cognitive behavioural therapies to claimants of disability benefits.

In its shift away from material redistribution towards a concern with the moral and spiritual welfare of the individual, New Labour social policy inevitably came to focus on the section of society that appeared to be both most vulnerable to the 'manufactured uncertainties' of the postmodern world and most susceptible to state intervention: children. In the early days of the New Labour government, the newly established Social Exclusion Unit took the lead in advancing Giddens' 'positive welfare' agenda, aiming to promote economic growth and individual well-being through 'positive prevention and early intervention' in family life. For the government's pioneering welfare initiative, 'social exclusion' occurred when 'people or areas suffer from a combination of problems such as unemployment, poor skills, low income, poor housing, high crime, bad health and family breakdown' (Social Exclusion Unit, 2001b, p 11). While recognising that it was difficult to distinguish risk factors that were causes or effects, for New Labour, 'the primary and original cause of many problems associated with crime, education and employment is seen to reside with poor parenting' (Parton, 2006, p 93). New Labour's focus on the risks facing children and young people led inexorably to its policy focus on professional intervention to improve parenting.

In Tony Blair's first term in office as prime minister, the drive to reform personal social services, as in other areas of the welfare state, proceeded hesitantly and unevenly. The 1998 White Paper *Modernising Social Services* indicated the government's determination to persist with the agenda of managerialism and the promotion of a mixed economy of welfare provision that had been initiated by the previous Conservative government (Department of Health, 1998). However, following Blair's second general election victory in June 2001, the pace of reform accelerated and the focus shifted towards measures to improve parenting and early intervention to prevent later difficulties. The 2003 Green Paper, *Every child matters,* proclaimed a 'new approach to the well-being of children and young people from birth to age 19' specifying as its 'aims and objectives' that 'every child, whatever their background or their circumstances' should have the support they needed to 'be healthy; stay safe; enjoy and achieve; make a positive contribution; achieve economic well-being' (Chief Secretary to the Treasury, 2003, p 9). These policies 'would not only bring about major organisational change but would also reconfigure the relationship between children, parents, professionals and the state well beyond concerns about child abuse (Parton, 2006:2).

Increased therapeutic intervention in children's lives through social care services was accompanied by parallel initiatives in other areas: in education ('early years', 'extended schools' and 'social and emotional aspects of learning' programmes), in criminal justice (through the wider use of 'anti-social behaviour orders' and the 'respect' agenda), in health (through campaigns against teenage pregnancy and obesity, such as the Change4Life programme to promote healthy lifestyles) (Earnshaw, 2008). The common theme was that 'linked-up' government agencies and appropriately qualified professionals could work with children and their families to encourage individual well-being and promote social cohesion. The key assumptions underlying New Labour social policy were that children were uniquely at risk in contemporary society, that they had been betrayed by existing services and professions and that early intervention was the key to their future happiness (and to the stability of society).

Government family policies now assumed the breakdown of the family and the divergent needs of different family members: 'No longer was the traditional patriarchal nuclear family seen as an adequate instrument of government. Increasingly the interests and identities of children and parents (both mothers and fathers) were disentangled and disaggregated' (Parton, 2006, p 5).

Parenting now became a public concern. For New Labour policy makers, parents – 'both mothers and fathers' – needed professional support to help them to grasp and fulfil their parental responsibilities and children relied on professionals to guarantee their safety and well-being.

Soft cop, hard cop

The Sure Start programme for parents and young children is New Labour's flagship social policy initiative. Modelled on the US Head Start program – part of President Lyndon Johnson's 'great society' and 'war on poverty' policies of the 1960s – Sure Start began with 250 local programmes in the most deprived neighbourhoods in 1999 and subsequently expanded to cover the entire country. Sure Start was consolidated in 2004 with the establishment of a network of Children's Centres, offering 'seamless integrated services and information' for parents and children of all ages, at first in the poorest areas, but rapidly spreading outwards, with a target of 3,500 centres throughout the country by 2010. Children's Centres offer a combination of 'early education and childcare' (incorporating elements of health as well as education and social care) together with 'support for parents', including help to get paid employment, and advice of a more or less systematic character on parenting. With a budget of £1.8 billion a year in 2006, the Sure Start programme amounted to a 'massive state investment in parenting and childhood' (Frost and Parton, 2009, p 125).

There were some tensions within the Sure Start programme between different aspects of the New Labour social policy agenda, tensions which unfolded as the programme expanded in scope (Glass, 2005; Hodge, 2005). On the one hand, they had a role to play in the 'welfare to work' policy of encouraging parents, in particular mothers, to participate in the labour market rather than relying on benefits, in part by providing affordable child care. On the other hand, they provided the opportunity for early intervention in childhood development and for the promotion of approved styles of parenting. The fact that the maternal employment rate remained 'almost static' between 1994 and 2004 suggests that the latter policy remained the dominant influence (Lloyd, 2008).

For authorities in social services preoccupied with failures of child protection, Sure Start programmes provided a means of targeting children at risk and pursuing preventive strategies; for those taking a wider view of child development, a universal service appeared to offer a less stigmatising and more comprehensive approach.

In practice, internal tensions in Sure Start were largely resolved by wider developments. On the one hand, the vogue for formal instruction in parenting popularised by successful television programmes such as Channel Four's *Supernanny* and numerous popular books and internet sites meant that government initiatives in this area were more likely to be welcomed than regarded as intrusive (Bristow, 2009). On the other hand, the success of Sure Start in the context of the parallel government campaign against 'anti-social behaviour' paved the way for parenting initiatives that were explicitly authoritarian (Waiton, 2008).

For example, Family Intervention Projects, launched in 2006 within the framework of the Respect Action Plan designed to tackle anti-social behaviour, offered an approach described as 'assertive' and 'persistent' to improve parenting skills in targeted families (White et al, 2008). These projects involve support workers engaging with parents in intimate family activities such as washing, dressing and feeding children, either through 'outreach' teams or in residential units. Though disparaged as 'sin-bins' in the tabloid press, these programmes were welcomed as offering hope to 'chaotic families' in a feature in a broadsheet newspaper on one pioneering scheme in Dundee (Gentleman, 2009). Within three years of their launch, some 2,600 families had voluntarily attended schemes in 170 centres, in which they are treated 'primarily as victims' even though they may display anti-social behaviour. According to the senior project worker in Dundee, 'a lot of residents find it prison-like to begin with, initially they find it quite intrusive' (Gentleman, 2009, p 12).

In 2007 the government launched the Family Nurse Partnership, through which specialist nurses (linked to local Sure Start programmes/ Children's Centres) visit 'vulnerable, first time, young parents' from early pregnancy until the child is two years old (Department for Children Schools and Families (DCSF), 2007a; Cabinet Office, 2009). Immediately dubbed 'foetal asbos' in the tabloids, this programme is directly derived from the US Nurse Family Partnership scheme, an anti-poverty initiative developed more than 30 years ago in Colorado. The idea is that 'through building a close, supportive relationship with the whole family', the nurse guides the mother 'to adopt healthier lifestyles, improve their parenting skills and become self-sufficient' (Cabinet Office, 2009).

Following the transfer of power from Tony Blair to Gordon Brown in July 2007, the government pressed ahead with its radical early childhood intervention agenda. Brown immediately signalled his priorities with the establishment of a new ministry, the Department for Children, Schools and Families, headed by his long-standing ally, Ed Balls. In December Balls launched the Children's Plan, to be implemented by newly established local Children's Trusts, bringing together education and social care, and incorporating some community health services (and in some areas, youth offending teams). 'Extended schools' are a key part of the programme for 'delivering' the '*Every child matters* outcomes' of improved well-being (Teachernet, 2009). Open from 8 am to 6 pm, 48 weeks a year, these offer 'a varied menu of activities' for children as well as 'parenting support' and access to specialist services. By 2008 some 2500 such schools were in operation. Children's Trusts were given a 'new leadership role' in coordinating children's services 'so that together they can engage parents and tackle all the barriers to the learning, health and happiness of every child' (DCSF, 2007b, p 3). The key themes in this ambitious programme were early intervention, multi-agency working, integration of services and sharing of information.

Positive psychology

The therapeutic content of New Labour's interventions in childhood is a synthesis of the 'positive psychology' and cognitive behavioural therapies associated with the programmes that have been imported from the US for deployment in British schools and children's centres. A major influence is the psychologist Martin Seligman, the author of numerous popular self-help and motivational books such as *Authentic happiness: Using the new positive psychology to realize your potential for lasting fulfilment* (Seligman, 2004) and *The optimistic child: A proven program to safeguard children against depression and build lifelong resilience* (Seligman, 1996). Seligman's Penn Resiliency Program, developed in Pennsylvania, has been promoted in the UK by New Labour's 'happiness tsar', Richard Layard, as part of his drive to cultivate 'emotional literacy' (Layard, 2007). This programme has been translated (apparently with some difficulty) into 'British English' and piloted in schools in Tyneside, Manchester and Hertfordshire (Challen et al, 2009). Another influential US model is the 'Incredible Years Program', developed by the nurse and clinical psychologist Carolyn Webster-Stratton in her Seattle parenting clinic. This has been widely implemented in parenting programmes in Wales (Hutchings et al, 2007; Bywater et al, 2009).

The cult of 'positive psychology' flourished in the US in the 1990s in the context of the ascendancy of speculative finance capitalism (Ehrenreich, 2009). It marked a revival of the theories of 'positive thinking' that first emerged in reaction to the punitive Calvinism of 19th-century America. In its modern form and often legitimised in the language of cognitive psychology, the new ideology appeared both to justify charismatic, intuitive, flamboyant corporate leadership and to help employers in 'managing the despair' of the millions of workers who lost their jobs in restructuring. In what Ehrenreich refers to as 'the years of magical thinking', New Age mysticism linked up with 'quantum flapdoodle pseudoscience' and penetrated deeply into middle-class America and its business culture. It also became a major influence on the new megachurches which preach the 'prosperity gospel' rather than old-style religious austerity: 'churches became more like corporations, corporations became more like churches' (Ehrenreich, 2009, p 144). Yet the main appeal of 'positive psychology', for elites on both sides of the Atlantic, is the way in which it preserves the 'toxic features' of evangelical Protestantism – its 'harsh judgmentalism' and its 'insistence on the constant interior labour of self-examination' (Ehrenreich, 2009, p 89).

A new approach requires new professionals, especially given the low esteem in which social workers have often come to be regarded. Richard Layard is explicit on the need for a 'new cadre' of specialist teachers 'acting as standard bearers of the movement' struggling to achieve an 'educational revolution' (Layard, 2007). New cohorts of specially trained 'early years' teachers and 'family support workers' are emerging as the 'barefoot doctors' of the Sure Start revolution. For the more specialised tasks of intensive family intervention, nurses, midwives and health visitors are preferred. According to a report on parenting policy by the think tank, Demos, health visitors are 'trusted and liked' (unlike social workers) and are an 'underused resource' (Lexmond and Reeves, 2009, p 63). However, the authors insist that they will need 'more training on parenting styles' and 'motivational interviewing'.

Intrusive and authoritarian

The authoritarianism of New Labour's therapeutic initiatives is most apparent in the more coercive programmes, such as Nurse–Family Partnerships and Family Intervention programmes. The controlling character of government policy was also apparent in the deployment of a wide range of what have been described as 'enforcement counsellors' in both traditional social work contexts and (more widely) in the novel agencies (Social Exclusion Unit, Connexions, and others) established under New Labour (Jordan, 2000). However, while Sure Start and the Children's Centres tend to be exempted from the strictures of radical commentators on New Labour neoliberal social policies, an authoritarian dimension is implicit in mainstream social care schemes for children. The scope of intervention extends from children 'in need' or 'at risk' to children in general, who became the target of professional assistance from an earlier and earlier age. Children may now receive professional assistance with all aspects of their development, in 'wrap around' facilities covering all the spaces between home and school, at every stage of their lives from infancy to further education. Parents, too, are offered professional support in carrying out their parenting responsibilities – and everybody comes under monitoring and surveillance. The danger of New Labour's interventionist approach towards children is that, by assuming the disaggregation of family relationships, it may exacerbate the process of fragmentation it seeks to contain. Third party interventions in the family, however well-intentioned and supportive, tend to undermine parental authority further and render children more reliant on professional mediation. The expanding range of surveillance intensifies mistrust and weakens adult solidarity in relation to the socialisation of the younger generation.

The process of what Jurgen Habermas described as the 'colonisation of the life world' of the private citizen by public authorities is made possible by the disorganisation of the public sphere and the weakening of informal relationships (Habermas, 1987). He warned that the 'juridification of everyday life' – which has advanced much further with New Labour's positive welfare policies – could cause the 'disintegration of life relations' and the consolidation of dependence on state services (Habermas, 1987, pp 364, 369).

Here we can turn to the legacy of radical social work. In the 1970s the radical social work movement had an acute awareness of the repressive consequences of the incorporation of Freudian psychological theories and techniques into 'casework', the prevalent form of social work practice (another import from the US) (Epstein, 1994). The radical movement was critical of the ways in which the casework approach redefined social problems as individual problems and, through the deployment of psychoanalytic jargon, pathologised social work clients. Radical social work writers explicitly disparaged an earlier version of the sort of psychologising that has now become widely accepted, characterising it as the 'pseudoscience' of traditional 'casework': 'The influence in particular of psychology has led to an over-emphasis on pathological and clinical orientations to the detriment of structural and political implications' (Bailey and Brake, 1975, p 145).

Indeed, in the quest to reclaim the humanity as well as the radicalism of social work, we can go further back to one of social work's most trenchant critics – the sociologist and social commentator Barbara Wootton. Writing in 1959, Wootton anticipated Brake and Bailey, pointing out that 'The root of the trouble seems once again to be traceable to the habit of confusing economic difficulties with personal failure or misconduct' (Wootton, 1959, p 291).

Her observation that 'the terminology is ultra modern but the concept is suspiciously reminiscent of older models' could readily be applied to much of New Labour's policy (notably its revival of 'cycle of deprivation' theories).

An initiative in 2009 by Alcohol Concern encouraging social workers to discreetly record families' alcohol consumption while visiting their homes provoked little comment (Fitzpatrick, 2009). Yet more than half a century ago Wootton raised concerns about social workers who 'blandly ignore the ethical questions raised by practices which suggest that they take advantage of other people's poverty, sickness, unemployment or homelessness in order to pry into what is not their business' (Wootton, 1959, p 279). For Wootton, professional intrusion into intimate personal matters was regarded as being corrosive of individual freedom. For the radical tradition that followed her it was understood as being inimical to any concept of collective resistance. Today, the first step towards reviving the radical tradition must involve challenging the violations of individual autonomy presented in the diverse guises of 'support', 'mentoring', 'guidance', 'counselling' in contemporary therapeutic social policy.

Radical social work today

The re-emergence of capitalist recession – with the return of mass unemployment, homelessness and other social manifestations of economic crisis – has raised the question of whether radical social work can be revived in the new millennium. Some, recognising the loss of progressive vision in contemporary social work practice, have called for social work to be 'repoliticised' along the lines of the radical model (Ferguson, 2008; Ferguson and Lavalette, 2009; Ferguson and Woodward, 2009). Recalling the attempts of the earlier movement to seek alliances with organisations of benefits claimants, housing activists, trade unionists and others, they have proposed linking up with contemporary movements of 'service users' (largely in mental health and disability) and wider 'anti-capitalist' campaigns, such as protests against globalisation, war and world poverty.

Others, pointing out that social work has been recruited to the distinctive modes of therapeutic governance promoted by New Labour, leading to the 'micromanagement of human interaction', insist that we need instead to 'get politics out of social work and therapy out of politics' (McLaughlin, 2008). This approach starts from a recognition of the need to challenge the way in which social work has been politicised by New Labour over the past decade (in part through the incorporation in a distorted form of some of the concepts of the radical movement, such as 'empowerment' and 'anti-discrimination') (Langan, 2002). Recognising the ascendancy of a pathologising psychological dynamic in New Labour social policy suggests a number of ways in which we can move forward.

The first and most obvious way of moving forward lies through mounting a challenge to psychological theories and their deployment in social policy. It is remarkable that the theories of positive psychology and the practices of the new wave of therapeutic entrepreneurs have received so little critical attention despite their pervasive influence in contemporary social (and educational) policy. An exposure of these theories – what Barbara Wootton characterised as the 'lamentable arrogance' of an earlier generation – would provide a sound basis on which to defend both the autonomy of the social work client and the professional autonomy of the social worker. It would also provide some foundation for solidarity between client and worker in the face of forms of state intervention that are corrosive of both family and professional relationships.

In terms of strengthening the position of social workers as a profession, it is vital to mount some resistance to the parallel process of colonisation of social work training by the nostrums of mentoring, coaching and leadership derived from US corporations (where such theories appear to have contributed to the current crisis of the financial sector). In terms of forging closer relations between social workers and clients, a common challenge to the use of IT surveillance systems purporting to reduce risk while merely intensifying distrust point the way forward.

Is radical social work still possible? Yes, if it rediscovers its humanistic roots in the defence of the principles of individual liberty and human rights.

TEN

Re-gilding the ghetto: community work and community development in 21st-century Britain

Sarah Banks

Introduction

The theory and practice of community work is bedevilled by debates around terminology, identity and ideology – just as much as, if not more than, social work. The term 'community' (noun), while often dismissed as meaningless, nevertheless has much more substantive content than the term 'social' (adjective) as it occurs in 'social work'. While 'community' tends to have a positive evaluative meaning (associated with warmth and caring), it also has a number of descriptive meanings (Plant, 1974) and can be used to describe groups of people that are exclusive, hierarchical, homogeneous and conservative, as well as groups that are inclusive, egalitarian, heterogeneous and challenging. As Purdue et al (2000, p 2) suggest, the contested nature of the concept of 'community' allows differing interests to 'manipulate a term with multiple meanings to their own ends'. In so far as community workers tend to support groups of people with common experiences of disadvantage and oppression to take collective action, they can easily adopt a radical rhetoric linked with a social change agenda. Yet community workers are also very aware of how vulnerable they are to cooption, as governments and service delivery agencies appropriate the radical-sounding discourse of 'community empowerment' and 'social justice'. Community workers have been, and some still are, intensely ambivalent about the mainstreaming of community work as a state-sponsored activity, about moves towards professionalisation and about whether community work should be regarded as a profession, occupation, social movement or a set of skills. To add to the confusion, 'community work' as a generic term for a range of practices is being superseded in Britain by the terms 'community development work' or 'community development' (traditionally regarded as just one of several approaches to community work).

This chapter will first explore the nature of 'community work' – outlining an analysis that regards 'community development' as one of several approaches to community work. Referring back to Mayo's (1975) chapter, we will consider her conclusion that community development as an intervention has limited radical potential. It is argued that this conclusion is equally valid 35 years later, as the more radical 'community action' approaches to community work have been marginalised and community development has become mainstreamed within policies and practices concerned with promoting citizen participation and neighbourhood renewal. Nevertheless, examples are offered of locally based action for political change (based on community organising and critical pedagogy), which keep alive the radical community work tradition.

The focus of this chapter is on community work as an occupation and set of practices in Britain, where it has developed separately from social work. Although identified in the 1960s and 1970s as the third method of social work (alongside group work and case work) and early social services departments had community development officers and neighbourhood workers based within them, from the 1980s, community work became marginalised in social work education and practice (Stepney and Popple, 2008). The discussion in this chapter centres on community work as an occupation in its own right, outside the framework of social work (see Mark Baldwin's chapter in this volume for discussion of the possibilities for a radical community-based social work).

Community work and community development

The title of this chapter includes reference to *community work* as well as *community development*, which was the subject of Mayo's (1975) chapter in *Radical social work* ('Community development: a radical alternative?'). This is a deliberate move to broaden the discussion, just as Mayo's focus on community development was a conscious choice to subject 'the most seductive form of community work' to critical analysis. I am using the term 'community work' in a broad sense to encompass a range of different types of work that are oriented towards social change with residents in neighbourhoods and with identity and interest groups. In this generic sense the term 'community work' covers practice approaches ranging from community-based planning and service delivery to community action and campaigning, with community development (focusing on self-help and citizen participation) somewhere in the middle, as shown in Table 10.1.

Table 10.1: Approaches to community work

	Community service and planning	Community development	Community action/community organising
Aims	Developing community-oriented policies, services and organisations	Promoting community self-help and citizen participation	Campaigning for community interests and policies
Participants	Organisations and service users/residents as partners	Residents and group members defining and meeting their own needs	Structurally oppressed groups organising for power
Methods	Maximising resident/service user involvement, inter-agency links and partnerships	Creative and co-operative processes	Campaign tactics on concrete issues
Key roles	Organiser, planner	Enabler, educator	Activist, leader
Possible ideological underpinnings	Liberal reformist; or even conservative; consensus seeking	Participatory democracy; liberal democratic; communitarian;or even conservative; consensus seeking	Marxist; anti-oppressive; or other structural theories of social problems; conflict theory

This table summarises and simplifies some of the main categories of community work drawn and developed from various key texts written in the 1970s, 1980s and 1990s (Gulbenkian Study Group, 1968; Gulbenkian Foundation, 1973; Thomas, 1983; Banks and Noonan, 1990; Popple, 1995). Although presented in tabular form, the boundaries between these approaches are not hard and fast, and, indeed, as Thomas (1983, p 107) points out, practitioners do not necessarily conceive of their work in this way. Nevertheless some kind of categorisation like this can be a helpful analytical tool to differentiate the wide range of functions, methods, and (implicitly) ideologies embodied within the generic term 'community work'.

Figure 10.1 presents the approaches in the form of overlapping circles, to indicate the fluidity of the boundaries.

Figure 10.1: Overlapping approaches to community work

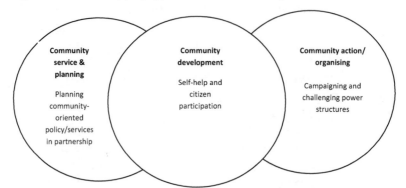

In this model, community development is at the centre of community work, and arguably is the dominant approach within community work as an occupation. The activities and practices identified in Table 10.1 as community development constitute the focus of much of what community workers did in the 1970s, 1980s and 1990s and what they have been doing in the first decade of the 21st century. Arguably community development is the approach with which most community workers feel comfortable. As Mayo (1975) argues in her chapter in *Radical social work*, it is 'attractive to those professionals in search of an alternative to the more directly hierarchical and paternalistic traditional approach of the helping professions'. It is also the type of work that is acceptable to employers and funders and can meet some of the service delivery and citizen participation objectives of central and local government and other agencies, especially if it merges into community service/planning.

This may partly explain why, during the first decade of the 21st century, the term 'community development' or 'community development work' is beginning to be used more frequently than 'community work' as the generic term covering social change oriented work in communities in Britain. This is most clearly demonstrated in the changing title of the occupation for which national occupational standards have been developed: the term 'community work' was used in 1995; 'community development work' in 2002; and 'community development' in 2009 (Federation of Community Work Training Groups and Mainframe Research and Consultancy Services, 1995; Paulo, 2002; Lifelong Learning UK, 2009). The network that has been most active in developing these standards has also changed its name from the Federation of Community Work Training Groups to the Federation for Community Development Learning. The Association of Community Workers, founded in 1968, was wound up in the mid-2000s, with its members being redirected to the Community Development Exchange (a membership organisation for individuals and agencies, officially established in 1991 as the Standing Conference on Community Development with funding from the Home Office).

What is the rationale for this change in terminology, and does it reflect changes in ideology, theory and practice, or is it merely semantic? The shift from 'community work' to 'community development' reflects a complex array of motivations and trends, some of which are contradictory including:

- a desire on the part of certain key players in the field to gain credibility and recognition for the work as a specialist occupation. The concept and practice of community development might be regarded as more specialist and mainstream than the all-embracing and rather diffuse concept of community work;
- uncertainty about the identity of the occupation or even whether it is an occupation at all, at the same time as a desire for the recognition of community work as an occupation in its own right. The latest national occupational standards, which ostensibly refer to a recognised occupation, conflate the development process that communities go through with community development work as an occupation; they also include as community development practitioners members of other professions using a 'community development approach'; a stretching of the term 'community development'. Not only is the term 'community development' inclusive of process and practice and a range of occupations and practitioners, it is being used in a generic sense to cover the ground previously covered by 'community work'. In theory, at least, the middle circle of Figure 10.1 is widening; a narrowing of focus of the activities of community workers – although the concept of 'community development' has stretched and statements of purpose and values are framed in the language of structural inequalities, the practice of community workers has moved away from community action/organising and more towards community service/planning.

However, before attempting to justify and elaborate on this analysis in more detail, let us return to Mayo's original chapter written in 1975 in which she subjected community development to some rather honest and rigorous critical analysis.

An historical perspective

In her chapter in *Radical social work*, Marjorie Mayo explores the question of whether community development is a radical alternative to casework. Not surprisingly, her answer is broadly speaking in the negative, with one of her conclusions being:

> If radical social change is the prime objective, community development is not a specially favourable starting point at all: nor does it have any automatic advantage over social work of the casework variety – indeed in some instances it may be, and has been, *more* repressive. (Mayo, 1975, p 142)

Although she qualifies this comment in the next paragraph, allowing that community (development) work does have some radical potential (small local campaigns can build up local capacity and link to the wider labour movement), the point she is making is that community development is not inherently radical. This is as true, if not more so, in 2010 as it was in 1975. Indeed, according to some analyses of community work (see Table 10.1), it is almost true by definition, as 'community development' is the term used to refer to an essentially reformist consensus-based approach to community work that focuses on the promotion of self-help and participation in civic life on the part of residents in local neighbourhoods and groups of citizens with common interests or identities. As depicted in Table 10.1, it is often distinguished from community action and community organising, which are more conflict-oriented and campaigning approaches, with the aim of building alliances and coalitions between people with common experiences of oppression and challenging existing power structures.

Mayo traces the history of term 'community development' and the practices associated with it to the British Colonial Office, which introduced educational programmes in the 1940s and 1950s in colonised countries to encourage self-help and local participation in anticipation of their independence. Similar approaches were also promoted in the US, in attempts to 'develop' the black minority population and in the war on poverty of the 1960s. The term was also in the title of the first British area-based anti-poverty programme, the Community Development Project (CDP), launched by the Home Office in 1969 in 12 areas, based on a notion of improving local areas by coordinating the efforts of national and local government, local services and local people. As Mayo (1975, p 137) comments about community development:

> As a relatively cheap and typically ideological attempt to resolve various economic, social and political problems it has clearly been attractive to governments and voluntary agencies both national and international for use not just in the Third World but also among racial minorities and indigenous poor at home.

The CDP and its aftermath is the subject of Mayo's chapter in the second collection on radical social work (Mayo, 1980). This later chapter is in some ways more optimistic, despite being written following the premature closure of the community development projects during the mid-1970s and in a time of recession and public expenditure cuts. The reason for the closure of the CDPs was because many of the community workers came into conflict with their sponsoring local authorities, having worked alongside local people to engage in community action – campaigns, protests and rent strikes; and many of the action researchers (of which Mayo was one) had contributed to numerous reports outlining the structural causes of unemployment, poverty and inequality and the futility of attempting to tackle such major social and economic problems piecemeal at local level (CDP Inter-Project Editorial Team, 1977; Benwell Community Project, 1978; Corkey and Craig, 1978; North Tyneside CDP, 1978; CDP Political Economy Collective, 1979; Loney, 1983). Mayo (1980, p 194) argues, however, that some progressive potential managed to survive the first round of public expenditure cuts of the mid- and late 1970s, leaving workers and community activists more experienced to make use of the limited room for manoeuvre and seeing one of the legacies of the CDPs as the broad alliance between community organisations and the labour movement. The CDPs are an example of a programme designed within a community development model (self-help and participation), which moved into community action (conflict and campaigning).

Arguably this progressive potential was hard to realise in the following period of neoliberal policies promoted by the Conservative government elected in 1979, as public spending was further cut and the welfare state came under increasing attack. As Mayo comments in a later chapter (Mayo and Robertson, 2003, p 27), in the subsequent area-based programmes introduced by the Conservative administration (such as Urban Development Corporations in 1981 and Enterprise Zones), there was 'less interest in opening the Pandora's box of community participation' and a much stronger emphasis on economic development and private sector involvement. Yet the problems of concentrations of poverty, especially in the inner cities, remained and as new area-based programmes were introduced (such as City Challenge in 1991 and the Single Regeneration Budget in 1994), it was recognised that social and economic problems needed to be tackled together and the involvement of local residents in planning and implementing some of these projects was part of the 'solution'. Community development workers were employed to work on these programmes and, especially in the later phases of Single Regeneration Budget programmes, increasingly took on roles in 'community capacity building' – that is, preparing residents to take part in partnership boards and to run projects (Banks and Shenton, 2001).

Nevertheless, in the 1980s the employment of generic neighbourhood-based community development workers by local authorities and voluntary organisations declined, as more specialist posts (for example, in community enterprise, community care and community health) began to grow – linked very much to the promotion of self-help, care in the community, volunteering and business development (Francis et al, 1984; Glen and Pearse, 1993). During the 1980s there was also a growing awareness among community workers themselves (as among other social welfare workers) of the importance of identity communities – with a particular stress on anti-racist and anti-sexist work (Dixon et al, 1982; Dominelli, 1990; Ohri et al, 1982) – a feature reflected in the chapter in the third British collection on radical social work, this time written by Ian Smith (1989). Smith also offers an account of the successful action on the part of grassroots community workers to fend off attempts to establish a national institute for community work in the mid-1980s, which would have been a move towards the professionalisation of community work – with the aim of giving it a clearer identity, stronger voice, recognised training and qualifications. Following a consultation exercise in 1986, a Standing Conference on Community Development was established instead, with space for regional groupings of workers and activists as well as national bodies. This is an example of the long-standing resistance on the part of community workers towards what was regarded as professionalisation – a position that was maintained for much longer than in social work or youth work. Smith (1989, p 276) characterises the debate during the 1980s as one between those who wanted to see community work establish itself as a profession and those who regarded it as a 'core set of skills that aims to enable local community groups to achieve their own objectives'. The terms 'profession' and 'professionalisation' were used loosely, with positive connotations for proponents (recognition and status for work alongside disadvantaged groups) and negative connotations for opponents (incorporation into the mainstream with loss of independence and critical edge).

Ironically, having resisted professionalisation, the Federation of Community Work Training Groups (a national federation of regional groups of community workers founded in 1982 that offered training for community activists and workers) became concerned in the late 1980s to offer recognition to people undertaking training in community work skills and to establish alternative routes to qualification for experienced activists (see Banks, 1990). This led to the active and early participation of the Federation in the development of National Vocational Qualifications in community work – a move resisted by many other occupational groups as entailing increasing government and employer control, simplification of complex practices, a focus on training at the expense of education and a sidelining of theory (Jones, 1989, pp 212–15). However, the Federation saw this as an opportunity to get community work qualifications recognised in their own right. By this time the links with social work were tenuous, with very few professional qualifying programmes for social work offering any significant community work input. Although the Central Council for Education and Training in Youth and Community Work had endorsed a route to community work qualification through accreditation of experience, this was not resourced and rarely used. By the mid-1990s, youth work became much more dominant, as The National Youth Agency took over the professional endorsement functions for youth and community work qualifications and community work was left on the margins.

Mainstreaming community development

With the national occupational standards in place (Federation of Community Work Training Groups and Mainframe Research and Consultancy Services, 1995), community work was ready to take advantage of the changing climate when New Labour came to power in Britain in 1997 and central government began to develop policies and programmes with an increasing focus on issues of social justice, inclusion and neighbourhood renewal. A whole range of policy initiatives was introduced to promote active citizenship, community capacity building, community plans, community leadership, community engagement and community empowerment, to name but a few (Department of the Environment, Transport and the Regions, 1998; Social Exclusion Unit, 1998; Social Exclusion Unit, 2001a; Home Office, 2004a, 2004b; Communities and Local Government, 2008). Those active in national community development organisations began to work hard to raise the profile of community work (specifically community development work) and to demonstrate its effectiveness in working with communities to develop the voices of the people traditionally excluded and to contribute to democratic and neighbourhood renewal. In 2006 several national bodies concerned to promote community development work formed a working party under the aegis of the Community Development Foundation and produced a report for the Department of Communities and Local Government called *The community development challenge* (Communities and Local Government, 2007). This report (p 11) comments that 'the focus [of New Labour] on tackling inequalities and striving for social justice aligned well with the core values and ideals of community development, which, as a profession, unexpectedly found itself largely in tune with government thinking.'

It also makes the point that (p 13) 'there is a CD profession, defined by national occupational standards and a body of theory and experience going back the best part of a century.'

The use of the term 'profession' in both these quotations is noteworthy. Mainly the term 'occupation' is used, but the fact that 'profession' has slipped into one or two places in the document is indicative of the bid for status and recognition represented by this report.

In the *Community development challenge* report we can, perhaps, find some clues to help elaborate on the answers to the questions posed earlier, about the rationale for the move from 'community work' to 'community development'. Community development as described by Mayo (1975) had its immediate origins in the desire for containing and controlling the move of the former British colonies towards independence. It was a managed way of giving control to local people, developing sustainable local systems of governance and service provision. Similarly the British Community Development Project was intended to be a relatively cheap way of tackling poverty and diverting attention from inequality by offering some degree of local participation in planning and building new housing, services and community projects – a means of 'gilding the ghetto' to use the evocative title of one of the CDP reports (CDP Inter-Project Editorial Team, 1977). According to the back cover of this report, the title comes from comments made by Miss Cooper, chief inspector in the children's department of the Home Office, as recorded in the minutes of a 1969 conference on poverty initiatives: 'There appeared to be an element of looking for a new method of social control – what one might call an antivalue, rather than a value. "Gilding the ghetto" or buying time, was clearly a component in the planning of CDP and Model Cities.'

However, as Mayo argues (1975), although community development is not inherently radical, it does have radical potential. The process of citizens engaging in collective action and participating in decision-making is a two-edged sword. It can bring people to political consciousness, stimulate protest, conflict, unease and unrest as well as contribute to developing community-based services and consensual partnership working. The potential of community development work to generate conflict is acknowledged in the *Community development challenge* report under the heading of 'managing tensions'. However, it is not highlighted as a main or desired outcome, rather as a by-product to be managed on the road to developing a responsible community:

> As disadvantaged communities begin to gain confidence and assert themselves, they frequently go through a stage of becoming more articulate in their grievances against whatever authorities they have to deal with. In mature CD theory and practice there is a well recognised journey from powerlessness through blame and protest to confidence, responsibility, negotiation and partnership. But this requires on the one hand that CD workers are very skilled and far-seeing, and on the other, that authorities themselves have an understanding of this process and do not react to the initial stages with denial or repression. (Communities and Local Government, 2007, p 31)

This statement highlights a vital role for community development workers – not only to bring 'disadvantaged' community participants to the negotiating table, but to educate them in the art of civilised participation, the making of moderate claims and to enable them to engage in constructive dialogue and partnership and to take responsibility.

In this account of community development, the concept is being stretched in the direction of what we identified as community service and community planning in Table 10.1. This is a move in the opposite direction to that taken by many of the CDP workers in the 1970s, who shifted the discourse and practice of community development very rapidly into the arena of community action, underpinned by a Marxist analysis of social problems. In the mid-2000s, the opportunity to mainstream the occupation of community development under New Labour was clearly regarded as a moment to be seized. This was a time when the occupation and its practice had become less radical and was partially incorporated, and when radical government rhetoric made it easier to meet in the comfortable, consensual middle ground. This is in stark contrast to the period of the late 1970s and early 1980s, which those concerned to mainstream and professionalise community work regarded as a lost moment. According to Thomas (1983), the CDP was a missed opportunity to establish community work as a profession with a discrete set of practice skills. Instead the chance was squandered as community workers turned into political analysts and central and local government beat a hasty retreat. With a Conservative government in power from 1979, the gap between the radical analysis of many community workers and neoliberal government policies was much too wide to bridge. The *Community Development Challenge* represents a sustained attempt to bridge a much narrower gap in the first decade of the 21st century.

Reclaiming the radical potential

Shaw (2008) argues that the much-evoked dichotomy between community development as a technical, 'objective' profession and community development as a radical, passionate social movement may be a useful conceptual distinction, but is not a real distinction in practice: 'It is important to remember that the contradictory provenance of community development with its roots in both benevolent welfare paternalism and autonomous working-class struggle ... has created a curiously hybrid practice' (Shaw, 2008, p 26).

Arguably such contradictions are at the heart of most of the state-sponsored welfare professions, including social work. However, in community development work, the fact that practice takes place at the level of the collectivity and is oriented towards social change means that it can be easier for the realities of an essentially reformist practice to be viewed through a radical lens.

As Shaw (2008, p 26) comments again,

> Part of the problem is that while the socialist discourse of transformation and empowerment has tended to operate at a rhetorical level, it has generally concealed a much more conformist and conservative reality.

Despite these cynical comments, Shaw's conclusion (p 34) is that community development does have the potential to contribute to radical change – as it embodies within it a choice about whether to act to maintain the status quo and reinforce existing inequalities in power, or whether to critique existing structures and work towards creating a more equal alternative 'world as it could be'. Community development is, she claims, both a professional practice and a political practice.

Similar points are made by recent commentators about the relationship between community development and community action/community organising. There is a tendency to regard these as mutually exclusive approaches. Yet DeFilippis et al (2007) point to a number of examples of established community-based projects in North America that engage in high profile, effective community organising and political campaigning (beyond their own neighbourhoods), while also undertaking locally-based community development and casework with individuals in relation to housing, employment or other legal disputes with the authorities. Bunyan (2010, p 13) in his account of the growth of broad-based organising in Britain notes the tendency of community work theory to 'divide into two broad camps based on the micro-level and the macro-level ... at the expense of what has been termed the meso-level'. Drawing on Goehler (2000), Mills (1970) and Shaw (2008, p 32), he argues that community or neighbourhood can be regarded as the meso-level where the micro-politics of personal troubles meets the macro-politics of public issues – a key arena for connecting people beyond the local into political activity.

Community organising

The growth of community organising in Britain, which developed in the 1990s and has slowly gained momentum over the first decade of the 21st century, is a good example of strategic community-based radical action – built from the grassroots; maintaining independence from the constraints of state funding; connecting local, national and global issues and networks; and coordinated by highly skilled workers. Community organising is derived from the work of the Industrial Areas Foundation set up by Saul Alinsky in the US in 1940, made popular by his books published in the 1960s and 1970s and still continuing today (Alinsky, 1969; Alinsky, 1989; Chambers, 2003; Pyles, 2009). Alinsky's method was based on the idea of organising people and money for power through building coalitions of dues-paying institutions (including places of worship, community organisations, schools and trades unions) that could then mobilise around carefully framed issues to challenge large corporations or state organisations on unjust practices, policies and laws. Some of Alinsky's provocative tactics to agitate residents, to frame winnable issues and to create conflict may seem as manipulative as those of the organisations being challenged. For example, he urges organisers to 'rub raw the resentments of the people of the community', 'fan the latent hostilities' and 'search out controversy' (Alinsky, 1989, p 116). This led to critiques of his tactics from the more moderate sections of the community work field, while his lack of a class-based Marxist political analysis also made many on the left wary of his approach (Henderson and Salmon, 1995; Mayo, 2005, p 106). Nevertheless the tactics have proved very effective, and have kept alive a tradition of radical, challenging community-based work.

While the tradition of community organising has never been strong in Britain, in the last decade people's organisations have been developing in several urban areas, often with major input from faith-based organisations and many under the aegis of the Citizen Organising Foundation (Bunyan, 2010). The most well-established is London Citizens, comprising three broad-based organisations: the East London Communities Organisation, South London Citizens and West London Citizens (www.cof.org.uk). Recent successful campaigns have included demands for a living wage, affordable housing, the rights of migrants and ethical guarantees for the 2010 Olympics, which have involved well-planned and high profile conflict tactics such as camping outside City Hall and marches and demonstrations in Trafalgar Square.

Smaller scale examples of community organising can be found in a growing number of other parts of Britain, including Birmingham, Manchester, Wales and Stockton-on-Tees. A good example of a small-scale local network that is supported under a national umbrella and has links with other groups nationally and internationally is the Thrive project in Thornaby, Stockton (www.church-poverty.org.uk/projects/thrive). This project developed under the aegis of a national body, Church Action on Poverty, which in turn is linked to the US-based Gamelial Foundation – a body that mentored Barack Obama when he worked as an organiser in Chicago and which has facilitated community organising training in Stockton and other parts of Britain. Thrive has built its capacity to engage in well-publicised actions on issues such as debt and predatory lending, by starting from research into the realities of people's everyday lives, based on in-depth household interviews (Orr et al, 2006), and then offering peer mentoring and support on debt and health-related matters. Despite tensions related to receiving financial support for some of the work from a variety of sources (including the local Primary Care Trust, which required strict outcome measures) Thrive has maintained a critical mix of individual casework, group support and strategic campaigning. The involvement of several Durham University staff and students has also boosted its capacity for mentoring and research work.

Critical pedagogy

Community organising is just one example of community-based oppositional politics supported by paid community workers. As already mentioned, it is not without its critics and there is a danger, as with all types of community action, that people who are living in poverty or experiencing injustice may be used as means for political ends. There are other styles and ideologies of community working that have a radical edge, including those using a critical pedagogy framework (derived from the work of Brazilian educator Paulo Freire) based on a process of conscientisation (developing people's awareness and understandings of their oppression and its sources) leading to collective action (Freire, 1972; Freire, 1993; Freire, 2001; Ledwith, 2005; Ledwith and Springett, 2010). Yet despite the profound influence of Freire's thinking on community work and community development theory, there are few examples of systematically Freirean approaches in Britain. The most notable is the long-running Adult Learning Project in Gorgie Dalry, Edinburgh, which started in 1979. Here programmes of learning are constructed with residents around locally defined themes, leading on to action programmes, based in a radical tradition of popular (of the people) education which links adult education with community action (Kirkwood and Kirkwood, 1989). As Colin Kirkwood (2007, p 7), one of the early tutors and a longstanding unpaid consultant for this project, commented in an interview: "In Freire's writing we found explicit confirmation of our view that poverty and exploitation could not be understood with reference to circumscribed localities but in terms of larger totalities; but equally that this did not invalidate starting from where people live and work."

For Freire, the agenda for learning derived from issues relevant to people's own lives, not from demands made on citizens by politicians:

> The emerging themes, the meaningful thematics, of any Freirean learning programme derive not from the current priorities of national governments or the European Union, although these may be powerfully influential ... It is not a matter of being 'in and against the state' but of being

simultaneously inside and beyond the state. (Kirkwood, 2007, p 6)

ALP has been funded by Edinburgh City Council from its inception, and workers are employees of the council. This may have caused tensions from time to time, but ALP has consistently maintained its Freirean ethos, mounting actions on a variety of themes from democracy in Scotland to land reform and sustaining international links and exchanges. This is a good example of state-sponsored practice that seems to have retained control over its own agenda.

State-controlled community development practice

Community-based projects, such as those described above, that are supported by community development workers to mount campaigns and engage in radical education are still in existence and some are part of local authority services. However, much community development work is constrained by the requirements of funders (especially central and local government) where the obsession with meeting targets, measuring outcomes and impact serves to divert the focus, time and effort of community participants, activists and paid workers. A recent survey showed that community development workers were spending much less time in face-to-face work (Glen et al, 2004). This is particularly true for local authority workers, many of whom have been drawn into corporate roles to support policy requirements for community planning, engagement and empowerment. The experience of Durham County Council's community development team provides an interesting example of the tensions faced by workers between engaging in strategic policy-level work (including advising all council departments on community engagement) and undertaking locally-based community development work on issues of concern to residents (Banks and Orton, 2007). Even those workers able to undertake local community development work were doing it at a distance, covering a relatively large geographical area and offering support to specific groups as required. The demise of generic neighbourhood work in this and many other councils means that long-term relationship building in a specific locality is less possible, which dramatically reduces the role of community development workers in building sustained action or protest-oriented groups.

Some of the biggest opportunities for neighbourhood level work have come through the national area-based regeneration schemes implemented from the 1990s. The most recent of these, New Deal for Communities, was launched in 1998 as a 'showcase for state of the art regeneration' (Social Exclusion Unit, 1998, p 55). It has focused on smaller areas (39 localities of not more than 4,000 households) over a longer timescale (10 years) with even more intense demands for community partnership. Some of the chosen New Deal for Communities (NDC) areas have been subject to a series of area-based initiatives since the 1960s (for example, the west end of Newcastle) and were still categorised as some of the most deprived neighbourhoods after more than 30 years of government-sponsored serial regeneration and community development programmes (Lupton, 2003). Many residents in the Newcastle NDC area were cynical and some recalcitrant. As Dargan (2009) suggests, this is not surprising, since the limited timescale for bidding for funding had meant that outside consultants were employed to develop the bid to determine a 10-year programme that was supposedly a genuine partnership with residents.

The impact of NDC on various indicators (levels of crime, educational achievement and so on) has been limited (Lawless, 2006), although the extent to which cause and effect can be measured, the validity of the measures used and the obsession with measurement itself are all open to question. While in some areas the levels of resident participation have been disappointing and expectations have been dashed (Dinham, 2005), in other areas large efforts have been made, working partnerships developed and improvements in housing, services and cultural provision made (see, for example, Hartlepool New Deal for Communities, 2010).

The work done with local residents on partnership boards and to develop new projects has generally been community work in the community development paradigm – with radical rhetoric and reformist practice. While many of the government programmes speak in the language of power-sharing and equal partnerships between residents, private, voluntary and public sector bodies ('power-with') or even of 'residents in control' with power to act and power over the agenda, the reality is somewhat different. The agendas are already shaped by central government and the scope for manoeuvre is severely limited, as the very definition of 'community empowerment' in the supposedly radical White Paper *Communities in control* so clearly shows: '"Community empowerment" is the giving of confidence, skills, and power to communities to shape and influence what public bodies do for or with them' (Communities and Local Government/Local Government Association, 2007, p 12).

Some of the language of the critiques of the new Labour initiatives is very telling. The spaces for community control are 'invited', not created, invented or demanded by people themselves; active citizenship is 'manufactured' rather than organic (Cornwall, 2002; Hodgson, 2004; Banks and Vickers, 2006). The language of the *Community development challenge* report makes it very clear that, despite the radical rhetoric, the 'community development offer' is one of controlled community involvement. Therefore, if some residents express anger when invited to participate, this is not surprising. In one NDC area, the poor quality of participation by some residents was noted, with examples of confrontational behaviour, abusive language, hostile looks and aggressive tones of voice (Dargan, 2009). This kind of behaviour may simply be regarded as irrational or a 'storming' phase on the road to residents taking responsibility, but equally it may be a rational response to an invitation to take responsibility without real power. Gardner (2007, p 3) suggests in relation to NDC generally, and indeed all community-based regeneration, that most community engagement is 'shallow and ephemeral' and local views can be 'parochial and illiberal'. The implication is that residents may not be ready or able to take responsibility. Yet if past government regeneration schemes have been experienced by residents as shallow and ephemeral, it is not surprising that recent experiences of community participation are often in the same vein. This should not be taken to imply that meaningful community participation is not possible, just that it needs to be approached differently – as a grassroots process. There are plenty of examples of sustained participatory community-based projects in very poor areas based on locally defined agendas and organic community action – such as the ALP project mentioned earlier.

Community development as a long-term value-based practice

So, what is the state of community work and community development in 2010? The latest iteration of the national occupational standards for what was called community work and is now called community development make a much stronger statement than previous versions about the value-based nature of community development and the primacy of values relating to challenging structural inequalities through collective action. For example, the key purpose of community development is expressed as follows (Lifelong Learning UK, 2009, p 3):

> Community Development is a long-term value-based process which aims to address imbalances in power and

bring about change founded on social justice, equality and inclusion.

The process enables people to organise and work together to:

- identify their own needs and aspirations
- take action to exert influence on the decisions which affect their lives
- improve the quality of their own lives, the communities in which they live, and societies of which they are a part.

The values underpinning the work are identified as:

1. *Equality and anti-discrimination* Challenging structural inequalities and discriminatory practices.
2. *Social justice* Identifying and seeking to alleviate structural disadvantage and advocating strategies for overcoming exclusion, discrimination and inequality.
3. *Collective action* Working with and supporting groups of people, to increase their knowledge, skills and confidence so they can develop an analysis and identify issues which can be addressed through collective action.
4. *Community empowerment* Supporting people to become critical, creative, liberated and active participants, enabling them to take more control over their lives, their communities and their environment.
5. *Working and learning together* Promoting a collective process which enables participants to learn from reflecting on their experiences.

These are hard-hitting, radical-sounding values, clearly expressed to give community development workers a mandate to tackle structural inequalities and challenge discrimination through collective action. However, their critical edge is somewhat muted by their placement in a document outlining a set of standards that conflates community development as a process, with community development as a set of activities and practices and community development as an occupation. This is a serious shortcoming and detracts from the power of the strong statement about values. As it is very obvious that the range of processes, activities, practices and professionals to which these values are supposed to apply is so all-embracing that either lip service will be paid to a weak version of these values (rather like the government version of community empowerment) or they will be ignored altogether. By trying to be inclusive, the values (and the national occupational standards of which they are a part) become less powerful. For these standards apparently apply not only to paid community development workers with generic or specific briefs, but also to community development activists/volunteers, other professionals taking a community development approach to their role and managers of community development practice. This would imply, for example, that a police officer, health visitor or architect who takes on a community-based role with a brief to undertake participatory practice, should subscribe to the values and practise with the knowledge and skills as laid down in the national occupation standards for community development.

Conclusion: from value statements to value commitments

If community workers are serious about values, then much more work needs to be done to turn the value statements in the various manifestos that have emerged from community development organisations in recent years (which are now coalescing largely around the national occupational standards) into value commitments that are believed in by workers and enacted in practice. As well as statements of principles (promoting of social justice, equality, community empowerment), we need workers to be motivated by passion and anger at injustice and to develop courage to challenge injustices, inequalities and work towards genuine power-sharing in very heterogeneous neighbourhoods or communities of interest and identity. Many workers do have these motivations and commitments and they are implementing them in the micro-processes of their practice (Banks, 2007; Hoggett et al, 2008), but much less so at the meso- or macro-level. Collective organisations and coalitions of those involved in community work that are independent of government funding can be more effective at challenging the current model of controlled community development (for example, the National Coalition for Independent Action, www. independentaction.net). There is a need to offer a constant critique of, and to move beyond, the empty rhetoric of 'healthy', 'safe', 'sustainable' communities, however seductive and tempting this discourse may be, to return to communities as sites of struggle, where issues of individual and social justice meet (Cooke, 1996; Hoggett, 1997; Shaw, 2008). Reminding ourselves that community work involves more than just community development may be an important step to reclaiming some of the radical potential that Mayo remarked on in 1975 and has worked for and written so much about in the subsequent 35 years.

ELEVEN

Resisting the EasyCare model: building a more radical, community-based, anti-authoritarian social work for the future

Mark Baldwin

Introduction

Social workers generally come into the profession wanting to make a difference in people's lives. They may be motivated to use their advantages to improve the wellbeing of those they see as less fortunate than themselves (social worker as helper) or by a sense of social justice and desire to change the world (Payne, 2005). The third part of Malcolm Payne's (2005) model for understanding social work is social work as control of resources. I have never met anyone who came into the profession with the latter as their inspiration or aspiration.

Despite this, we are living in a world where social workers are mainly engaged in resource control. In adult care, services have been reduced to a minimum available for people whose needs have reached 'substantial' or 'critical' on the eligibility criteria (DH, 2002; Henwood and Hudson, 2008). Anything else which people require will have to be paid for, or provided by relatives. This creates a two-tier system in which those who can pay for services will receive them before their circumstances reach eligibility requirements. For those who cannot afford to pay for services, there is the depressing wait for the moment when personal, family or community resources finally give out and they are required to go cap-in-hand for whatever services are available in their area. Their own individual crisis is not prevented and they are not in a position to make use of the twin policy imperatives of New Labour's Transformation agenda – choice and control. This has, in anecdotal terms, been referred to as the EasyCare model, with a nod towards low-cost airlines that reduce services to the minimum and charge for extras.

Radicalism is mostly associated with resistance to authoritarian imposition or discrimination and this has been the case with radical social work as long as there have been people with a critical perspective on social work (Powell, 2001; Ferguson and Woodward, 2009). One of the key areas of resistance at the moment is the imposition of market driven approaches to the delivery of social care services (Ferguson et al, 2005; Ferguson, 2008a). This is the political context in which ruling politicians have constructed a system which is rhetorically defined as choice and control, but, in reality is far from that.

Resistance to this system is essential for radical social work because EasyCare constructs a system which is outside of the values, traditions and ethos of professional social work. It is also outside of the expressed wishes of service users who, according to the government policy that created Transformation and Personalisation (DH, 2006; DH, 2007), desire choice and control of services to meet their expressed needs. Social workers, service users and, apparently, the government, are at one on this, but it has not prevented the rapid erosion of services for vulnerable service users.

Radical approaches should be more than this, however. It is not just about resistance to the negativity of social welfare within a capitalist system as it was presented to us 35 years ago by Bailey and Brake (1975). Radical social work should offer a positive alternative to what is currently on offer. For the sake of our profession, and, what is more important, for the sake of people who are reliant on services, we need to demonstrate that there is a way of understanding the social work role other than servicing a shift of resources to the private sector, administering financial management systems within a receding resource pool, and passing the responsibility for managing risk back to vulnerable service users and their families.

This chapter will, in addressing the future possibilities for radical approaches within social work, say a fair deal about opportunities for resistance. It will also discuss the positive alternatives to the defensive practice required of (in particular) local authority-based social workers. In the work that I have done for the Social Work Action Network (see www.socialworkfuture.org), both nationally and regionally, I have been struck by how many social workers and students are unhappy with the system which they are required to service. They want to resist but also model constructive practice. This chapter is intended to provide those practitioners with some tools which they can utilise both individually and collectively.

I will approach these areas – radical resistance and positive radical practice – from the starting point of the seminal work in the UK – Bailey and Brake's *Radical social work* (1975). I will pick out the main themes from this edited book, bringing them into the contemporary context. What opportunities are there for understanding Bailey and Brake's themes for radical practice in current social work? These ideas require some critique because, even though the ideas are still relevant, they do now require further consideration. In addition, they provide a powerful framework for thinking about and proposing a radical approach to both resistance and positive practice.

In the second half of the chapter I will advocate examples of radical practice for today, including ideas for action that are feasible in most organisations where social workers are employed and students carry out their practice learning. It is important also, in looking at radical practice as both resistance and positive practice to place this in the broader context of political campaigning and action.

Themes from Bailey and Brake

Individualism

Roy Bailey (foreword, this volume) tells us that the idea for the book came about because student social workers in the early 1970s were crying out for theories that would allow them to argue against the restrictive knowledge base offered by social work programmes. So from the outset of *Radical social work* it is argued that social work has an over-reliance on psychology, particularly with its emphasis on 'pathological and clinical orientations to the detriment of structural and political implications' (Bailey and Brake, 1975, p 1).

This focus on individual pathology will be familiar to most social workers now as the medical model (Oliver and Sapey, 2006; Payne, 2009), favouring individual explanations for presenting problems, and requiring individual treatment responses. The more favoured social model of disability (Oliver and Sapey, 2006; Payne, 2009) provides better understanding of the way individuals are constructed by this medicalised approach to service users. While the medical model constructs service users as flawed individuals requiring services to alleviate their individual impairment, we now have a system of assessment in which service users are, in addition, constructed as individuals within a market of care. This is often referred to as commodification (Ferguson et al, 2005) and has the adverse effect for service users of tying them in to systems on which they become dependent, much like the medical model.

Making alliances with new movements

Bailey and Brake stressed the importance of social workers making alliances with new movements. In the 1970s they listed the Women's Movement, Gay Liberation, the Mental Patients' [sic] Union, Claimants and Tenants' Unions. There was a strong argument that such alliances would make social work practice more in tune with the needs of those people who use services, but would also ensure that the oppression experienced by the groups the organisations represented could be more readily resisted through alliances.

In the contemporary context we have a prevailing rhetoric about involving service users in service development and delivery and it feels as if the opportunities are potentially more positive than they were in the 1970s. There is an argument that the rhetoric on service user involvement has become tokenistic consumerism, in which organisations tick boxes to indicate service users have been consulted rather than attempt to equalise the power differentials that ensure services are resource driven.

While there is some scepticism about this rhetoric (Baldwin and Sadd, 2006), it does provide an imperative to turn tokenism into a real and irresistible alliance for change. This notion of collective action is a fundamental aspect of radical practice and one that I will return to later in the chapter. I argue that making alliances with service users and the service user movement is the key aspect of a radical social work practice.

Radical social work as a critique of the history of the welfare state

Peter Leonard's (1975) chapter make a strong play for a radical critique of the welfare state and its contradictions within a capitalist mode of production. It is argued that the welfare state was set up to 'resolve the contradictions between certain aspects of production and consumption' (Bailey and Brake, 1975, p 2). These contradictions revolve around the cycles of production and consumption that create unemployment and inequalities within the labour market and which have a disproportionate effect on the working class. While the welfare state is constructed to alleviate these contradictions it does not 'challenge ideologically the fundamental nature of capitalist democracy' (Bailey and Brake, 1975, p 2).

This Marxist structural analysis, with the addition of a critique of globalisation and neoliberal values, is still a key intellectual factor for radical social work (Ferguson et al, 2005; Ferguson, 2008a; Ferguson and Woodward, 2009). This is important because of the dearth of critique of this position from contemporary mainstream political parties, all of whom seem content to maintain a social services system that does no more than manage the negative outcomes of these contradictions.

It is important for social workers to adopt a critical and reflective stance to their practice, noting whom their service users are, and how they came to be constructed as users within the welfare state system. Noting, recording and challenging the nature of capitalist democracy and the way in which it creates and perpetuates inequalities is a key aspect of radical practice.

The persistence of poverty

In Bailey and Brake, the fairly dated figures for poverty tell us that 12% of the population lived at subsistence level with the majority of these people in employment. In the 21st century nearly 20% of the population live below the official poverty line. Of those living in poverty, 54% live in working households (Toynbee and Walker, 2008). So it is still the case that most people live in poverty not because of an over-reliance on public benefits (as right-wing newspapers would argue), but because of poverty wages. This is despite the introduction of the minimum wage by New Labour in 1999.

These factors are important because so many users of social work services live in poverty. To work with these individuals and families on the basis that their difficulties are separate from structural factors is to collude with the social system that constructs poverty and marginalisation and does little to alleviate the effects of it.

Cultural diversity

It is notable that Bailey and Brake explored the importance of 'cultural diversity' (1975, p 8) in the development of radical practice. This predated the debates around anti-racist (Dominelli, 1988), anti-discriminatory (Braye and Preston-Shoot, 1995), and anti-oppressive (Dalrymple and Burke, 1995) practice in social work by several years. Their concern was that social work education in the 1970s made 'evaluative assumptions of normality' in the knowledge base for social work practice, and that this inevitably individualised and pathologised service users at the expense of 'an examination of class struggles and interests' (p 8) which, they argued, was a more fruitful way of understanding the position of service users. Indeed, their argument, that 'radical social work is essentially understanding the position of the oppressed in the context of the social and economic structures they live in' (p 9), leads them to state that the most human approach for social workers to adopt is a socialist one.

The continuing need for social work to develop anti-racist (Williams, this volume) and anti-sexist (Penketh, this volume) practices indicates that this is an area for radical practice now just as much as it was in the 1970s. We have, since the 1970s, continued to see examples of institutional discrimination (Macpherson, 1999; Blofeld, 2003), as well as individual disabling attitudes by social workers (Baldwin, 2006). The value base of anti-racist and anti-discriminatory practice is still an area of importance to service users experiencing marginalisation on the grounds of disability, age, sexuality, ethnicity, gender and class. It is concerning that the curriculum for social work education is largely devoid of values statements to combat these forms of oppression.

In the 1970s there was a major problem of community-based racism from the National Front, a factor challenged by radical social workers among others at the time. The re-emergence of the British National Party (BNP) and other fascist organisations such as the English Defence League creates a similar context for contemporary social work which we ignore at our peril. Fascist organisations have a history of attempting to mobilise the working class by telling lies about one section in relation to another. Racism and homophobia are commonly understood as the ethos of the BNP. Less known is a chilling attitude towards disabled children, as expressed by Jeffrey Marshall, senior organiser for the BNP's London European election campaign, that 'we live in a country today which is unhealthily dominated by an excess of sentimentality towards the weak and unproductive … no good will come of it.' He is also alleged to have added 'there is not a great deal of point in keeping these people alive after all' (Doward, 2009). These comments should be a stark reminder of the ways in which fascism can affect the lives of people with whom social workers engage.

Social work education

Geoffrey Pearson in Bailey and Brake (1975) argued that social work education existed largely in a moral and political vacuum and it was not enabling students to understand the political nature of social work. In the current context we can see that there is an interest from social work students in alleviating social injustice. This is demonstrated in their attendance at SWAN conferences nationally and regionally, with the South West of England Social Work Activists' Network having social work students as the single largest category of members when it was set up in 2008. More recently a conference run by students for students was organised at London South Bank University with the title Neoliberalism versus Social Justice.

My own experience with recent recruits is of a commitment to social justice, but with little understanding of the political processes involved in achieving this. There is a misguided belief that alleviating social injustice ought to be achievable through individual practice. This has clearly led to disillusionment and burn-out when students and recent graduates have assumed that it is their incompetence at carrying out assessments which prevents them from getting costed packages of care approved, when actually the panels are set up to manage finances and not to meet the needs of potential service users. While the stories we hear of recent graduates leaving the profession for these reasons are anecdotal, it is the case that retention of qualified staff is in crisis, with retention levels having fallen by 50% in the past year (LGA, 2009).

Community work

The chapter by Marj Mayo is interesting in that it argues that the opportunity for radical practice through community approaches has largely been a missed opportunity. By suggesting that community development has been more about 'community psycho-therapy' (Mayo, 1975, p 136) than challenging deprivation, Mayo places community orientations to practice in the 1970s in much the same quarter as Bailey and Brake do social work in the introductory chapter.

She argues for a radical community practice and the rejection of romantic notions of community and what 'the people' can achieve. A radical practice would instead offer an 'analysis of actual potential' (p 136) within communities. These are similar to arguments made in the contemporary community work literature (Stepney and Popple, 2008) with government looking to the profession to provide an impression of interest in community development when it actually fits better the more authoritarian New Labour approach to dealing with antisocial behaviour.

That said, community approaches do provide a radical alternative to the individualising and pathologising nature of care management and risk assessment. The revisiting of community orientations to policy and practice, and the significance of 'social capital' as one part of the framework for transforming adult social care (DH, 2007) may be rhetorical, but it does provide an opportunity for a radical approach, along with user involvement. Social capital is a contestable concept in government policy, but, in the context of the policy on shifting emphasis to prevention, mainstreaming universal services and participation, it does provide an opportunity for furthering community and service user participation, collaborative rather than market driven and needs- rather than resource-led approaches to service provision.

Theory and critical reflection

Leonard (1975) noted in Bailey and Brake that radical practitioners in the 1970s were suspicious of theory, feeling that it served the purposes of the status quo rather than a radical practice. Leonard urged the avoidance of an 'unreflective activism in radical practice' (p 47). His chapter charts the useful theoretical concepts that are available to explain, inform and evaluate radical practice.

This suspicion of theory is still evident today with a largely anti-intellectual approach from much of social work education. The centrality of practice-based learning in social work degrees is going to be offset by the proposed reduction in placement days back from 200 to 130, but there is a feeling that these days should not be filled with more theory. What we have here is the danger of an apprenticeship model of social work education. Students are required, in this model, to learn how to do *this* job in *this* organisation. Such an approach avoids the requirement of professional practice to challenge the otherwise unquestioned customs and routines of organisational procedures that can construct an unwitting institutional discriminatory regime (Macpherson, 1999). Much of what contemporary social workers find difficult (Jones, 2005) about the expectations on their practice is that these expectations are built into well-established customs and routines which become authoritarian when they are not open to challenge.

Bailey and Brake spoke of the importance of developing 'critical action' (p 10) and Leonard of the need to develop 'critical consciousness' (p 47). In the contemporary era we talk of critical reflection (Fook, 2002) as the approach required to question the broader context in which we practice. Fook argues that critical approaches see knowledge as situated in social, economic and historical contexts (Fook, 2002), that knowledge is subjective and reflects power relationships and that critical reflection challenges dominant knowledge and social relations. This sociological perspective argues that knowledge is socially constructed and not a fixed reality on which we can all agree. The powerful nature of some knowledge reflects the manner in which some ways of making sense of the world are more powerful than others. A critical reflective approach questions the nature of dominant knowledge and asks whose interests it serves and whose it oppresses.

A good example of this is the case of people with learning difficulties. When I first practised as an unqualified social worker, most adults with learning difficulties (we did not then use that terminology) who were not living with their parents lived in institutions. The knowledge that informed this practice was based on the powerful medical model of 'mental handicap' which was specific to that era, and which constructed relationships that dominated people with learning difficulties in their daily lives.

Since then the knowledge that informs practice with people with learning difficulties has been transformed out of all recognition. Gone are the beliefs, based on the previously repressive knowledge system, that people with learning difficulties are unable to make decisions, hold opinions, hold down jobs, live independently, and so on. They are the same people, but the knowledge that informs practice with them has shifted. Adopting a critical and reflective approach to other powerful forms of knowing that dominate our profession is an essential aspect of radical practice.

This critical reflection is essential to expose the contradictions and perverse incentives of contemporary managerial systems. People associated with housing will know that the target for rough sleepers is zero. Housing authorities are required to count rough sleepers (and no, they are not rough sleepers if they sleep sitting up or are under a bench), and make returns on the numbers. When government inspectors visit it is not unusual for an authority to set up a night shelter to house rough sleepers so the box marked zero can be ticked. The following day the shelter is closed. The need has been met. This is not the needs of vulnerable street homeless people but the need to tick that box marked zero. There are other examples of perverse incentives, for example 'quick win assessments' in which managers send social workers out to assess the needs of service users with low priority for non-existent services in order to boost the number of assessments being completed (another target determining LAs star rating).

Again we are seeing the importance of radical practice in resisting oppressive functions of state organisation, but there is also an aspect of positive practice here, too. The concept of critical consciousness was borrowed from Paolo Freire's notion of praxis in which critical reflection leads to action which enables powerless people to transform their reality. The social work role here is to enhance the creative, determining potential of people. In the contemporary era this includes making the most of systems for involving service users in decision-making. It also enhances models for empowering practice (Dalrymple and Burke, 1995). The legacy of Leonard's list of empowering practices is still highly relevant: interdependence not dependence, equality not hierarchy, dialogue not indoctrination, and collective action to resist dehumanisation and assert humanity (Leonard, 1975, p 57).

There is a problem here for radical activists, however. By blowing the whistle on such oppressive institutional practices they can lay themselves open to criticism or even disciplinary action. In the final section of this chapter I will return to the importance of collective action of organisations such as Unions and the Social Work Action Network in speaking on behalf of practitioners, and service users against such practices to avoid exposing individuals to discipline.

Educating the public about the social work role

Stuart Rees (1975) makes a strong case for clarifying the role of social work with the general public, and also for senior managers to advocate on behalf of the social worker voice in local and national policy debates. This is an aspect of social work professionalism which has been around for 35 years, with the leaders of our profession having achieved very little in the way of educating the public and politicians about the nature of our role and responsibilities. As a consequence, we have been buffeted by anti-professional tendencies of successive governments, particularly in the Thatcher and post-Thatcher era of managerialism. Now, when the horse has bolted, the Taskforce (Social Work Taskforce, 2009b) has belatedly taken up the task of explaining to the public the role and tasks of social work.

Facing up to the task: The interim report of the Social Work Taskforce included a 'public description of social work' (p 50). This definition is descriptive, providing the public with little idea of the complexity of the role, the knowledge base for practice, let alone the values and political nature of professional practice, including the implications of working in partnership with marginalised people.

There is a historic opportunity for radical perspectives in social work to assert an alternative view of our profession, one based on an understanding of social justice, of empowerment, of service user control and of resistance to the authoritarian political social and economic forces that oppress the people with whom social workers work. This is a description of social work that would educate the public and have great resonance with both service users and social workers. I need now to turn to that practice and define the actions necessary to engage in radical social work practice.

Five actions for a contemporary racial social work practice

I now want to focus this discussion into a number of specific areas for practice and actions in which social workers could engage individually and/or collectively. These are areas for action which I feel are both important and feasible. Any radical practice in the current climate of managerial control and a defensive organisational ethos is going to be hard to achieve and most will require collaborative approaches, preferably in conjunction with a collective organisation such as a Union or a radical campaigning organisation such as SWAN. Action in concert with service users, individually or with organisations run by and for service users will always reflect a powerful alliance for resistance.

The five action areas for a contemporary radical social work practice are:

* making the political nature of social work explicit
* developing a critically reflective approach to organisation and practice
* making alliances with service users
* developing a practice based on social justice
* acting collectively.

Making the political nature of social work explicit

Definitions of politics in text books focus on a number of different aspects of the concept, emphasising that politics occurs in conflictual circumstances (Axford et al, 1997). Definitions also note that the phenomena of diversity (many differing beliefs and values) and scarcity (not enough resources to satisfy everyone) means that political practice could involve conflict or cooperation (Heywood, 2000). This leads to the concept of power which means the 'ability to achieve a desired outcome' (p 34). In our context the desired outcome is the allocation of scarce resources (Heywood, 1994). For our purposes, therefore, politics can be defined as the manipulation of power to determine access to scarce resources.

So in what sense is it important to make the political nature of social work explicit? The social welfare arena is one in which access to scarce resources is contested on a daily basis. Social workers, in assessing individuals' needs, in presenting them to decision-makers, and in advocating on behalf of those individuals in this decision-making process (or not), are at the centre of political decision making in social welfare.

So, whether they like it or not, social workers are a key element of state power when it comes to making decisions about who gets access to scarce resources. Every time a social worker decides how they are going to explain a service user's right to be assessed for a Direct Payment, for instance, means they are taking a political decision. Every time they decide that this service user's needs requires them to write a powerful assessment report, they are making decisions that are within the political arena, utilising their power to determine access to scarce resources. Assessment is an event in a political process of deciding who gets access to the scarce resources which will meet needs.

A radical perspective that is intent on making the political nature of social work explicit will note and expose the tendency for social work to be used by organisations to manage scarce resources rather than enable choice and control which is the rhetoric of national and local government. Every time a social worker is required to make a decision on access to services within an authority that only provides services to people qualifying at the highest rate of the eligibility criteria (critical) they are undermining the supposed policy of choice and control, for service users, because when your needs reach the 'critical' level, there is little opportunity or ability left to make choices or take control.

The perverse incentives of managerial practice noted above are organisational ploys to manage scarce resources while at the same time giving the impression of responsiveness. Again, adopting a political perspective on social work practice enables us to expose the way in which these actions favour resource management rather than meeting need.

Advocacy, in this context, can be classed as radical practice. To advocate on behalf of service users with managers and decision-making panels is to make a political statement about the rhetoric of choice and control – the gap between how decisions *ought* to be made, and how they *are* made. Social workers tell us that managers do not read assessment reports when making decisions about care packages. They will more often look at the amount of money it will cost and base their decision on that. This practice needs to be exposed.

For these reasons, it is important that students should be taught about the political nature of social work practice, otherwise they are unlikely to survive decision-making processes which appear to reject their professional practice in writing assessment reports, when actually decisions are based on eligibility and the availability of resources and not the needs of individuals.

Developing a critically reflective approach to organisation and practice

If, as social workers, we have a commitment to social justice inherent within the definition of social work (www.ifsw.org; IFSW, 2000) and which was accepted by the Taskforce Committee and, by accepting their recommendations, the government, then we need to evaluate the policies and practices of our organisations to gauge whether practice fits with intentions. This involves adopting a questioning approach to organisational practice. It means we must analyse the powerful forms of knowledge that are inherent within policy and organisation, and make judgements about what this knowing tells us and whom or what it favours. Personalisation, for instance, involved an ethos of service delivery that emphasised choice and control, for the service user. It originated within the disability and service user movements. It has, following the extensive consultation with patients and service users that resulted in the policy document *Our health, our care, our say* (DH, 2006), been accepted as government policy. At this point, however, the implementation of something called personalisation diverts from the original ethos. Instead of service users being given choice and control, although the language is still used, we have vulnerable adults being required to act as individual consumers in a market of care.

In recognising that service users tend to live in or on the edges of poverty, it is important that we have explanations for both how and why this happens. Blaming service users for the personal consequences of being poor is less easy if we adopt a critical and analytical stance that recognises that some behaviour is actually logical given the circumstances, rather than pathological, which is how it is often assessed (Baldwin, 1996). Peter Leonard (1975) argues powerfully that it is social systems creating poverty and class-based oppression which are pathological, not the individuals whose presenting problems of mental ill-health, offending behaviour or social isolation are so often focused on by social workers.

The same thing can be said for other social consequences of structural disadvantage such as racism. Rocky Bennett's outburst that led to his death while being restrained came as a result of a long period of being subjected to racial abuse in the NHS Mental Health establishment where he was living, and which was not dealt with (Blofeld, 2003). Having a set of theoretical tools for evaluating context and behaviour can help us avoid the kind of stigmatisation and labelling that led to this man's death.

Making alliances with service users

I argue that this is the key aspect of radical action for social work practice in the current context. It was a key argument for Bailey and Brake in the 1970s, but the context for involvement by service users in the process of social work and social service development just was not there in that era. It may well be largely tokenistic (Baldwin and Sadd, 2006) in many contemporary settings, but it is clear government policy and a requirement on public bodies at a number of different levels. This requirement gives the social work profession the opportunity to engage in powerful alliances with people whose voice the government claims counts (DH, 2006), and to utilise this alliance to both resist managerial excess, and to promote a different approach to social work practice.

Social workers can think about their individual practice with service users, reminding themselves of their legal duty (in children and families work) to work in partnership with parents and young people. It is clear government policy guidance (DH, 1990) in adult services that social workers should adopt the same approach with disabled and older people. The maxim of 'good' practice that is based on the values of respect for uniqueness and diversity, recognition of strengths, rights to choice and protection, control, countering discrimination, avoiding stigmatisation and partnership working (VRs) could still be used to inform practice. Reminding ourselves of the positive practices of active listening, demonstrating interest and respect, advocacy and acknowledging strengths is a part of getting back to the roots of positive, radical, practice.

On a collective basis social work practitioners can use current systems for involving service users wherever they are working. In universities, academic staff and students are urged to work in alliance with service users. There is an opportunity here for radical academics and students to put pressure on programmes to take this requirement seriously and to make broad alliances with service users. There is money available for this work and it needs to be used in developmental ways to maximise the sort of involvement that results in programmes adopting critical and reflective practices. This is another area where professional power which discriminates against service users could be challenged. Where students learn the value of this fundamental approach to social work practice in their degree programmes they are much more likely to practise in a way that minimises the harmful effects of power relationships in subsequent professional practice.

Developing practice based on social justice

Another area where a critically reflective and questioning approach to organisation and practice is appropriate is in evaluating organisations that employ social workers. There is an authoritarianism and misuse of power associated with custom and practice which is often not questioned. An example of this is institutionalised racism where everyday routines are not questioned and they construct a way of working that favours some at the expense of others.

The recent classic case of this is institutional racism within the Metropolitan Police Force (Macpherson, 1999) in which the Report into the death of Stephen Lawrence noted the unwitting nature of organisational racism that led to the case being mishandled. The tool that has been developed to root out such practices is the Impact Assessment tool. Under their duty to promote racial equality (this has now been extended to cover all forms of equality) all public bodies and, through commissioning, all service providers, are required to carry out an assessment of all policies and procedures to assess the possibility of unwitting discrimination. It would be a radical approach within your organisation to ask where the results of the impact assessment are, what it found and what changes have been made. My own enquiries through some organisations suggest that these assessments are done, if at all, at arm's length from practitioners who are not consulted.

A practice based on social justice will also, as Leonard (1975) argued in Bailey and Brake, shift the basis for such practice from individual pathology to the pathology of social systems. An understanding that recognises that some behaviour is logical within pathological social systems is much less likely to result in stigmatising and scapegoating approaches to individuals and families within their communities.

Acting collectively

There are many opportunities for acting collectively as noted above. Social workers can build alliances that reflect mutual interests and which resist more powerful perspectives practice. Collectively, social work can speak more effectively and, as noted above, will do so with considerable authority if it is in alliance with service users. In the radical social work organisation SWAN (www.socialworkfuture.org) there is a fundamental principle that we work collectively and in alliances. Conferences and now the national steering group reflect the principle, with conference platforms always including a service user, an activist practitioner and an academic.

Six actions for a radical practice

There are many activities in which social workers and students could engage that could be referred to as radical, but I wanted to end this chapter with just six actions that would constitute radical practice and which could be engaged in by practitioners in alliance with others, notably, with service users.

1. Record every decision that you and colleagues in your team are required to make, where decisions favour resource control over meeting the needs of service users. This data could be collected and analysed by an organisation such as SWAN and then used in a collective argument with specific employers about the way in which professional practice is being used for rationing purposes and not the stated purpose of meeting service user needs. Examples would be managers only looking at the 'bottom line' of care packages and not the needs assessed, 'quick win' assessments, and other examples of the pursuit of targets that do not have service user needs at their heart.

2. Advocacy, as argued above is a key aspect of radical practice as, to advocate on behalf of service users with decision makers is to make a political statement about how decisions *ought* to be made, and expose how they *are* made. It will require a confident, well-argued, and assertive approach to assessment report writing. It is the managers who make the decisions on resource expenditure and they ought to be made aware of the basis on which they are making those decisions and not be allowed to get away with sloppy and oppressive custom and routine.

3. Identify the systems available within organisations that are there to deal with oppression, such as impact assessments. Ask management who is responsible for carrying them out and what the results are. What lessons have been learnt for individual and organisational policy, procedure, protocol and practice? A practitioner or student in a team could offer to carry out an impact assessment in their team which could expose the discriminatory nature of many procedures that social workers are required to carry out.

4. A potential project of great learning worth for a student on placement would be one that profiles the expressed needs of the local community (of need or geographical patch). A community needs assessment could provide a great deal of useful information about how the community the team is serving perceive their own needs as well as examples of the positive strengths within the community,

both informal and formal. Such projects can also have the effect of building alliances around areas of mutual interest.

5. Teams could invite service user-led organisations to attend a team meeting to express their needs and concerns and to debate areas of mutual interest. If the team is not clear about such organisations it is likely that the local university will have these details, if they have a social work degree programme and have been utilising the money provided by the General Social Care Council for the development of user and carer involvement in their programme.

6. Professionals could join or reactivate their involvement in collective action organisations such as Unison or SWAN. National SWAN is now a membership organisation and joining it, attending conferences, engaging with the website and starting a local or regional network is a method for building a strong alliance of activist social workers, students and service users.

Conclusions

In 2007 a group of social workers, service users, academics and students from the South West of England attended the second annual conference of SWAN, in Glasgow. It was a hugely uplifting conference in which we heard powerful arguments about the state of social work today. We left the conference and headed to the airport to fly back to Bristol buoyed up by the collective feeling that we were not alone in feeling that something should and could be done to resist these tendencies which were not giving service users the 'empowerment' the rhetoric promises. We felt there was a powerful lobby to resist but that it was also possible to model something different within social work – cooperation rather than competition, social justice rather than blame and stigma, human needs of people before profit.

We decided to put on a regional conference, booking a venue for up to 300 people but secretly each of us thought even 50 people coming to discuss these issues would be a good start. In the event we had 300 people asking to be added to our South West regional network and 250 people attending the conference. It was another uplifting day for all of us and we had added many more people to our list of those who understood that they were not alone in their professional or personal despair at the way social welfare was developing.

Since then we have had many regional meetings of activists, planned campaigns, and provided input to the national organisation, including running a successful conference in Bath in 2009. Sub-regional groups now meet to discuss issues and plan action. It is early days but there is a feeling of mutual aid which encourages us to feel that there are alternatives to what we are all experiencing at present.

So what can we conclude about the future for radical social work in 2010? Given the enthusiasm for radical alternatives born out of desperation that social workers are demonstrating regionally and nationally, this would seem to be a very good time to be organising, making alliances and campaigning for a radical alternative to the social work that is on offer at the moment. In order to achieve this, however, and in order to avoid the marginalisation of radical ideas or the marginalising of those who are expressing them, there are some important tactics which we must follow.

- We need to develop our understanding and our skills in acting in sophisticated political fashion wherever we are.
- We should not be afraid of exposing the powerful knowledge and ideology that underpins current policy and practice, and which debases professional practice and the values of social work.
- We should get used to judging our own and our organisations' practice on the values of social justice, rather than the values of resource control, privatisation and profit. Our profession is here to make the social work – not the markets work.
- We need to make alliances wherever we can and especially with service users. These alliances, when it comes to both resistance and to modelling a more empowering practice, will be powerful and irresistible.
- We should not wait for this to happen, looking to others, but should act assertively and with conviction in the collective defence of our profession. We are acting in this way, we need to remind ourselves and our detractors, because of the needs of service users, and not self interest. If that is a motivation that is strange to others and does not fit with the dominant ideology of greed and individualisation then I think that the arguments will resonate strongly with people who are currently responding with distaste and rejection of these values when they are expressed elsewhere – in the banking industry and in parliamentary practices.

Bibliography

Acheson, D. (1998) *Independent inquiry into Inequality in Health Report*, London: The Stationery Office.

Age Concern (2002) *Opening doors to the needs of older lesbians, gay men and bisexuals*, London: Age Concern.

Alcabes, P. (2008) *Dread: How fear and fantasy have fuelled epidemics from the Black Death to Avian Flu*, New York: Public Affairs.

Alinsky, S. (1969) *Reveille for radicals*, New York: Vintage Books.

Alinsky, S. (1989) *Rules for radicals*, New York: Vintage Books (1st published in 1971 by Random House).

Allen, K. (2004) *Max Weber: A critical introduction*, London: Pluto Press.

APA (American Psychiatric Association) (2002) *Diagnostic and statistical manual of mental disorders* (4th edn), Washington DC: APA.

Atkin, K. and Chattoo, S. (2007) 'The dilemmas of providing welfare in an ethnically diverse state: seeking reconciliation in the role of a "reflexive practitioner"', *Policy & Politics*, vol 35, no 3, pp 377–93.

Axford, B., Browning, G., Huggins, R., Rosamond, B. and Turner, J. (1997) *Politics: An introduction*, London: Routledge.

Bailey, R. and Brake, M. (1975) *Radical social work*, London: Edward Arnold.

Baldwin, M. (1996) 'White anti-racism: is it really no-go in rural areas?', *Social Work Education*, vol 15, no 1, pp 18–33.

Baldwin, M. (2006) 'Helping people with learning difficulties into paid employment: will UK social workers use the available Welfare to Work system?', *Journal of Policy Practice,* vol 5, nos 2/3.

Baldwin, M. and Sadd, J. (2006) 'Allies with attitude: service users, academics and social services agency staff learning how to share power in running a social work education course', *Social Work Education*, vol 25, no 4, pp 348–59.

Banks, S. (1990) 'Accrediting prior learning: implications for education and training in youth and community work', *Youth and Policy*, no 31, pp 8–16.

Banks, S. (2007) 'Becoming critical: developing the community practitioner', in H. Butcher, S. Banks, P. Henderson with J. Robertson (eds) *Critical community practice*, Bristol: The Policy Press, pp 133–52.

Banks, S. and Noonan, F. (1990) 'The poll tax and community work', *Association of Community Workers: Talking Point*, nos 117 and 118.

Banks, S. and Orton, A. (2007) '"The grit in the oyster": community development in a modernising local authority', *Community Development Journal*, vol 42, no 1, pp 97–113.

Banks, S. and Shenton, F. (2001) 'Regenerating neighbourhoods: a critical look at the role of community capacity building', *Local Economy*, vol 16, no 4, pp 286–98.

Banks, S. and Vickers, T. (2006) 'Empowering communities through active learning: challenges and contradictions', *Journal of Community Work and Development*, vol 8, pp. 83–104.

Banyard, K. and Lewis (2009) *Corporate sexism: The sex industry's infiltration of the modern workplace*, London: The Fawcett Society.

Barnard, A., Horner, N. and Wild, J. (eds) (2008) *The value base of social work and social care*, Maidenhead: Open University Press.

Barnes, C., Mercer, G. and Shakespeare, T. (1999) *Exploring disability: A sociological introduction*, Cambridge: Polity Press.

Basketter, S. (2009a) 'Where next after the Lindsey strike?', *Socialist Worker*, 4 July (www.socialistworker.co.uk/art.php?id=18322).

Basketter, S. (2009b) 'Total victory for Lindsey strikers', *Socialist Worker*, 4 July (www.socialistworker.co.uk/art.php?id=18354).

BBC (British Broadcasting Corporation) News (2010) 'Bilin marks five years of West Bank barrier protest', 19 February.

Behan, T. (2009) *The Italian resistance*, London: Pluto.

Bellamy, K., Bennett, F. and Millar, J. (2006) *Who benefits? A gender analysis of the UK benefits and tax credit system*, London: The Fawcett Society.

Benwell Community Project (1978) *Permanent unemployment*, Benwell Community Project, final report series, no 2, Newcastle-on-Tyne: Benwell Community Project.

Beresford, P. (1999) 'Making participation possible: movements of disabled people and psychiatric system survivors', in T. Jordan and A. Lent (eds) *Storming the millennium: The new politics of change*, pp 34–50, London: Lawrence and Wishart.

Beresford, P. (2005) 'Theory and practice of user involvement in research: making the connection with public policy and practice', in L. Lowes and I. Hulatt (eds) *Involving service users in health and social care research*, pp 6–17, London: Routledge.

Beresford, P. (2006a) 'Service user values, in Community Care/Nottingham Trent University: confirming our value base in social work and social care', *Community Care*, 16 March.

Beresford, P. (2006b) 'Nottingham meeting gladdens the heart', Opinion, Stand Up for Social Care campaign, *Community Care*, 16 March.

Beresford, P. (2007a) *The roles and tasks of social workers: Report of service user consultation, for the England Review, 28 February 2007, carried out by Shaping Our Lives*, London: General Social Care Council.

Beresford, P. (2007b) *The changing roles and tasks of social work from service users' perspectives: A literature informed discussion paper*, for the Review of Social Work Roles and Tasks in England, London: General Social Care Council.

Beresford, P. (2010) 'Learning from history: beyond current controversy to achieving a truly strong voice for social work', Blog, Community Care www.communitycare.co.uk/blogs/social-care-the-big-picture/2010/03/learning-from-history-basw-the-national-college-and-a-strong-social-work-voice.html.

Beresford, P. and Croft, S. (1980) *Community control of social services departments*, London: Battersea Community Action.

Beresford, P. and Croft, S. (1989) 'Decentralisation and the personal social services', in M. Langan and P. Lee (eds) *Radical social work today*, London: Unwin Hyman.

Beresford, P. and Croft, S. (1992) 'The politics of participation', *Critical Social Policy*, no 35, Autumn, pp 20–44.

Beresford, P. and Croft, S. (1993) *Citizen involvement: A practical guide for change*, Basingstoke: Macmillan.

Beresford, P. and Croft, S. (2004) 'Service users and practitioners reunited: the key component for social work reform', *British Journal of Social Work*, vol 34, pp 53–68.

Beresford, P. and Harding, T. (eds) (1993) *A challenge to change: Practical experiences of building user led services*, London: National Institute for Social Work.

Beresford, P., Adshead, L. and Croft, S. (2007) *Palliative care, social work and service users: Making life possible*, London: Jessica Kingsley.

Beresford, P., Shamash, O., Forrest, V. Turner, M. and Branfield, F. (2005) *Developing social care: Service users' vision for adult support* (Report of a consultation on the future of adult social care) Adult Services Report 07, London: Social Care Institute for Excellence in association with Shaping Our Lives.

Bergsten, B., Beresford, P. and Nambiar, N. (2009) *Brukarsamverkan I Utbildningen Av Socionomer*, April, Lund: School of Social Work, Lund University.

Bessell, B. (1978) 'A matter of principles', *Community Care*, 13 September

Beveridge, W. (1942) *Social Insurance and Allied Services*, Cm 6404, London: HMSO.

Bhanti, R. (2001) *Social development: Analysis of some social work fields*, Chennai: MCC Press.

Biestek, F. (1957) *The casework relationship*, London: Allen & Unwin.

Birchall, I. (1974) *Workers against the monolith*, London: Pluto.

Birchall, I. (1986) *Bailing out the system: Reformist socialism in Western Europe 1944–1985*, London: Bookmarks.

Bloch, A. and Solomos, J. (eds) (2010) *Race and ethnicity in the 21st century*, Basingstoke: Palgrave Macmillan.

Blofeld, J. (2003) *Independent inquiry into the death of David Bennett*, Cambridge: Norfolk, Suffolk and Cambridgeshire Strategic Health Authority.

Boltanski, L. and Chiapello, E. (2007) *The new spirit of capitalism*, London: Verso.

Bourne, J. (2010) 'Comment: putting John Denham's speech in context', Institute for Race Relations, 21 January 2010, www.irr.org.uk/2010/january/ha000024.html.

Brake, M. and Bailey, R. (eds) (1980) *Radical social work and practice*, London: Edward Arnold.

Branch, T. (1988) *Parting the waters: America in the King Years*, New York: Simon and Schuster.

Branch, T. (1998) *Pillar of fire: America in the King Years*, New York: Simon and Schuster.

Branch, T. (2006) *At Canaan's edge: America in the King Years*, New York: Simon and Schuster.

Branfield, F., Beresford, P., Danagher, N. and Webb, R. (2005) *Independence, wellbeing and choice: A response to the Green Paper on Adult Social Care. Report of a consultation with service users*, London: National Centre for Independent Living and Shaping Our Lives.

Braverman, H. (1976) *Labour and monopoly capital: The degradation of work in the twentieth century*, New York: Monthly Review Press.

Braye, S. and Preston-Shoot, M. (1995) *Empowering practice in social care*, Buckingham: Open University Press.

Brewer, C. and Lait, J. (1980) *Can social work survive?*, London: Temple.

Bristow, J. (2009) *Standing up to supernanny*, Exeter: Societas.

Brittan, S. (2008) 'Auguries for a "vile" decade', *Financial Times*, 1 May.

Bromley, C., Curtice, J. and Given, L. (2007) *Attitudes to discrimination in Scotland 2006: Scottish Social Attitude Survey*, Edinburgh: Scottish Centre for Social Research.

Brown, T. and Hanvey, C. (1987) 'A spirit of the times', *Community Care*, 30 July.

Bryan, B., Dadzie, S. and Scafe, S. (1985) *The heart of the race: Black women's lives in Britain*, London: Virago Press.

Bunyan, P. (2010) 'Broad-based organizing in the UK: reasserting the centrality of political activity in community development', *Community Development Journal*, vol 45, no 1, pp 111–27.

Burrows, R. (2003) *Home ownership and poverty in Britain*, York: Joseph Rowntree Foundation.

Bywater, T., Hutchings, J., Daley, D. and Whitaker, W. (2009) 'Long-term effectiveness of a parenting intervention for children at risk of developing conduct disorder', *The British Journal of Psychiatry*, no 195, pp 318–24.

Cabinet Office (2009) Family Nurse Partnership, http://webarchive. nationalarchives.gov.uk/+/http:/www.cabinetoffice.gov.uk/social_ exclusion_task_force/family_nurse_partnership.aspx

Callinicos, A. (1999) *Social theory: A historical introduction*, Cambridge: Polity.

Callinicos, A. (2006) *The resources of critique*, Cambridge: Polity.

Callinicos, A. (2010a) *The bonfire of illusions: The twin crises of the liberal world*, Cambridge: Polity.

Callinicos, A. (2010b) 'Obituary of Daniel Bensaid', *Socialist Worker*, no 23, p 10.

Campbell, J. and Oliver, M. (1996) *Disability politics: Understanding our past, changing our future*, London: Routledge.

Campbell, P. (1996) 'The history of the user movement in the United Kingdom', in T. Heller, J. Reynolds, R. Gomm, R. Muston and S. Pattison (eds) *Mental health matters*, Basingstoke: Macmillan.

Cannan, C. (1975) 'Welfare rights and wrongs', in R. Bailey and M. Brake (eds) *Radical social work*, London: Edward Arnold.

Care Leavers' Association (2010) 'LGBT care leavers' (www.careleavers. com-lgbt-care-leavers).

Carlin, N. (1989) 'The roots of gay oppression', *International Socialism*, no 42, pp 63-113.

Carpenter, E. (1908) *The intermediate sex*, London: Echo.

Carson, G. (2009a) 'Social workers say "we are underpaid and over worked"', *Community Care*, 30 July.

Carson, G. (2009b) 'Exclusive research: aging workforce threatens staff shortage', *Community Care*, 30 July.

Case Con manifesto (1975) in R. Bailey and M. Brake (eds) *Radical social work*, London: Edward Arnold.

CCETSW (Central Council for Education and Training in Social Work) (1976) *Guidelines to social work training rules*, London: CCETSW.

CCETSW (1975a) 'Education and training for social work', *Discussion paper 10*, February, London: CCETSW.

CCETSW, (1975b) 'A new form of training: the certificate in social service', *Paper 9.1*, March, London: CCETSW.

CDP (Community Developmewnt Project) Inter-Project Editorial Team (1977) *Gilding the ghetto: The state and the poverty experiments*, London: CDP Inter-Project Editorial Team.

CDP Political Economy Collective (1979) *The state and the local economy*, Newcastle: CDPPEC.

Centre for Longitudinal Studies (2007) *Millennium Cohort Study*, London: Institute of Education.

Centre for Social Justice (2008) *Breakthrough Glasgow: Ending the costs of social breakdown*, London: Centre for Social Justice.

Challen, A., Noden, P., West, A. and Machin, S. (2009) *UK resiliency programme evaluation*, Interim Report, Research Report No DCSF–RR094, DCSF/LSE.

Chambers, E. (2003) *Roots for radicals*, New York: Continuum.

Charlton, J.I. (1998) *Nothing about us without us: Disability, oppression and empowerment*, California: University of California Press.

Chief Secretary to the Treasury (2003) *Every child matters* (Cm 5860). London: The Stationery Office.

Chu, W.C.K., Ming-sum Tsui and Miu-chung Yan (2009) 'Social work as moral and political practice', *International Social Work*, vol 52, no 3, pp 287–98.

Clarke, J. (1993) (ed) *A Crisis in Care: Challenges to social work*, London: Sage.

Close, D.H. (2004) 'War, medical advance and the improvement of health in Greece, 1944–53', *South European Society & Politics*, vol 9, no 3, pp 1–27.

Coates, K. and Silburn, R. (1970) *Poverty: The forgotten Englishman*, Harmondsworth: Penguin.

Cochrane, K. (2008) 'Now, the backlash', *G2, The Guardian*, 1 July.

Cohen, S. (1975) 'It's alright for you to talk: political and sociological manifestos for social work', in R. Bailey and M. Brake (eds) *Radical social work*, London: Edward Arnold.

Coleman, N. (2009) 'This is the modern world! Working in a social services contact centre', in J. Harris and V. White (eds) *Modernising social work: Critical considerations*, Bristol: The Policy Press.

Communities and Local Government (2007) *The community development challenge*, London: Communities and Local Government.

Communities and Local Government (2008) *Communities in control: Real people, real power*, www.communities.gov.uk/publications/communities/communitiesincontrol

Communities and Local Government/Local Government Association (2007) *An action plan for community empowerment: Building on success*, London: Communities and Local Government/Local Government Association.

Concannon, L. (2009) 'Developing inclusive health and social care policies for older LGBT citizens', *British Journal of Social Work*, no 39, pp 403–17.

Cooke, I. (1996) 'Whatever happened to the class of '68? The changing context of radical community work practice', in I. Cooke and M. Shaw (eds) *Radical community work: Perspectives from practice in Scotland*, Edinburgh: Moray House.

Cooke, R. (2008) 'How far have we come in 80 years', *The Observer*, 7 December.

Cooper, D. (1971) *The death of the family*, Harmondsworth: Penguin.

Corkey, D. and Craig, G. (1978) 'CDP: community work or class politics', in P. Curno (ed) *Political issues in community work*, London: Routledge and Kegan Paul.

Cornwall, A. (2002) 'Locating citizen participation', *IDS Bulletin*, vol 33, no 2, pp 49–58.

Craig, G. (2007) '"Cunning, unprincipled and loathsome": the racist tail wags the welfare dog', *Journal of Social Policy*, vol 36, no 4, pp 605–23.

CRE (Commission for Racial Equality) (2007) *A lot done, a lot to do: Our vision for an integrated Britain*, London: CRE.

Crine, A. (1979) 'News Focus', *Community Care*, 4 January.

CTSW (Council for Training in Social Work) (1971) *The teaching of fieldwork*, Discussion Paper, 4, CTSW, London.

Dalrymple, J. and Burke, B. (1995) *Anti-oppressive practice: Social care and the law*, Maidenhead: Open University Press.

Dargan, L. (2009) 'Participation and local urban regeneration: the case of the New Deal for Communities (NDC) in the UK', *Regional Studies*, vol 43, no 2, pp 305–17.

Darlington, R. and Lyddon, D. (2001) *Glorious summer*, London: Bookmarks.

Davis, M. (1999) *Sylvia Pankhurst: A life in radical politics*, London: Pluto.

DCSF (Department for Children, Schools and Families) (2007a) 'Government's parenting strategy: putting parents in control', Press Release 2007/0020, 8 February.

DCSF (2007b) *The Children's Plan: Building brighter futures*, London: The Stationery Office.

DCSF/DH (Department for Children, Schools and Families/Department of Health) (2009) *Building a safe confident future: The final report of the Social Work Task Force*, November, London: DCSF/DH.

Dedoulis, E. and Caramanis, C. (2006) 'Imperialism of influence and the state–profession relationship: the formation of the Greek auditing profession in the post-WWII era', *Critical Perspectives on Accounting*, vol 18, no 4, pp 393–412.

Dee, H. (2010) *The red in the rainbow: Sexuality, socialism and LGBT liberation*, London: Bookmarks.

DeFilippis, J., Fisher, R. and Shragge, E. (2007) 'What's left in the community? Oppositional politics in contemporary practice', *Community Development Journal*, vol 44, no 1, pp 38–52.

Denham, J. (2010) 'Tackling race inequality: a statement on race', www.communities.gov.uk/publications/communities/tacklingrace inequalitystatement

Denham, Lord (2010) *The Guardian*, 14 January.

Department of State (1947) 'The immediate need for emergency aid to Europe', 29 September, President's secretary's files, Truman Papers, www.trumanlibrary.org/hstpaper/psf.htm

DETR (Department of the Environment, Transport and the Regions) (1998) *Modernising local government: Local democracy and community leadership*, London: DETR.

DH (Department of Health) (1990) *Caring for people: Policy guidance*, London: HMSO.

DH (1998) *Modernising social services: Promoting independence, improving protection, raising standards*, White Paper (Cm 4169), London: The Stationery Office.

DH (2002) *Fair access to care services: Guidance on eligibility criteria for adult social care* (LAC (2002) 13), London: DH.

DH (2006) *Our health, our care, our say: A new direction for community services*, London: DH.

DH (2007) *Putting people first: A shared vision and commitment to the transformation of adult social care*, London: DH..

Dinham, A. (2005) 'Empowered or over-powered? The real experiences of local participation in the UK's New Deal for Communities', *Community Development Journal*, vol 40, no 3, pp 301–12.

Dixon, G., Johnson, C., Leigh, S. and Turnbull, N. (1982) 'Feminist perspectives and practice', in G. Craig, N. Derricourt and M. Loney (eds) *Community work and the state*, London: Routledge and Kegan Paul.

Dominelli, L. (1988) *Anti-racist social work: A challenge for white practitioners and educators*, Basingstoke: Palgrave.

Dominelli, L. (1990) *Women and community action*, London: Venture Press.

Doogan, K. (2009) *New capitalism? The transformation of work*, London: Polity.

Dorling, D. (2010) *Injustice: Why social inequality persists*, Bristol: The Policy Press.

Doward, J. (2009) 'Exposed: ugly face of BNP's leaders', London: *The Observer*.

Dunn, B. (2009) 'Myths of globalisation and the new economy', *International Socialism*, no 121, pp 75–97.

Earnshaw, M. (2008) 'Communities on the couch', in D. Clements, A. Donald, M. Earnshaw and A. Williams (eds) *The future of community: Reports of a death greatly exaggerated*, London: Pluto.

Edinburgh Support Workers' Action Network (2010) 'Controversial care and support tender collapses', Press release, 1 February (www.swanedinburgh.blogspot.com).

Editorial (1978a) 'A new dawn rises for BASW', *Community Care*, 20 September.

Editorial (1978b) 'Time to resolve BASW's crises', *Community Care*, 13 September.

Editorial (1981) '....and a not-too-bad new year', *Community Care*, 1 January.

Ehrenreich, B. (2009) *Smile or die: How positive thinking fooled America and the world*, London: Granta.

Eilers, K. (2003) 'Social policy and social work in 1928', in S. Hering and B. Waaldijk (eds) *History of social work in Europe (1900–1960): Female pioneers and their influence on the development of international social organizations*, Opladen: Leske und Budrich.

Elliot, L. (2010) 'A few strikes don't make a spring of discontent', *The Guardian*, 29 March.

Engels, F. (1884 [1978]) *The origins of the family, private property and the state*, Beijing: Foreign Language Press.

Epstein, L. (1994) 'The therapeutic idea in contemporary society', in Adrienne S. Chambon and Allan Irving (eds) *Essays in postmodernism and social work*, Toronto: Canadian Scholars' Press.

Equalities Review, The (2007) *Fairness and freedom: The final report of The Equalities Review*, London: The Cabinet Office.

Equality Challenge Unit (2009) 'The experience of lesbian, gay, bisexual and trans staff and students in HE' (www.ecu.ac.uk).

Family Law Review (2009) *Breakthrough Britain: Every family matters*, London: Centre for Social Justice.

Fanshawe, S. and Sriskandarajah, D. (2010) *'You can't put me in a box': Super-diversity and the end of identity politics in Britain*, London: Institute for Public Policy Research.

Farrell, M. (1980) *Northern Ireland: The Orange State*, Londo: Pluto.

Fawcett Society (2010) *Equal pay day 2 November 2010 – Join Fawcett to demand women's equal rights to equal pay*, Campaign document, London: Fawcett Society.

Federation of Community Work Training Groups and Mainframe Research and Consultancy Services (1995) *Community work S/NVQ project: National occupational standards and proposed award specifications*, Sheffield: FCWTGs and Mainframe.

Feinberg, L. (1998) *Trans liberation: Beyond pink or blue*, Boston, MA: Beacon Press.

Ferguson, I. (2008a) *Reclaiming social work: Challenging neoliberalism and promoting social justice*, London: Sage.

Ferguson, I. (2008b) 'Neoliberalism, happiness and well-being', *International Socialism*, no 117, pp 87–121.

Ferguson, I. and Barclay, A. (2002) *Seeking peace of mind: The mental health needs of asylum seekers in Glasgow*, Stirling: University of Stirling.

Ferguson, I. and Lavalette, M. (2007) '"The social worker as agitator": the radical kernel of British social work', in M. Lavalette and I. Ferguson (eds) *International social work and the radical tradition*, Birmingham: Venture Press.

Ferguson, I. and Lavalette, M. (2009) *Social work after Baby P: Issues, debates and alternative perspectives*, Liverpool: Hope University.

Ferguson, I. and Woodward, R. (2009) *Radical social work in practice: Making a difference*, Bristol: The Policy Press.

Ferguson, I., Lavalette, M. and Whitmore, E. (2005) (eds) *Globalisation, global justice and social work*, London: Routledge.

Finch, J. (1988) 'Whose responsibility? Women and the future of family care', in J. Allen, J. Wicks, J. Finch and D. Leat (eds) *Informal care tomorrow*, London: Policy Studies Institute.

Fitzpatrick, M. (2009) 'Don't turn social workers into police', *Community Care*, 17 September.

Fook, J. (2002) *Social work: Critical theory and practice*, London: Sage.

Francis, D., Henderson, P. and Thomas, D. (1984) *A survey of community workers in the United Kingdom*, London: National Institute for Social Work.

Freire, P. (1972) *The pedagogy of the oppressed*, London: Penguin.

Freire, P. (1993) *Education for critical consciousness*, New York: Continuum.

Freire, P. (2001) *Pegagogy of freedom: Ethics, democracy and civic courage*, Lanham, Maryland: Rowman and Littlefield.

Frost, N. and Parton, N. (2009) *Understanding children's social care: Politics, policy and practice*, London: Sage.

Fukuyama, F. (1989) 'The end of history', *The National Interest*, Summer.

Gardner, G. (2007) 'Recognising the limits to community-based regeneration', Paper presented at 'What is the added value of the community-based partnership approach', School of Oriental and African Studies, 16 July, http://extra.shu.ac.uk/ndc/ndc_presentations.htm

Garrett, M. (1973) 'By whose authority?', *Case Con*, April, pp 3–6.

Garrett, P.M. (2009) *Transforming children's services? Social work, neoliberalsim and the 'modern' world*, Maidenhead: Open University Press.

Gentleman, A. (2009) 'How do you solve a problem like 50,000 chaotic families?', *The Guardian*, 2 November.

Gentleman, A. (2010) 'It makes you feel like you are a failure', *Society Guardian*, 13 January.

Giddens, A. (1998) *The Third Way: The renewal of social democracy*, Cambridge: Polity.

Gilroy, P. (1987) *There ain't no black in the Union Jack: The critical politics of race and nation*, London: Hutchinson.

Glass, N. (2005) 'Some mistake surely', *The Guardian*, 8 January.

Glen, A. and Pearse, M. (1993) *A survey of community practitioners*, Bradford: Bradford and Ilkley Community College.

Glen, A., Henderson, P., Humm, J., Meszaros, H. and Gaffney, M. (2004) *Survey of community development workers in the UK*, London: Community Development Foundation/Community Development Exchange.

Gluckstein, D. (1999) *The Nazis, capitalism and the working class*, London: Bookmarks.

Glynn, M., Beresford, P., Bewley, C., Branfield, F., Butt, J., Croft, S., Dattani, K. and Pitt, T. (2008) *Person-centred support: What service users and practitioners say*, York: Joseph Rowntree Foundation.

Goehler, G. (2000) 'Constitution and the use of power', in H. Goverde, P. Cerny, M. Haugaard and H. Lentner (eds) *Power in contemporary politics: Theories, practices, globalisations*, London: Sage.

Goldthorpe, J.H. and Lockwood, D. (1968) *The affluent worker in the class structure*, Cambridge: Cambridge University Press.

Gough, I. (1979) *The political economy of the welfare* state, London: Macmillan.

Gould, J. (1977) *The attack on higher education: Marxism and radical penetration*, London: Institute for the Study of Conflict.

Graham, H. (1987) 'Being poor: perceptions and coping strategies of lone mothers', in J. Brannen and G. Wilson (eds) *Give and take in families*, London: Allen & Unwin.

Gulbenkian Foundation (1973) *Current issues in community work*, London: Routledge and Kegan Paul.

Gulbenkian Study Group (1968) *Community work and social change*, London: Longman.

Habermas, J. (1987) *The theory of communicative action. Vol 2. Lifeworld and system: A critique of functionalist reason*, Cambridge: Polity.

Hadjis, T. (1981) *The victorious revolution that was lost*, Athens: Dorikos.

Halifax, N. (1988) *Out, proud and fighting: Gay liberation and the struggle for socialism*, London: SWP.

Halliday, J. (1975) *A political history of Japanese capitalism*, New York: Monthly Review Press.

Halmos, P. (1978) *The personal and the political: Social work and political action*, London: Hutchinson.

Handler, J. (1968) 'The coercive children's officer', *New Society*, 3 October.

Harding, T. and Beresford, P. (eds) (1996) *The standards we expect: What service users and carers want from social services workers*, London: National Institute for Social Work.

Harman, C. (1988) *The fire last time: 1968 and after*, London: Bookmarks.

Harman, C. (2009) *Zombie capitalism: Global crisis and the relevance of Marx*, London: Bookmarks.

Harris, J. (2003) *The social work business*, London: Sage.

Harris, J. and White, V. (eds) (2009) *Modernising social work: Critical considerations*, Bristol: The Policy Press.

Hartlepool New Deal for Communities (2010) *Hartlepool New Deal for Communities succession strategy*, Hartlepool: Hartlepool New Deal for Communities.

Harvey, D. (2005) *A brief history of neoliberalism*, Oxford: Oxford University Press.

Haynes, M. (2009) 'Capitalism, health and medicine', *International Socialism*, no 123, pp 137–60.

Healy, L.M. (1987) 'International agencies as social work settings: opportunity, capability and commitment', *Social Work*, vol 3, no 5, pp 405–9.

Healy, L. (2001) *International social work: Professional action in an interdependent world*, Oxford: Oxford University Press.

Heath, A., Rothon, C. and Ali, S. (2010) 'Identity and public opinion', in A. Bloch and J. Solomos, *Race and ethnicity in the 21st century*, London: Palgrave Macmillan.

Hekimoglou, E. (2005) 'Waiting for the allies', *E Istorika*, no 288, pp 6–10.

Henderson, P. and Salmon, H. (1995) *Community organising: The UK context*, London: Community Development Foundation.

Henwood, M. and Hudson, B. (2008) 'Checking the facts: the government's current system of delivering social care will seriously limit the potential benefits of personalised budgets', London: *The Guardian*, 13 February.

Heraud, B.J. (1967) 'Teaching of Sociology in professional social work courses', unpublished paper to Sociology Teachers Section, British Sociological Association Annual Conference.

Hering, S. (2003) 'A soldier of the 3rd International: the social activities of the Swiss communist Mentona Moser', in S. Hering and B. Waaldijk (eds) *History of social work in Europe (1900–1960): Female pioneers and their influence on the development of international social organizations*, Opladen: Leske und Budrich.

Heywood, A. (1994) *Political ideas and concepts: An introduction*, Basingstoke: Macmillan.

Heywood, A. (2000) *Key concepts in politics*, Basingstoke: Palgrave.

Hills, J. (2010) *An anatomy of economic inequality in the UK: Executive Summary*, January, London: National Equality Panel.

Hills, J., Brewer, M., Jenkins, S., Lister, R., Lupton, R., Machin, S., Mills, C., Modood, T., Rees, T. and Riddell, S. (2010) *An anatomy of economic inequality in the UK*, January, London: National Equality Panel.

HMSO (1972/76) *Health and Personal Social Services Statistics*, London: HMSO.

Hodge, M. (2005) 'A reply to Norman Glass', *The Guardian,* 8 January.

Hodgson, L. (2004) 'Manufactured civil society: counting the cost', *Critical Social Policy*, vol 24, no 2, pp 139–64.

Hogan, M. (1991) 'The Marshal plan', in Charles S. Maier (ed) *The cold war in Europe: Era of a divided continent*, New York: Markus Wiener Publishing.

Hoggett, P. (1997) 'Contested communities', in P. Hoggett (ed) *Contested communities: Experiences, struggles, policies*, Bristol: The Policy Press.

Hoggett, P., Mayo, M. and Miller, C. (2008) *The dilemmas of regeneration work: Ethical challenges in regeneration*, Bristol: The Policy Press.

Home Office (2004a) *Building civil renewal: Government support for community capacity building and proposals for change*, London: Home Office.

Home Office (2004b) *Active learning for active citizenship: A report by the civil renewal unit*, London: Home Office.

Horgan, G. (2007) *The impact of poverty on young children's experiences of school*, York: Joseph Rowntree Foundation.

Hubbard, R. and Rossington, J. (2005) *As we grow older: A study of the housing and support needs of older lesbians and gay men*, London: Polari Housing Association.

Husband, C. (1980) 'Culture, context and practice: racism in social work', in M. Brake and R. Bailey (eds) *Radical social work and practice*, London: Edward Arnold.

Hutchings, J., Bywater, T., Daley, D., Gardner, F., Whitaker, C., Jones, K., Eames, E. and Edwards, R.T. (2007) 'Parenting intervention in Sure Start services for children at risk of developing conduct disorder: pragmatic randomised controlled trial', *British Medical Journal*, vol 334, no 7595, doi:10.1136/bmj.39126.620799.55.

Hutton, W. (2010) 'Of course class still matters – it influences everything we do', *The Observer*, 10 January.

IFSW (International Federation of Social Workers) (2000) *The definition of social work*, www.ifsw.org/f38000138.html

IFSW (2006) *50 year jubilee: making a world of difference*, www.ifsw.org/p38001381.html

Ioakimidis, V. (2008) *A critical examination of the political construction and function of Greek social work*, unpublished PhD thesis, Liverpool: University of Liverpool.

Ioakimidis, V. (2011) 'Welfare under warfare', in M. Lavalette and V. Ioakimidis (eds) *Social work in extremis*, Bristol: The Policy Press.

Jones, C. (1978) *An analysis of the development of social work education and social work 1869–1977*, unpublished PhD thesis, Durham: University of Durham.

Jones, C. (1983) *State social work and the working class*, Basingstoke: Macmillan.

Jones, C. (1989) 'The end of the road? Issues in social work education', in P. Carter, T. Jeffs and M. Smith (eds) *Social work and social welfare*, pp 204–16, Milton Keynes: Open University Press.

Jones, C. (1999) 'Social work and society', in R. Adams, L. Dominelli and M. Payne (eds) *Social work: Themes, issues and critical debates*, London: Macmillan.

Jones, C. (2005) 'The neoliberal assault: voices from the front line of British state social work', in I. Ferguson, M. Lavalette and E. Whitmore (eds) *Globalisation, global justice and social work*, London: Routledge.

Jones, C. and Lavalette, M. (2011) '"Popular social work" in the Palestinian West Bank: dispatches from the frontline', in M. Lavalette and V. Ioakimidis (eds) *Social work in extremis*, Bristol: The Policy Press.

Jones, C. and Novak, T. (1999) *Poverty, welfare and the disciplinary state*, London: Routledge.

Jones, C., Ferguson, I., Lavalette, M. and Penketh, L. (2004) *The social work manifesto*, www.socialworkfuture.org/index.php/swan-organisation/manifesto.

Jordan, B. (2000) *Social work and the Third Way: Tough love as social policy*, London: Sage.

Joyce, P., Corrigan, P. and Hayes, M. (1988) *Striking out: Trade unionism in social work*, London: Macmillan.

Keeley, M. (1962) 'Unitarian Universalist institutional records', Andover-Harvard Theological bMS 16121-2, Greek Program, p 5.

Kendall, K. (1978) 'The IASSW from 1928–1978: a journey of remembrance', in K. Kendall (ed) *Reflections on social work education 1950–1978*, New York: International Association of Schools and Social Work.

Kincaid, J. (1973) *Poverty and equality in Britain*, Harmondsworth: Penguin.

Kirkwood, C. (2007) 'Interview with Colin Kirkwood by Emilio Lucio', unpublished manuscript obtained from Colin Kirkwood, later published as: Kirkwood, C. (2010) 'Freirean approaches to citizenship: an interview with Colin Kirkwood by Emilio Lucio-Villegas', in E. Lucio-Villegas (ed) *Citizenship as politics: International perspectives from adult education*, Rotterdam: Sense Publishers.

Kirkwood, G. and Kirkwood, C. (1989) *Living adult education: Freire in Scotland*, Milton Keynes: Open University Press.

Kofas, J. (1989) *Intervention and underdevelopment: Greece during the cold war*, London: Pen State University Press.

Koliopoulos, J. and Veremis, Th. (2004) *Greece. The modern sequel: From 1831 to the present*, London: C. Hurst and Co Publishers Ltd.

Laing, R.D. (1965) *The divided self*, Harmondsworth: Penguin.

Laird, S.E. (2008) *Anti-oppressive social work: A guide for developing cultural competence*, London: Sage.

Lally, D. (1987) 'International social welfare organizations and services', in A. Minahan (ed) *Encyclopedia of social work* (18th edn), pp 969–86, Silver Spring, MD: National Association of Social Workers Press.

Langan, M. (1993) 'The rise and fall of social work', in J. Clarke (ed) *A crisis in care: Challenges to social work*, London: Sage.

Langan, M. (2002) 'The legacy of radical social work', in R. Adams, L. Dominelli and M. Payne (eds) *Social work: Themes, issues and critical debates*, London: Macmillan.

Langan, M. and Lee, P. (1989) (eds) *Radical social work today*, London: Unwin Hyman.

Larkin, P. (1988) *Collected poems*, London: Faber & Faber.

Lavalette, M. (2006a) 'Marxism and welfare', in M. Lavalette and A. Pratt (eds) *Social policy: Theories, concepts and issues* (3rd edn), London: Sage.

Lavalette, M. (2006b) *George Lansbury and the rebel councillors of Poplar*, London: Bookmarks.

Lavalette, M. (2007) 'Social work today: a profession worth fighting for?', in G. Mooney and A. Law (eds) *New Labour, hard labour*, Bristol: The Policy Press.

Lavalette, M (2011) 'Social work in extremis: disaster capitalism, "social shocks" and "popular social work"', in M. Lavalette and V. Ioakimidis, *Social work in extremis*, Bristol: The Policy Press.

Lavalette, M. and Ferguson, I. (eds) (2007) *International social work and the radical tradition*, Birmingham: Venture Press.

Lavalette, M. and Ioakimidis, V. (eds) (2011) *Social work in extremis*, Bristol: The Policy Press.

Lavalette, M. and Levine, B. (2011) 'Samidoun: grassroots welfare and popular resistance in Beirut during the 33 day war of 2006', in M. Lavalette and V. Ioakimidis (eds) *Social work in extremis*, Bristol: The Policy Press.

Lavalette, M. and Mooney, G. (2000) *Class struggle and social welfare*, London: Routledge.

Lawless, P. (2006) 'Area-based interventions. Rationale and outcomes: the New Deal for Communities programme in England', *Urban Studies*, vol 43, no 11, pp 1991–2011.

Layard, R. (2007) 'The teaching of values', Ashby Lecture, University of Cambridge, *CentrePiece*, Summer.

Ledwith, M. (2005) *Community development: A critical approach*, Bristol: The Policy Press.

Ledwith, M. and Springett, J. (2010) *Participatory practice: Community-based action for transformative change*, Bristol: The Policy Press.

Lent, A. (2002) *British social movements since 1945: Sex, colour, peace and power*, Basingstoke: Palgrave Macmillan.

Lentell, H. (1998) 'Families of meaning: Contempoary discourses of the family', in G. Lewis (ed) *Forming nation, framing welfare*, London: Routledge.

Leonard, P. (1975) 'Towards a paradigm for radical practice', in R. Bailey and M. Brake (eds) *Radical social work*, London: Edward Arnold.

Lewis, G. (2002) *Race, gender and social welfare: Encounters in a postcolonial society*, Cambridge: Polity Press.

Lewis, J. (1986) (ed) *Labour and love: Women's experiences of home and family 1850–1940*, Oxford: Basil Blackwell.

Lexmond, J. and Reeves, R. (2009) *Building character*, London: Demos.

LGA (Local Government Association) (2009) 'Challenges remain in social work retention and recruitment', London: Local Government Association, www.lga.gov.uk

Lifelong Learning UK (2009) 'National occupational standards for community development', www.lluk.org

Lindow, V. (2001) 'Survivor research', in C. Newnes, G. Holmes and C. Dunn (eds) *This is madness too: Critical perspectives on mental health services*, Ross-on-Wye: PCCS Books, pp 135–46.

Lister, J. (2008) *The NHS after 60: For patients or profits?*, Middlesex: Middlesex University Press.

Lloyd, E. (2008) 'The interface between childcare, family support and child poverty strategies under New Labour', *Social Policy and Society*, vol 7, no 4, pp 479-94.

London–Edinburgh Weekend Return Group (1979) *In and against the State*, London: Collective of Socialist Economists.

Loney, M. (1983) *Community against government: The British Community Development Project 1968–78*, London: Heinemann Educational Books.

Lorenz, W. (1994) *Social work in a changing Europe*, London: Routledge.

Lowes, L. and Hulatt, I. (eds) (2005) *Involving service users in health and social care research*, London: Routledge.

Lupton, R. (2003) *Poverty street: The dynamics of neighbourhood decline and renewal*, Bristol: The Policy Press.

Macpherson, W. (1999) *Report into the death of Stephen Lawrence*, London: The Stationery Office.

Marshall, T.H. (1965) *Social policy*, London: Hutchinson.

Martínez-Brawley, E. and Vázquez Aguado, O. (2007) 'The professionalization of Spanish social work: moving closer to Europe or away from its roots?', *European Journal of Social Work*, 1468–2664, vol 11, no 1, pp 3–13.

Mayer, J.E. and Timms, N. (1970) *The client speaks: Working class impressions of casework*, London: RKP.

Mayo, M. (1975) 'Community development: a radical alternative?', in R. Bailey and M. Brake (eds) *Radical social work*, London: Edward Arnold.

Mayo, M. (1980) 'Beyond CDP: reaction and community action', in M. Brake and R. Bailey (eds) *Radical social work and practice*, London: Edward Arnold.

Mayo, M. (2005) *Global citizens: Social movements and the challenge of globalisation*, London: Zed.

Mayo, M. and Robertson, J. (2003) 'The historical and policy context: setting the scene for current debates', in S. Banks, H. Butcher, P. Henderson and J. Robertson (eds) *Managing community practice: Principles, policies and programmes*, Bristol: The Policy Press.

Mazower, M. (1993) *Inside Hitler's Greece*, New Haven and London: Yale University Press.

McCann, E. (1974) *War and an Irish town*, London: Pluto.

McLaughlin, K. (2005) 'From ridicule to institutionalisation: anti-oppression, the state and social work', *Critical Social Policy*, vol 25, pp 283–305.

McLaughlin, K. (2008) *Social work, politics and society: From radicalism to orthodoxy*, Bristol: The Policy Press.

McLennan, G. (2010) 'Progressivism reinvigorated', in J. Pugh (ed) *What is radical politics today?*, London: Palgrave Macmillan.

Michael, G. (1976) *Content and method in fieldwork teaching*, unpublished PhD Thesis, Edinburgh: University of Edinburgh.

Michaels, W.B. (2009) 'What matters: review of *Who cares about the white working class?*' edited by K.P. Sveinsson, *London Review of Books* [Online] vol 31, no 16, pp. 11–13; www.lrb.co.uk/v31/n16/walter-benn-michaels/what-matters

Mickel, A. (2009) 'Exclusive survey reveals workforce that is dedicated but less than happy', *Community Care*, 30 July.

Millar, M. (2008) 'Anti-oppressiveness: critical comments on a discourse and its context', *British Journal of Social Work*, vol 38, no 2, pp 362–75.

Milligan, D. (1975) 'Homosexuality: sexual needs and social problems', in R. Bailey and M. Brake, *Radical social work*, London: Edward Arnold.

Mills, C.W. (1970) *The sociological imagination*, Harmondsworth: Pelican.

Mooney, G. (1998) 'Class and social policy', in G. Lewis, S. Gewirtz and J. Clarke (eds) *Rethinking social policy*, London: Sage.

Morris, J. (ed) (1996) *Encounters with strangers: Feminism and disability*, London: Women's Press.

Morton, D. and Angel, N. (2010) A report on the Neoliberalism vs Social Justice social work student conference, 17 February, London: London South Bank University, www.bathstudent.com/pageassets/socs/societies/socialworkandsocials/student-social-work-conference.pdf

Munday, B. (1972) 'What is happening to social work students?', *Social Work Today*, 15 June.

Mynott, E. (2005) 'Compromise, collaboration and collective resistance: different strategies in the face of the war on asylum seekers', in I. Ferguson, M. Lavalette and E. Whitemore, *Globalisation, global justice and social work*, London: Taylor and Francis.

Nadasen, P. (2005) *Welfare warriors: The welfare rights movement in the US*, New York: Routledge.

Neale, J. (2001) *The American war: Vietnam 1960–1975*, London: Bookmarks.

Newman, J. (2007) 'Rethinking "the public" in troubled times: unsettling state, nation and the liberal public sphere', *Public Policy and Administration*, vol 22, no 1, pp 55–75.

North Tyneside CDP (1978) *North Shields: Organising for change in a working class area*, North Tyneside CDP, final report, vol 3, Newcastle: Newcastle-on-Tyne Polytechnic.

Novak, T. (1988) *Poverty and the state*, Milton Keynes: Open University Press.

Oakley, A. (1976) *The sociology of housework*, London: Martin Robert.

O'Connor, J. (1973) *The fiscal crisis of the state*, New York: St Martin's Press.

Ohri, A., Manning, B. and Curno, P. (1982) *Community work and racism*, London: Routledge and Kegan Paul.

Oliver, M. (1983) *Social work with disabled people*, Basingstoke: Macmillan.

Oliver, M. (1990) *The politics of disablement*, Basingstoke: Macmillan.

Oliver, M. (1996) *Understanding disability: From theory to practice*, Basingstoke: Macmillan.

Oliver, M. (2009) *Understanding disability: From theory to practice* (2nd edn), Basingstoke: Palgrave Macmillan.

Oliver, M. and Barnes, C. (1998) *Disabled people and social policy: From exclusion to inclusion*, London: Longman.

Oliver, M. and Sapey, B. (2006) *Social work with disabled people* (3rd edn), Basingstoke: Palgrave.

Orr, J. (2007) *Sexism and the system: A rebel's guide to women's liberation*, London: Bookmark.

Orr, S., Brown, G., Smith, S., May, C. and Waters, M. (2006) *When ends don't meet: Assets, vulnerabilities and livelihoods*, Manchester/Oxford: Church Action on Poverty/Oxfam GB.

Parekh Report (2000) *The future of multi-ethnic Britain*, London: Profile Books.

Parton, N. (2006) *Safeguarding childhood: Early intervention and surveillance in late modern society*, Basingstoke/New York: Palgrave Macmillan.

Patel, N. (1995) 'In search of the Holy Grail', in R. Hugman and D. Smith (eds) *Ethical Issues in Social Work*, London: Routledge.

Paulo (2002) *National occupational standards for community development work*, www.lluk.org

Payne, M. (2005) *Modern social work theory* (3rd edn), Basingstoke: Palgrave Macmillan.

Payne, M. (2009) 'Adult services and health-related work', in R. Adams, L. Dominelli and M. Payne (eds) *Social work: Themes, issues and critical debates* (3rd edn), Basingstoke: Macmillan.

Pearson, G. (1975a) 'Making social workers: bad promises and good omens', in R. Bailey and M. Brake (eds) *Radical social work*, London: Edward Arnold.

Pearson, G. (1975b) *The deviant imagination*, London: Macmillan.

Penketh, L. (2000) *Tackling institutional racism*, Bristol: The Policy Press.

Perlman, H.H. (1957) *Social case work: A problem solving process*, Chicago, IL: University of Chicago Press.

Phillips, M. (1994) 'An oppressive urge to end oppression', *Observer*, 1 August.

Phillips, M. and Phillips, T. (1998) *Windrush: The irresistible rise of multiracial Britain*, London: HarperCollins.

Phillips, T. (2005) 'After 7/7: Sleep walking into segregation', Speech given to the Manchester Council for Community Relations, 22 September, www.humanities.manchester.ac.uk/socialchange/research/social-change/summer-workshops/documents/sleepwalking.pdf

Plant, R. (1974) *Community and ideology*, London: Routledge and Kegan Paul.

Popple, K. (1995) *Analysing community work: Its theory and practice*, Buckingham: Open University Press.

Powell, F. (2001) *The Politics of Social Work*, London: Sage.

Powell, M. (ed) (2002) *Evaluating New Labour's welfare reforms*, Bristol: The Policy Press.

Prison Reform Trust (2007) *Women's imprisonment: Corston review provides blueprint for reform*, 14 March.

Purdue, D., Razzaque, K., Hambleton, R. and Stewart, M. (2000) *Community leadership in area regeneration*, Bristol: The Policy Press.

Pyles, L. (2009) *Progressive community organising: A critical approach for a globalising world*, New York: Routledge.

Reardon, C. (2009) 'Family acceptance project: helping LGBT youth', *Social Work Today*, vol 9, no 6, November/December.

Reed, B., Rhodes, S., Schofield, P. and Wylie, R. (2009) 'Gender variance in the UK: Gender identity research and education' (www.gires.org.uk/assets/Medpro-Assets/GenderVarianceUK-report.pdf).

Rees, S. (1975) 'How misunderstanding occurs', in R. Bailey and M. Brake (eds) *Radical social work*, London: Edward Arnold.

Reisch, M. and Andrews, J. (2002) *The road not taken: A history of radical social work in the US*, New York: Brunner–Routledge.

Rex, J. (1975) *Race, colonisation and the city*, London: Routledge and Kegan Paul.

Rex, J. and Moore, R. (1967) *Race, community and conflict*, London: Oxford University Press.

Rex, J. and Tomlinson, S. (1979) *Colonial immigrants in a British city*, London: Routledge and Kegan Paul.

Rivers, I. (2000) 'Social exclusion, absenteeism and sexual minority youth', *Support for Learning*, no 15, pp 13-18.

Runciman, D. (2009) 'How messy it all is', *London Review of Books*, 22 October, pp 3–6.

Sakamoto, I. and Pinter, R.O. (2005) 'Use of critical consciousness in anti-oppressive social work practice: disentangling power dynamics at personal and structural levels', *British Journal of Social Work*, vol 35, no 4, pp 435–52.

Salford National Union of Teachers (2010) Prevalence of Homophobia Survey: May 2010 (Primary and Secondary), (www.schools-out.org.uk).

Salomon, K. (1990) *'The cold war heritage: UNRRA and the IRO as predecessors of UNHCR'*, in G. Rystad (ed) *The uprooted: Forced migration as an international problem in the post war era*, Lund: Lund University Press.

Save the Children (2010) *Measuring severe child poverty in the UK*, London: Save the Children/New Policy Institute.

Saville, J. (1957/58) 'The welfare state: an historical approach', *New Reasoner*, vol 3, Winter.

Scottish Home and Health Department and Scottish Education Department (1966) *Children and young persons (Scotland)*: Report by the Committee appointed by the Secretary of State for Scotland, [the Kilbrandon Report] Edinburgh: HMSO.

Seebohm, F. (1968) *Report of the Committee on Local Authority and Allied Personal Services* [the Seebohm Report] London: HMSO.

Seligman, M. (1996) *The optimistic child: A proven program to safeguard children against depression and build lifelong resilience*, New York: Harper.

Seligman, M. (2004) *Authentic happiness: Using the new positive psychology to realize your potential for lasting fulfilment*, New York: Simon and Schuster.

Shakespeare, T. (ed) (1998) *The disability reader: Social science perspectives*, London: Cassell.

Shaw, M. (2008) 'Community development and the politics of community', *Community Development Journal*, vol 43, no 1, pp 24–36.

Sherry, D. (2010) *Occupy! A short history of workers' occupations*, London: Bookmarks.

Simon, B. (1967) 'The nature and objectives of professional education', unpublished paper to the Annual Conference of the Association of Social Work Teachers.

Simpkin, M. (1979) *Trapped within welfare*, London: Macmillan.

Sivanandan, A. (1985) 'RAT and the degradation of black struggle', *Race and Class*, vol 26, no 4, pp 1–33.

Sivanandan, A. (1990) *Communities of resistance*, London: Verso.

Smith, I. (1989) 'Community work in recession: a practitioner's perspective', in *Radical social work today*, pp 258–78, London: Unwin Hyman.

Smith, M. (2007) 'The shape of the working class', *International Socialism*, no 117.

Social Exclusion Unit (1998) *Bringing Britain together: A national strategy for neighbourhood renewal*, London: Cabinet Office.

Social Exclusion Unit (2001a) *A new commitment to neighbourhood renewal: National strategy action plan*, London: Cabinet Office.

Social Exclusion Unit (2001b) *Preventing social exclusion*, London: The Stationery Office.

Social Perspective Network (2006) 'Meeting the mental health needs of the LGBT community', (www.spn.org.uk/index.php?id=1023).

Social Work Taskforce (2009a) *Building a safe, confident future: The final report of the Social Work Taskforce*, London: Department for Children, Schools and Families; www.dfcs.gov.uk

Social Work Taskforce (2009b) *Facing up to the task: The interim report of the Social Work Taskforce.* London: DCFS.

Statham, D. (1978) *Radicals in social work*, London: Routledge and Kegan Paul.

Stedman Jones, G. (1971) *Outcast London*, Oxford: Clarendon Press.

Stepney, P. and Popple, K. (2008) *Social work and the community: A critical context for practice*, Basingstoke: Palgrave Macmillan.

Stevenson, O. and Parsloe, P. (1993), *Community care and empowerment*, York: Joseph Rowntree Foundation.

Stone, E. (ed) (1999) *Disability and development: Learning from action and research in the majority world*, Leeds: The Disability Press.

Stratton, A. (2010) 'Women bear the brunt of budget cuts', *The Guardian*, 5 March.

Stubbs, P. (1985) 'The employment of black social workers: from 'ethnic sensitivity' to anti-racism?', *Critical Social Policy*, vol 12, pp 6–27.

Sunderland, R. (2010) 'Cameron's right about marriage, but he offers the wrong remedy', *The Observer*, 10 January.

Sveinsson, K.P. (ed) (2009) *Who cares about the white working class?*, London: The Runnymede Trust.

SWAN (Social Work Action Network) (2010) Website of the Social Work Action Network: www.socialworkfuture.org.

Syed, A., Craig, G. and Taylor, M. (2002) *Black and minority ethnic organisations' experience of local compacts*, York: Joseph Rowntree Foundation.

Tarrow, S. (1994) *Power in movement*, Cambridge: Cambridge University Press.

Tawney, R.H. (1949/1964) 'Social democracy in Britain', in *The Radical Tradition*, London: Pelican.

Taylor, I. (1972) 'Client refusal: a political strategy for radical social work', *Case Con*, No 2, pp 59–68.

Teachernet (2009) *Extended Services*, www.teachernet.gov.uk/wholeschool/extendedschools/

Teloni, D. (2011) 'Grassroots community social work with the "unwanted": the case of Kinisi and the rights of refugees and migrants in Patras (Greece)', in M. Lavalette and V. Ioakimidis (eds) *Social work in extremis*, Bristol: The Policy Press.

Thomas, C. (2007) *Sociologies of disability and illness: Contested ideas in disability studies and medical sociology*, Basingstoke: Palgrave Macmillan.

Thomas, D. (1983) *The making of community work*, London: Allen & Unwin.

Thompson, N. (1998) *Promoting equality: Challenging discrimination and oppression*, Basingstoke: Palgrave Macmillan.

Thompson, N. (2006) *Anti-discriminatory practice* (4th edn), Basingstoke: Macmillan.

Timmins, N. (1995) *The five giants: A biography of the welfare state*, London: Fontana Press.

Titmuss, R.M. (1974) *Social policy*, London: George Allen & Unwin.

Tomlinson, D.R. and Trew, V. 2002 (eds) *Equalising opportunities, minimising oppression: A critical review of anti-discriminatory policies in health and social welfare*, London: Routledge.

Townsend, P. and Abel-Smith, B. (1966) *The poor and the poorest*, Occasional Papers in Social Administration, London: Bedford Square Press.

Toynbee, P. (2010) 'Little by little, the blue seeps through Cameron's silky skin', *The Guardian*, 22 January.

Toynbee, P. and Walker, D. (2008) *Unjust rewards: Exposing greed and inequality in Britain today*, London: Granta.

Unison (2009) *Still slipping through the net? Front-line staff assess children's safeguarding progress*, London: Unison.

Unison (2010) *Not waving but drowning: Paperwork and pressure in adult social work service*, London: Unison.

UPIAS (Union of the Physically Impaired Against Segregation)/Disability Alliance (1976) *Fundamental principles of disability: Being a summary of the discussion held on 22nd November, 1975 and containing commentaries from each organization*, London: The Union of the Physically Impaired Against Segregation and the Disability Alliance.

Vertovec, S. (2007) 'Super-diversity and its implications', *Ethnic and Racial Studies*, vol 30, pp 1024–54.

Viney, M. (2009) 'Bending the rules', *Society Guardian*, 28 October.

Waiton, S. (2008) *The politics of anti–social behaviour*, Abingdon: Routledge.

Walby, S., Armstrong, J. and Humphreys, L. (2008) *Research report 1: Review of equality statistics*, London: Equality and Human Rights Commission (www.lancs.ac.uk/fass/doc_library/sociology/Walby_review_of_equality_statistics_241008.pdf).

Walter, N. (2010) 'I believed sexism in our culture would wither away. I was entirely wrong', *G2, The Guardian*, 25 January.

Weber, M. (2001) *The Protestant ethic and the spirit of capitalism*, London: Routledge.

Weeks, J. (2009) *Sexuality: Key ideas* (3rd edn), London: Routledge.

Weinstein, J. (1986) 'Angry arguments across the picket lines: Left labour councils and white collar trade unionists', *Critical Social Policy*, no 17, pp 32–6.

Weinstein, J. (1989) *Child abuse and the Tyra Henry dispute: A case study of the impact of social policy on social workers and social workers on social policy*, Goldsmiths College unpublished masters dissertation.

Weintraub, P. (1945) 'UNRRA: an experiment in international welfare planning', *The Journal of Politics*, vol 7, no 1, pp 1–24.

Westergaard, J. (1995) *Who gets what? The hardening of class inequality in the late twentieth century*, London: Polity Press.

White, C., Warrener, M., Reeves, A. and La Valle, I. (2008) *Family intervention projects: An evaluation of their design, set-up and early outcomes*, Research Report No DCSF–RW047, London: National Centre for Social Research.

White, S., Hall, C. and Peckover, S. (2009) 'The descriptive tyranny of the Common Assessment Framework: technologies of categorization and professional practice in child welfare', *British Journal of Social Work*, vol 39, no 7, pp 1197–217.

Whitehead, M., Townsend, P. and Davidson, N. (1988) *Inequalities in health: The Black Report and the health divide*, Harmondsworth: Penguin.

Widgery, D. (1988) *The national health: A radical perspective*, London: Hogarth Press.

Wilkinson, R. and Pickett, K. (2009) *The spirit level: Why more equal societies almost always do better*, London: Penguin.

Williams, R. (2009) 'Gender pay gap still as high as 50%, UK survey says', *The Guardian*, 30 October.

Williams, C. (2010) 'The extent and nature of cultural diversity training within social work education in Wales', www.wedhs.org.uk

Williams, C. and Johnson, M. (2010) *Race and ethnicity in a welfare society*, Maidenhead: Open University Press.

Williams, C. and Soydan, H. (2005) 'When and how does ethnicity matter? A cross-national study of social work responses to ethnicity in child protection cases', *British Journal of Social Work*, vol 35, no 6, pp 901–20.

Williams, F. (1989) *Social policy. A critical introduction: Issues of race, gender and class*, Cambridge: Polity Press.

Wilson, A. and Beresford, P. (2000) 'Anti-oppressive practice: emancipation or appropriation?', *British Journal of Social Work*, no 30, pp 553–73.

Wilson, C. (2007) 'LGBT politics and sexual liberation', *International Socialism*, no 114, pp 137–70.

Wilson, D. (1974) 'Uneasy bedfellows', *Social Work Today*, vol 5, no 1, pp 6–8.

Witner, L. (1982) *American intervention in Greece, 1943–1949*, New York: Columbia University Press.

Witte, E.F. (1960) 'Developing professional leadership for social programs', *Annals of the American Academy of Political and Social Science*, no 329, pp 123–36.

Woodhouse, C.M. (1976) *The struggle for Greece*, London: Hart-Davis MacGibbon.

Woodroffe, J. (2009) *Not having it all: How motherhood reduces women's pay prospects*, London: Fawcett Society.

Woodword, K. (2006) 'Feminist critiques', in M. Lavalette and A. Pratt (eds) *Social policy: Theories, concepts and issues*, London: Sage.

Wootton, B. (1959) *Social science and social pathology*, London: Allen & Unwin.

Wootton, B. (1978) 'The social work task today', *Community Care*, October, no 4.

Wright, E.O. (2009) 'Class patternings', *New Left Review*, no 60, pp 101–16.

Yellolly, M. (1987) 'Why the theory couldn't become the practice', *Community Care*, vol 9, no 7.

Index

Page references for figures are in *italics*